FASCISM, ARCHITECTURE,
AND THE CLAIMING OF
MODERN MILAN, 1922–1943

FASCISM, ARCHITECTURE, AND THE CLAIMING OF MODERN MILAN, 1922–1943

LUCY M. MAULSBY

UNIVERSITY OF TORONTO PRESS
Toronto Buffalo London

Library and Archives Canada Cataloguing in Publication

Maulsby, Lucy M., 1973–, author
Fascism, architecture, and the claiming of modern Milan, 1922–1943 /
Lucy M. Maulsby.

(Toronto Italian studies)
Includes bibliographical references and index.
ISBN 978-1-4426-4625-4 (bound)

1. Architecture – Italy – Milan – History – 20th century.   2. Fascism and architecture –
Italy – Milan – History – 20th century.   3. Architecture and state – Italy –
Milan – History – 20th century.   4. Public buildings – Italy – Milan – History –
20th century.   5. Milan (Italy) – Buildings, structures, etc. – History –
20th century.   I. Title.   II. Series: Toronto Italian studies

NA1121.M6M39 2014   720.945′21109041   C2013-905577-0

University of Toronto Press acknowledges the financial assistance to its publishing
program of the Canada Council for the Arts and the Ontario Arts Council.

Canada Council   Conseil des Arts
for the Arts   du Canada

ONTARIO ARTS COUNCIL
CONSEIL DES ARTS DE L'ONTARIO
50 YEARS OF ONTARIO GOVERNMENT SUPPORT OF THE ARTS
50 ANS DE SOUTIEN DU GOUVERNEMENT DE L'ONTARIO AUX ARTS

University of Toronto Press acknowledges the financial support of the Government
of Canada through the Canada Book Fund for its publishing activities.

SOCIETY OF
ARCHITECTURAL
HISTORIANS

Illustrations in this book were funded in part or in whole by a
grant from the SAH/Mellon Author Awards of the Society of
Architectural Historians.

To William and Tasker

Contents

Illustrations

Acknowledgments

There are many people to thank for their help and support in shaping this project and bringing it to the sort of completion that a book implies. I first became interested in the relationship between architecture and politics in interwar Italy as a graduate student at Cambridge University while working with Peter Carl. I remain indebted to Peter for having alerted me to many of the complexities of fascist-era Italy as well as for his critical insights as this project moved from research paper to doctoral dissertation to book. I have also benefited enormously from the generosity of Diane Ghirardo, Emily Braun, and Vittoria de Grazia, each of whom has each contributed in fundamental ways to the shaping of this project.

Research trips to Italy between 2000 and 2006 provided a necessary opportunity to spend time in Milan, visit archives and libraries, and participate in a variety of academic communities. I am grateful to Francesco Benelli, Maristella Casciato, Claudia Conforti, Gian Paolo Consoli, Caroline Goodson, Nadia Zonis, and others who contributed to making my stays in Rome as pleasurable as they were productive. Terry Kirk, whose absence I continue to feel sharply, deserves recognition not only for his friendship but also for his teaching and scholarship. Lucilla and Gabrielle Travaglini and their children were marvelous hosts and guides on countless occasions. Alessio Assonitis collected material for me from the Biblioteca Nazionale Centrale in Florence when I could not travel there myself. In Milan Chiara Baglione, Marina Demetra Casu, Fluvio Irace, Martino Marazzi, Luca Molinari, Paolo Nicoloso, Aldo and Maria Luisa Norsa, Renzo Riboldazzi, Claudio Sangiorgi, Jeffrey Schnapp, Pia Rigby, Augusto Rossari, and Massimiliano Savorra offered much-appreciated friendship, advice, and local knowledge. Particular thanks go to Ferruccio Luppi, who made introductions, helped with images, tracked down sources, and tirelessly responded to questions about a variety of topics. I thank

Savino Campanale and Maurizio Galliani at the Archivio Civico; Mirella Zevi Muzio and Giovanni Muzio at the Archivio Giovanni Muzio; Gianni Mezzanotte at the Archivio Mezzanotte; Luisa Spinatelli at the Archivio Tito Bassanesi Varisco; Letizia Castellini Baldissera at the Fondazione Portaluppi; and the staff at the Civica Raccolta delle Stampe Achille Bertarelli, the Civico Archivio Fotografico e Biblioteca, the Archivio Storico della Camera di Commercio, the Archivio Soprintendenza Beni e Artistici e Architettonici, and the Archivio Storico in Milan. In Florence Gianna Frosali assisted me with the Fondo Marcello Piacentini. In Rome Mariapina Di Simone and the staff at the Archivio Centrale dello Stato helped me to navigate state records and answered innumerable questions. I am also grateful to the librarians at the Biblioteca Sormani and the Biblioteca Nazionale Braidense in Milan and the Biblioteca di Archeologia e Storia dell'Arte in Rome.

I owe Barry Bergdoll, Mary McLeod, and Robin Middleton a substantial debt for their advice on and support of earlier versions of this project developed at Columbia University. I also appreciate the insights I gained from working with Hillary Ballon and Joseph Connors, whose writing about the urban role of architecture in Baroque Rome sparked some of the questions that drove my initial research. A regular reading group led by Vittoria de Grazia resulted in fertile intellectual discussions as well as lasting friendships. The opportunity to present some of this research in papers, lectures, and other forums allowed me not only to sharpen my focus but also to benefit from the questions and comments of colleagues, including Jesús Escobar, Gail Fenske, Mia Fuller, Brian McLaren, and Michelangelo Sabatino. I could not have completed this book without the support and council of many people, including Esra Akcan, Nuit Banai, Lucy Miller Creagh, Kate Isard, Kris Juncker, Bill Kaizen, Karen Kurczynski, Andrew Manson, Andrew McReynolds, Ken Tadashi Oshima, Fernando Quesada, and Kimberly Elman Zarecor. A very special thanks goes to David Rifkind.

I have also appreciated the support of friends and colleagues in Boston. In addition to my colleagues at the Department of Architecture at Northeastern University, I have benefited from conversations about this material with Daniel Abramson, Silvia Bottinelli, Paolo Scrivano, and Nancy Stieber. I am also enormously grateful to the staff of the Interlibrary Loan Department at Snell Library for tracking down books, periodicals, and various other odds and ends related to this project. Blake Coran helped to prepare a number of images for publication.

The University of Toronto Press and my editors Ron Schoeffel, who was not able to see this project completed, Siobhan McMenemy, and Leah Connor have contributed in essential ways to making this a better book. Terry Teskey was an excellent copyeditor. Steven Frankel's sharp eye and elegant touch improved an initial draft of this text enormously. Ruth Pincoe did an excellent job on the index. Augusto Rossari and Paolo Nicoloso kindly commented on early drafts of select chapters. I would also like to thank the two anonymous readers who offered insightful and thoughtful criticism of my manuscript.

An earlier version of some of the material contained in chapter 3 was presented at the European Association for Urban History in 2008 and subsequently published as "The Piazza degli Affari and the Contingent Nature of Urbanism in Fascist Milan" in *Urban History* (May 2011): 65–83.

This project has been supported by several grants, including a Wollemborg Fellowship, a Whiting Fellowship, a number of travel fellowships from Columbia University, a Wolfsonian-FIU Fellowship, and a research leave from Northeastern University.

My parents have provided unflagging moral support and spent more time with their grandchildren than they probably anticipated as I completed the manuscript. My husband John has supplied boundless encouragement and never failed to make me smile. My sons William and Tasker have helped me keep things in perspective. This book is dedicated to them.

Abbreviations

b.   busta
c.   cartella
f.   fascicolo
prot.   protocollo
s.   scatola

ACM   Archivio Civico, Milan
  PR   Piano Regolatore
  SG   Segreteria Generale
  LLPP   Servizi e Lavori Pubblici
ACS   Archivio Centrale dello Stato, Rome
  AABBAA   Antichità e Belle Arti
  PI   Pubblica Istruzioni
  PNF   Partito Nazionale Fascista
  SPD   Segreteria Particolare del Duce
AGM   Archivio Giovanni Muzio, Milan
ALL   Archivio Leone Lodi, Milan
APM   Archivio Paolo Mezzanotte, Milan
ASBAAM   Archivio Soprintendenza Beni Artistici
            e Architettonici, Milan
ASCC   Archivio Storico della Camera di Commercio, Milan
ASCM   Archivio Storico Civico, Milan
  AGR   Archivio Giuseppe Rivolta
  OF   Ornato Fabbriche

CSAC	Centro Studi Archivio della Comunicazione, Parma
AGD	Archivio Giuseppe De Finetti
FMP	Fondo Marcello Piacentini, Biblioteca della Facoltà di Architettura, Università degli Studi, Florence
FPP	Fondazione Piero Portaluppi, Milan

FASCISM, ARCHITECTURE,
AND THE CLAIMING OF
MODERN MILAN, 1922–1943

Introduction

Milan today epitomizes the modern Italian city. An important but relatively modest city in the nineteenth century, by the turn of the century it had become a vibrant commercial and industrial centre and a force in the cultural life of the nation. In the first decades of the twentieth century, however, Milan's reputation and prosperity were threatened by multiple failures to meet the challenges brought about by rapid social and economic change. In an effort to address these challenges and as part of a larger program to transform Italy, Mussolini's fascist government initiated a building campaign in Milan that, as in much of the rest of the country, brought about faster and more profound change than at any other time in the nation's modern history. In September 1923, the fascist-controlled municipal government announced its objective of radically transforming Milan – the birthplace of fascism and the primary gateway to Italy from northern Europe. In a letter sent to Benito Mussolini's newspaper *Il Popolo d'Italia*, the fascist sympathizer Mayor Luigi Mangiagalli explained that the newly appointed prime minister of Italy and head of the National Fascist Party (Partito Nazionale Fascista) "wanted the city to embody the 'greatness of Italy.'" Proposed changes included the "partial demolition and reconstruction of the center" to improve sanitary conditions and the creation of "new avenues, parks, and gardens" to connect the city centre with the surrounding territory recently placed under the city's administrative control.[1] The municipal government initiated the development of a master plan, an endeavour that called for substantial reshaping of the centre of the city as well as the undeveloped countryside within the city's territorial borders. Eager to take advantage of opportunities made possible by these anticipated reforms, businesses and speculators submitted designs for new construction throughout the city. Alongside these initiatives, the fascist regime sponsored the construction of a variety of new buildings, ranging from relatively modest local party headquarters to monumental civic structures constructed to house large government institutions, intended to burnish the city's image and solidify fascism's presence. My focus is the public buildings central to Mussolini's effort to secure his position and make Milan into an exemplary fascist city; these provide an opportunity to consider the symbolic concerns that shaped fascism's engagement with Milan as well as the multiple, and often contradictory, forces that defined the architectural and urban history of interwar Milan.

Despite the scale and significance of Milan's transformation, the current literature largely overlooks the city's architectural and urban history during the 1920s, 1930s, and 1940s. As a result, many of the general assumptions held about the fascists' attitudes towards architecture and urban planning are based on studies of Rome and, more recently, of provincial centres.[2] This is particularly true of the literature for English-speaking audiences. Milan, in many respects, presents a substantially different example. Fascism's orientation towards the Mediterranean basin and obsession with Roman antiquity – themes that drove the interwar transformation of Rome – had a different resonance in a city historically tied to northern Europe and whose major monument was, and remains, its soaring Gothic cathedral. Fascism's anti-urban policies and idealization of rural life, forces that resulted in legislation to curb the growth of large cities and in the development of new agricultural centres (most notably the new towns in Pontine Marshes), met resistance in a city whose image was intertwined with the modern metropolis. In a similar fashion, the regime's investment in architectural and urban interventions intended to highlight Italy's noble past and expand an emergent tourist industry (in towns such as Ferrara and Siena) had little traction in a city defined by strong commercial and industrial interests. Indeed, the particular economic structure, social composition, and cultural orientation of Milan, like other important urban centres,[3] had important consequences for its interwar architectural and urban culture. By focusing on Milan's transformation during the *ventennio nero* (the nearly twenty-year period of fascist rule), I hope to reopen questions about the ways in which fascism used architecture to substantially reconfigure urban areas, and thus interrogate its relationship to international debates about large cities.

Since the late nineteenth century, Milan had the reputation of being the Italian city most intimately associated with modern institutions and ways of life. Significant growth – the city grew from just over 240,000 to over 800,000 residents between 1860 and 1920 – manifested the effects of industrial expansion as people moved out of the countryside and into large cities in search of jobs.[4] Municipal leaders, concerned about competing with European centres of industry and commerce, sought to bring order and discipline to the medieval tangle of central Milan and to provide a coherent model for the enlargement of the city. The city's first comprehensive master plan and a number of new buildings, most notably the soaring glass Galleria Vittorio Emanuele II (Giuseppe Mengoni, 1862–1977), showed how the city's centre could be remade through planning and architecture. The construction of new passenger stations, the development of public transportation systems, grand residences, and the establishment of public art museums and exhibitions showcasing recent technological advancements were among the improvements that affirmed Milan's identity as a centre of industry and commerce defined by bourgeois tastes and habits. This new construction transformed the city centre and filled in open land beyond the city walls. However, by the first decades of the twentieth century the optimism that characterized the late nineteenth century had given way to profound unease as the municipal government struggled to address the problems associated with rapid population growth and industrialization.

Fascist leaders, when they first took charge of municipal affairs in 1922, inherited not only a depleted municipal budget but also a city with a flagging morale in need of improved and expanded civic services and infrastructure. As in the rest of Italy, the First World War left Milan crippled from the strain of military engagement and the pressures of reverting to a peacetime economy. Public works projects provided jobs for an unskilled work force and reinforced the notion that the new regime could reform a political system that was widely viewed as corrupt and inefficient. In 1926 the municipal government launched a competition to generate ideas for a new master plan. It was to provide for a population of two million, more than double the 836,000 residents in 1921,[5] and thus required radical changes. The municipal government's plans for Milan sought to impose a rational order on the city, to resolve persistent health and sanitary concerns, to augment the city's stature as a centre of trade and commerce, and to showcase the effectiveness of fascist leadership, which was manifest at the same time in the reorganization of municipal offices, the consolidation of services scattered throughout the city's centre, and improved infrastructure for the processing and distribution of food. These reforms, as well as the abolition of representative government and curtailment of free speech, provided an expedient means to limit opposition and centralize control. The regime's building projects, which included Fascist Party outposts as well as new public structures, aimed to communicate its growing authority and took advantage of the anticipated transformation of the city and region. This process of change initiated a debate between municipal leaders, ordinary citizens, architects, engineers, and planners over what kinds of urban and architectural changes would be appropriate in the making of fascist Milan. Together

these debates and projects can be understood as the initial phase of a comprehensive endeavour to renovate and redesign the urban fabric and, by extension,
to fashion a new Italian city.

Central Milan resembled a construction site by the early 1930s. Although
the city's master plan, prepared by the head of the city planning office, Cesare
Albertini, would not be ratified until 1934 (nearly a decade after he started
work on the project), his proposals for the reconfiguration of the city centre
were being executed well before then. Indeed Milan remains, as historians
Giancarlo Consonni and Graziella Tonon note, "the Italian city most marked
in absolute and relative terms by the fascist scalpel."[6] To make way for new
buildings, streets, and squares, the city authorized the demolition of churches,
palaces, and monasteries (as well as the unremarkable residential and commercial buildings that lined the city's narrow cobblestone streets) and the filling
in of canals that had once connected Milan to regional markets. This controversial master plan, though not carried out in full, led to the destruction of
approximately sixty thousand rooms (*vani*) in central Milan, and displaced a
hundred thousand people, who were disproportionally working-class and poor
residents.[7] They were relegated to the periphery, where residential housing
blocks, factory complexes, and a smattering of services had begun to spring
up. The regime's growing confidence and desire for control was manifest not
only in the ambitious scale of the urban plan, which required the demolition
and reconstruction of approximately 50 per cent of the city's centre,[8] but also in
the size, number, and character of accompanying architectural projects.

Architectural historians, influenced by the growing body of work of cultural historians and, in particular, Emilio Gentile's groundbreaking research
into fascism as a cultural religion, have sought to identify the intentions behind
that ideology and culture with the aim of understanding the role of architecture and urbanism – alongside discourse and ritual – in the project of making
fascist Italians.[9] In this effort, Mussolini regarded Rome, more than any other
city, as the symbolic and practical extension of his rule. The clearing of land
around monuments associated with Rome's Imperial past, the opening of a
new thoroughfare connecting the capital to the sea, the creation of a vast new
stadium (larger than the Coliseum) against the hills along the northern arch of
the city, and the construction of the long and broad Via Conciliazione linking
the Vatican to Rome, as well as a series of large public exhibitions (including the Mostra della Rivoluzione Fascista [1932] and Mostra Augustea della
Romantità [1937]), were all intended to position Mussolini as the inheritor of
a glorious past and the maker of a magnificent future.[10] The ideas that shaped
Rome were, to some extent, repeated in the Lombard capital. For example,
Milan devoted resources to the excavation of Imperial ruins,[11] the creation of

grandiose spaces with monumental new architecture, and the construction of new transportation networks and athletic facilities (though none so grand as those planned for Rome). The city's more limited artistic patrimony (particularly in comparison with Rome) justified vast demolitions in the city centre, and its geographical and historical ties to Northern Europe, among other factors, created a cultural, political, and economic environment that made Milan different from Rome.

Milan was a recognized centre of artistic criticism and production by the start of the twentieth century. In the early 1930s Milan's most important new cultural building was the brick and travertine Palazzo dell'Arte (1932–33) by Giovanni Muzio. The building was constructed to house the Triennale, an exposition dedicated to fostering alliances between industry and the arts established in 1923 and relocated from Monza to Milan in 1933. The exhibition hall is on the western edge of the sylvan landscape of Sempione Park in a position that is honorific but effectively removed from the symbolic centre of the city and oriented towards what was then (and still is today) a wealthy bourgeois district. It was an effective reminder that Mussolini favoured Rome as the nation's cultural capital even as he promoted the arts elsewhere. Exhibitions held at the Triennale throughout the interwar period introduced Italian audiences to a variety of innovative approaches to architecture and urban design, but the figures involved in these projects, many of whom were based in or around Milan, had little influence on the redevelopment of the Lombard capital in this period. Preoccupied with symbolic and financial concerns, the people most directly engaged with the city's transformation focused attention on Milan's role in fascism's founding history and its position as a vital centre of economic, commercial, and financial activity. Mussolini celebrated these aspects of Milan's identity during regular, well-publicized visits from government headquarters in Rome to Milan. Implying that improving the image of the nation's commercial centre was as important to fascism as the enhancement of the political and cultural centre, he surveyed works in process, inaugurated recently completed buildings, and reviewed the city's plans for growth.

Although Milan assumed a new shape within the context of the fascist political, social, and economic agenda, the form and character of the city were influenced by government officials, party leaders, urban planners, local administrators, private landowners, speculative developers, and cultural critics, each with their own often-conflicting set of priorities. Diane Ghirardo's analysis of the restoration of the Palazzo del Corte in Ferrara provides a striking example of the way in which local cultural elites – with agendas that were often substantially different from those that came from Rome – defined interwar urban and architectural activity there.[12] This work, not unlike Victoria de Grazia's earlier investigation of the regime's after-work leisure organization (the Opera Nazionale Dopolavoro) draws attention to the messy reality behind fascism's efforts to reconfigure Italian life and society and challenges the view that an authoritarian political system alone offers an adequate framework for analysing the complex, multifaceted forces that transformed Italy under fascism.[13] Certainly civic leaders in Milan, not unlike those described in D. Medina Lasansky's accounts of interwar Arezzo, recognized the value of positioning their endeavours within the context of national agendas; however, a close reading of newspaper and journal articles from that time reveals the tensions between local and national forces as well as the various agencies involved in the building process.[14] Further evidence for the range of opinions and priorities that existed about how best to shape the urban sphere can be seen in official correspondence, minutes of meetings, financial accounts, building records, personal letters, and other documents housed in state, municipal, and private archives, each of which holds different information and perspectives. The contents of Milanese newspapers and journals show that local narratives often took precedence over national ones, and correspondence between city and party leaders reveals competition for limited resources (above all, land and money) and disagreements about the symbolic goals of specific urban and architectural strategies. The minutes of meetings record the diversity of views held by municipal officials about architectural and urban priorities. Architects' archives provide a rich fount of visual information but are often less useful for reconstructing the context in which these works were created because of the sources' later efforts to distance their work from a discredited regime. Taken together, these documents also shed light on the limits of government's and party officials' ability to control the physical space of the city. The regime's financial and political dependence on Milan's powerful business community, the persistence of social structures forged in the pre-fascist period, the dominance of speculative interests, and the ability of influential figures to shape public opinion fostered an environment in which the city's transformation was contentious, divisive, and rarely straightforward. Indeed, despite the regime's ambitions, the character of architectural works was often determined by rather prosaic concerns, such as the desire for commercial gain and the need for practical and expedient solutions. A more thorough awareness of the factors that affected individual architectural and urban projects helps clarify the relationship between specific design decisions and the regime's totalitarian claims, and demonstrates that fascism was just one of a number of forces that shaped Milan.

The two most comprehensive accounts of the city's interwar history, Ferdinando Reggiori's *Milano, 1800–1943* (1947) and Dario Franchi and Rosa

Chiumeo's *Urbanistica a Milano in regime fascista* (1972), provide a critical foundation for investigating the events of that period and have been enriched by a number of more focused studies.[15] Reggiori, an active participant in urban and architectural debates during that time, traces the city's development from Napoleon to the fall of Mussolini. He is profoundly critical of the 1934 master plan and blames its failures (its lack of aesthetic considerations, for example) on the municipal government and, above all, on Albertini, who allowed the plan to "smolder and cook" behind closed doors.[16] Franchi and Chiumeo anchor their analysis in the political context of fascist Milan. They argue that the municipal government's decision to maintain the city's monocentric character was a direct consequence of fascism's desire to reinforce the authority of the central state.[17] However, their analysis, which directs attention to select urban examples, also recognizes the role speculative interests played in shaping the city.[18] Andrea Bona's excellent investigation of the ways in which the circle of architects associated with the Novecento sought to redirect the city's plans for the redevelopment of Milan sheds light on how personal relationships and professional alliances contributed to the city's interwar history.[19] Although I consider in some detail Milan's master plan of 1934 and its variants, and take into account the variety of buildings constructed during this period, I focus on a select number of public buildings in order to detail the long process through which some individual buildings were realized, and others not, and the consequences this had for the urban environment.

This work follows fascism's rise and fall in Milan from the early 1920s, when Mussolini was gathering support for his regime, to the outbreak of the Second World War and fascism's collapse in the early 1940s. The opening chapter, "Milan in Context," provides an overview of the city's social and spatial transformation during the late nineteenth and early twentieth centuries, the period in which Milan solidified her identity as a centre of modern life. The unique set of urban, economic, and social conditions produced by this environment and the patterns of change it set in motion played a determining role in shaping Milan's urban form and civic character in the first decades of the twentieth century and coloured fascism's operations in the Lombard capital. The next two chapters chart the regime's building activities in the first decade of fascist rule. Chapter 2, "Respectable Fascism: Fascist Party Headquarters, 1922–1931," looks closely at the Fascist Party's initial efforts to insinuate itself into the urban fabric through the strategic placement of provincial and neighbourhood party headquarters (*case del fascio*). These outposts created a local network for fascist operations and, along with rallies and processions, provided the most visible manifestation of party activity in the city. The architectural character, location, and interior appointments of these buildings demonstrate the Fascist Party's effort to present an image of legitimacy and respectability as Mussolini consolidated power during the first decade of fascist rule. Chapter 3, "The Commercial City: The Trading Exchange and Piazza degli Affari, 1928–1939," focuses on Paolo Mezzanotte's Trading Exchange (Palazzo delle Borse, 1928–1931) and a related plan for a new business district in central Milan. This project demonstrates how Mussolini sought to redirect the commercial life of the city by manipulating an established institution to serve new political ideas. It also exemplifies how competing interests among the various agencies involved in the building process altered a significant swathe of the city's medieval urban core in advance of Albertini's master plan.

By the early 1930s, the regime's commitment to architecture as a tool of persuasion had assumed a new character, a consequence of multiple factors, including the Great Depression, Mussolini's increased confidence in the stability of his regime, and new leadership within the Fascist Party. Chapter 4, "Fascist Authority: The Palace of Justice, 1932–1940" chronicles the central government's effort to make its mark on Milan through the construction of a massive new law court and the restructuring of the adjacent district. The stark and physically overwhelming Palace of Justice (Palazzo di Giustizia) by Roman architect Marcello Piacentini, the architect most closely associated with Mussolini, signalled a new attitude towards the expression of political authority in Milan. This building remains the most forceful architectural demonstration of state power in the city and continues to function as one of the most potent symbols of the Italian judicial system. Themes introduced in chapter 2 are continued in chapter 5, "Urban Networks: Fascist Party Headquarters, 1931–1940," which returns to the Fascist Party's activities in Milan and further documents party officials' efforts to manipulate public and private interests to secure property and funding for these endeavours. Representative examples of neighbourhood party centres at the edge of the traditional city and the new provincial party headquarters in the city's centre built by Piero Portaluppi show a fundamental shift in the Fascist Party's image and the civic role intended for these outposts. They also show how the formal innovations introduced by Giuseppe Terragni and other architects associated with the Modern Movement in Italian architecture were interpreted by a younger generation of architects.

Chapter 6, "Museum, Monument, and Memorial: The Palazzo del *Popolo d'Italia*, 1938–1942" focuses on the Palazzo del *Popolo d'Italia* by Milanese architect Giovanni Muzio. This project represents the regime's most completely expressed, though not fully realized, effort to connect its institutions to the physical and symbolic landscape of Milan. Ostensibly a new building to house the press and offices for Mussolini's mouthpiece, the newspaper *Popolo d'Italia*, it also functioned as the emblematic centre for that newspaper and its related publications. The structure occupied the eastern side of the capacious and irregularly shaped Piazza Cavour, a strategically and historically important plaza positioned between the urban core and the expanding periphery on the northern edge of the city, which was slated for significant redevelopment in the 1934 master plan. Muzio collaborated with artist Mario Sironi on the most symbolically charged elements of this project: the façade, entryway, exhibition space, and Mussolini's office. Together they crafted a building that fused the documentary and symbolic strategies of a museum, monument, and memorial into a single structure, although the symbolic program was never completed according to their plans. Indicative of its fascist associations, a mob of angry of anti-fascist groups attacked the building after Mussolini's regime collapsed.[20] The concluding section of the book explores the idea of Milan advanced by the fascist regime within the context of contemporary European debates about the modern city.

Milan presents a unique opportunity for analysing how fascism operated in a dynamic urban environment, due to its privileged position as the leading commercial and financial centre of Italy, a centre for industry, and its symbolic value as the birthplace of fascism. It also adds a new, Italian point of view to the growing body of literature that analyses the relationship between architecture and the modern European city.[21] In many respects, the radical reworking proposed by the fascist administration exemplifies the regime's campaign to use architecture and urban planning as a means of transforming Italian society. New streets, plazas, and public buildings not only gave the city a fundamentally new aspect but also changed the way residents moved through its streets, altered the kinds of activities that took place in its public spaces, and disrupted the traditional hierarchy of the urban core. To this extent, the urban transformation of Milan must be understood against the background of fascist politics. At the same time, the complicated nature of the conflicts that arose as a consequence of this process and the implications this had for the built environment suggest that Milan's transformation cannot be understood simply in fascist terms. This book aims to provoke a new understanding of twentieth-century Milan and of the ways in which fascism contributed to the formation of modern Italy.

CHAPTER ONE

Milan in Context

Milan [is] ... passionate with life, rich with initiative, with impulses, with various and fertile activities in the field of production and in art and culture. Of such cities it is necessary to follow point by point their rhythm and growth.[1]

Milan's position on the broad plains that extend south from the snow-capped Alps has shaped its modern history as a pivotal link between northern Europe and the Italian peninsula, and is closely tied to her status as a centre of trade, industry, and finance. Napoleon, aware of her strategic importance, made Milan the capital of the Kingdom of Italy (Regno Italico) in 1796 and proposed a series of urban initiatives commensurate with that official distinction, including the organization of the primary points of entry into the city, a grand government complex around Sforza Castle, and the formation of a building commission (Commissione d'Ornato, 1807). In 1814, Milan passed from French to Austrian hands. The Austrian court maintained many of the civic and administrative reforms begun under Napoleon but severely limited the city's local autonomy.[2] The struggle for Italian unification brought independence from Austria in 1859, but placed the regional capital under the authority of the nascent Italian state, centred first in Turin (1861–65), then in Florence (1865–70), and finally in Rome (1870). During this period, Milan's leaders began to define the role of the Lombard capital as a centre of financial and commercial activity within the context of the new nation.[3] At the same time, Italian as well as foreign businesses and investors laid the foundations for Milan's emerging industrial economy. By the final decades of the nineteenth century, Milan was the leading industrial, commercial, and financial centre of Italy and a major force in the cultural life of the nation. The urban, economic, and social conditions produced by this environment and the patterns of change that it set in motion were enormously influential in determining the city's urban form and civic identity. Until the very close of the nineteenth century, when Milan elected its first socialist government, a liberal city council and mayor oversaw much of this change.[4] When Mussolini came to power in the early 1920s, he sought to correct the perceived failures of earlier administrations, to solidify Milan's importance in the national hierarchy, to direct its affairs towards newly victorious fascist political and economic objectives, and to polish the image of the city where he had founded his political movement. Through this process, fascism confronted the successes and failures of the bourgeois capitalist project of the nineteenth century and its legacy.

In Milan during the period immediately following the *Risorgimento*, the movement that resulted in Italian unification in 1870, the city council led by Mayor Antonio Beretta (1860–7) advanced the idea that the key to the city's success (and, by extension, that of the newly formed republic) lay in the economic and intellectual expansion that had already begun to transform other European nations, most notably France. In every respect, Milan remained a modest city by European standards (figure 1.1). The 1861 census recorded that its population was just over 240,000.[5] Cities of comparable size included Amsterdam, Brussels, Dublin, Glasgow, and Lisbon. Vienna and Berlin were about twice as large, with populations of 476,000 and 548,000, respectively, and Paris had reached the two million mark while London had passed three million. Within Italy, Milan had only slightly more than half the population of Naples, which at 417,000 was the nation's most populous city. However, the Lombard capital was one-third larger than Rome, which had a population of 184,000 and was only just beginning to take on the character of a national capital.[6] Most of Milan's residents were clustered in the compact centre of the city, defined by a ring of canals that had once effectively tied the city to regional markets. It had just begun to expand beyond this inner boundary into an outer ring cultivated by the nobility and encircled by defensive walls built during the Spanish occupation in the sixteenth century. These walls marked the administrative limits of the city.[7]

Unable to provide public services and infrastructure that were common by now in major commercial centers in Europe, Milan's municipal government, anxious to meet the needs of its burgeoning population, formed partnerships with investors and private companies, many of which were held in foreign hands.[8] In 1864 the city council, dominated by a political and social elite of provincial landowners and businessmen, contracted with the French-owned Union Society of Gas (Union des gaz) to increase the city's gas lines.[9] Public and private partnerships also contributed to a host of civic initiatives that resulted in new construction. These included the new slaughterhouse (1861–3), the San

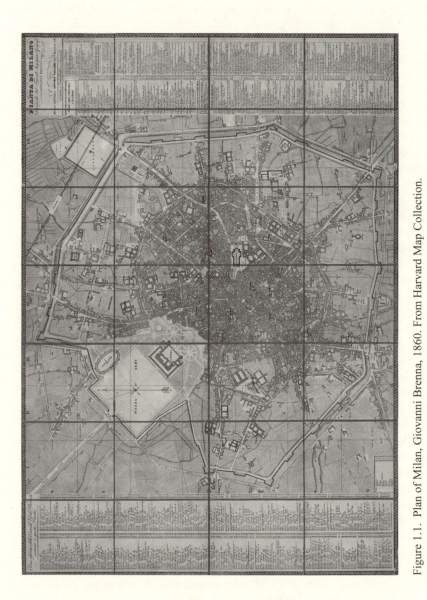

Figure 1.1. Plan of Milan, Giovanni Brenna, 1860. From Harvard Map Collection.

Figure 1.2. Central Station, Louis-Jules Bouchot, Milan, 1857–64. Demolished 1932. From *Ricordo di Milano: 32 Vedute*.

Vittore prison (1871), the Monumental Cemetery (Cimitero Monumentale, 1863), and the reorganization of the city's markets.[10] The establishment of the Milan Polytechnic (founded as the Regio Istituto Tecnico Superiore in 1863), the city's first university, demonstrated city leaders' commitment to developing a foundation for future growth in the technical sector. The municipal government also channelled resources into the development of transportation and communication networks in order to foster Milan's image as an efficient city and to broaden commercial opportunities.[11] In 1864, the Central Station, designed by French architect Louis-Jules Bouchot and located just beyond the Spanish walls along the northern edge of the city, provided a ceremonial entrance to the city for travellers arriving by rail for the first time (figure 1.2). The new station spurred speculative residential development in the district and connected the city to an existing but still fragmented national rail network.[12] Soon after, the city approved another passenger station (Stazione Genova, 1865) southwest of the city's centre, resulting in development for the growing working-class population in that area.[13] The Società anonima omnibus (1862) introduced Milan's first internal public transportation system, featuring horse-drawn carriages capable of travelling through the city's narrow streets. A decade later,

Figure 1.3. Piazza del Duomo, Milan, late nineteenth century. Giuseppe Mengoni's Galleria Vittorio Emanuele II (1862–78) is at the far left. Author's collection.

the service was extended to reach recently established residential communities beyond the urban core. These new transportation hubs and systems altered the relationship between the centre and the periphery and, together with new technologies, services, settlement patterns, and economic relationships, began to erode the largely agricultural foundation of the region's social fabric.

The project for the Piazza del Duomo and the Galleria Vittorio Emanuele II exemplifies the city's enthusiasm for unification and signalled the increased influence that Milan's emergent bourgeois culture – formed from a growing class of industrialists, businessmen, professors, doctors, and lawyers – began to exert over the landed aristocracy (figure 1.3).[14] The project was begun in 1862 according to the designs of the Bolognese architect Giuseppe Mengoni, but was based on ideas that had been discussed since the 1830s; it required the demolition of old buildings around the existing irregular piazza and a significant area north of Milan's medieval cathedral, the traditional heart of the city. In their place, Mengoni created a spacious, uniform piazza in front of the cathedral and, adjacent to it, a covered double arcade with glass-and-iron vaulted roofs. The arcade led pedestrians from the Piazza del Duomo past expensive shops and restaurants to the Piazza della Scala in front of the celebrated La Scala Opera

House and Palazzo Marino, the seat of the city council, which had been refurbished according to the designs of Luca Beltrami in 1892. Begun in partnership with an English company, the project absorbed a significant percentage of the city's resources: between 1860 and 1882 the council designated more than 50 per cent of its budget for monumental public works projects, while 4.9 per cent went to the construction of schools.[15] Covered arcades, which embodied the complexities of nineteenth-century urban life for German philosopher and literary critic Walter Benjamin (1892–1940), had been a feature of Milan's urban fabric since the opening of the modest Galleria de Cristoforis (Andrea Pizzala, 1831).[16] However, the scale and magnificence of this initiative were wholly new. Although uniform urban spaces had been a characteristic of other Italian cities since the Renaissance and had formed the rationale for restructuring European cities – most notably Paris – since the seventeenth century, such projects had never taken root in Milan. This was in part due to the city's history as a commercial rather than political centre. The new building complex next to the Piazza del Duomo transformed the urban core into a locus of commercial, cultural, and civic activity on a par with that of Italian and European centres of influence. At the same time, the venture – which unabashedly celebrated commerce, relied on foreign capital and technical expertise, and employed an architectural and urban order that had little relationship to local traditions – exposed the ruling classes' uncertainty about how best to express its newfound wealth and influence.

By the 1880s, Milan's reputation as a leading centre of business and industry had been firmly established. Within Italy, the city's only competition in the industrial sector came from the nearby port city of Genoa in Liguria and the manufacturing centre of Turin in the adjacent province of Piedmont. Milan's industrial economy had expanded from a traditional base of textile production (most notably silk) and luxury goods to include mechanical and chemical industries.[17] The opening of the Saint Gotthard Tunnel through the Swiss Alps in 1882, connecting Lucerne with Milan, improved rail connections between Milan and northern Europe and solidified the city's importance as a gateway between Italian and European markets.[18] Modelled in spirit on the nineteenth-century World's Fairs of Paris and London and held in Milan's Public Gardens (Giuseppe Piermarini 1783–86, Giuseppe Balzaretto 1857–62, Emilio Alemagna 1881), the 1881 National Exhibition of Arts and Industries (Esposizione Nazionale) showcased the nation's considerable achievements and highlighted the city's position as a national leader in the industrial sector.[19] Many of the displays featured heavy machinery, including a locomotive that was manufactured entirely in Italy, sophisticated optical instruments, agricultural equipment, textile machinery, and a hydraulic elevator.[20] All were the objects of considerable fascination. The exhibition as well as contemporary publications captured the city's confidence and optimism and celebrated Milan as a civil society based on the values of the wealthy bourgeoisie who fueled the city's economic growth and supported its numerous charitable organizations – the "moral capital of Italy." That phrase conveyed the extent to which French positivism and the English penchant for voluntary societies had found fertile ground among local business and community leaders.[21] It was also intended to draw attention to the differences between Milan and the corrupt bureaucracy of Rome. Disillusioned by the failed promise of the *Risorgimento* and frustrated by policies formed in Rome, the local elite felt that Milan had paid a particularly high price for unification and suffered from unnecessary government regulation.[22]

In this climate of civic pride and economic expansion, the liberal-controlled city council employed the municipal engineer Cesare Beruto to develop a master plan for Milan in 1884 (figure 1.4).[23] The council intended that the master plan would integrate the city's centre with the *Corpi Santi* – the substantial, irregularly shaped rural territory around the city, annexed in 1873 – and provide solutions to a growing number of urban problems related to sustained population growth and industrialization. By 1881, Milan's population had reached 321,839. Of these, 214,004 lived within the Spanish walls (constructed around the city's historical centre in the sixteenth century) and 108,000 in the surrounding towns and countryside. At that time, Rome had 244,000 residents and Naples 449,000.[24] The Beruto Plan, presented in December 1884 and later reworked by a commission headed by rubber manufacturer Giovanni Battista Pirelli, was designed to direct Milan's growth according to a coherent strategy and introduce urban features befitting the city's cosmopolitan aspirations. European cities of considerable size had used master plans since the mid-nineteenth century to regulate new construction in urban centres, to plan for growth, and to integrate public services. In Italy, the master plan for Florence developed by Giuseppe Poggi in 1865 and for Rome by Alessandro Viviani in 1873 showed how these ideas could be adapted to an Italian context in fashioning a capital city.[25] The Beruto Plan focused instead on the needs of a commercial and industrial centre, an aspect of the city's identity already found in much of its recent development, including the refashioning of Piazza del Duomo and the new Galleria.[26]

When Beruto started work on the master plan for Milan, the cathedral and its recently completed fronting piazza served as the ceremonial centre of Milan. Clustered nearby were major civic institutions such as the law courts and city hall. Around this symbolic centre, the urban core remained largely medieval in

Figure 1.4. Master Plan for Milan, Cesare Beruto, 1884. Civica Raccolta delle Stampe Achille Bertarelli, Castello Sforzesco, Milan.

character. Narrow, winding cobblestone streets were common between sizable blocks that housed businesses and residences, many of which were in deplorable condition. More comfortable homes and successful enterprises were scattered here and there and clustered around the city's few straight streets, as well as on Via Cappuccio, Via Borgonuovo, and Via Unione.[27] Small-scale factories or workshops, which produced such goods as clothing and leather and comprised just under half of Milan's industrial economy, took up the remainder of the traditional urban core.[28] The northern edge of the city between the inner ring and the Spanish bastions, where the land was higher and thus better suited to construction, had been developed in the nineteenth century; it accommodated the main train station, wealthy residential and commercial districts, and the city's first public garden. In contrast, most of the city's southern edge remained undeveloped. Mechanical and chemical industrial operations set up production centres near the major railway stations on the northern and southwestern border of the city.[29] Beyond the walls, occasional factories, slums, villages, farms, and medieval monasteries broke the otherwise flat landscape.[30]

With an engineer's eye for efficiency and with characteristic Milanese practicality, Beruto's plan strove to reconcile the existing urban fabric with the needs of a modern city. Beruto's use of regular streets and wide avenues and inclusion of green spaces showed the influence of nineteenth-century planning strategies and addressed contemporary anxieties about urban density and the social and sanitary problems common in heavily populated areas. To provide an armature for future growth and to facilitate the movement of traffic, the plan extended Milan's radial form. An interior ring, like Vienna's Ringstrasse (1860), preserved the contour of the city's former walls. However, the Milan example – unlike that of Vienna, which was lined by new institutional buildings in the service of the reformed state – did not need to accommodate the kinds of government buildings that were central to the operations of a capital city.[31] Between the interior ring and a new outer ring that would be constructed, Beruto proposed a band of large, contiguous urban blocks, each featuring a regular grid of straight streets broken by occasional plazas in various geometrical shapes, an arrangement that echoed nineteenth-century German planning techniques already employed in Berlin and other major European cities. Beruto looked to Europe's commercial centres, such as Frankfurt and Marseille, to develop his plan for Milan's growth.[32] Like Milan, these cities had been built up around ancient cores unable to support the pressures created by new populations, transportation and communication systems, commercial expansion, and other forces tied to modernization. Indicative of the extent to which financial imperatives shaped Milan's form, the Pirelli Commission altered the plan over the following decade to create greater opportunities for profit. For example, the

Figure 1.5. View looking down Via Dante towards the Castello Sforzesco, Milan, early
twentieth century. From *Ricordo di Milano: 32 Vedute.*

commission eliminated most of the proposed parks and increased the amount
of land available for speculative development.[33] Finally approved in 1889, the
plan represented a substantial triumph for the business community, reinforced
the monocentric order of the city, and laid a foundation for the uniform extension of Milan over the countryside into the following century.

   Fulfilling the city council's desire to give the centre of the city a more harmonious and grander appearance, the Beruto Plan provided a blueprint for
altering Milan's urban core. To improve circulation and to create visual and
spatial unity, Beruto inserted into the tangle of ancient streets at the city's
centre broad and, where possible, straight streets leading to historically and
artistically significant monuments. The new streets also provided an ordered
and gracious context for the city's commercial activities. The most prominent example of this effort is Via Dante, constructed between 1886 and 1892
(figure 1.5).[34] Although it had its origins in Napoleonic-era plans, its final form
comported fully with late-nineteenth-century expectations for urban design as
established by Haussmann's plans for Paris. Via Dante connects two of the
principal historical monuments of Milan: the medieval Castello Sforzesco
(which had recently been converted to house a public museum and library)

Figure 1.6. Stock Exchange, Luigi Broggi, Milan, 1901. Reggiori, *Milano*, 394.

and the cathedral. In the manner of Paris, the city required builders to construct buildings with regular façades along the straight Via Dante as it ran southeast from the Castello, to frame the oval Piazza Cordusio half a mile away. Within a decade, the piazza held Luigi Broggi's ornate Stock Exchange (1901) as well as several leading credit and insurance companies (figure 1.6).[35] Other financial institutions and related commercial activities soon sprang up along the adjacent streets in handsome new buildings. These showpieces sought to capture something of what Broggi had argued should be the "eminently commercial character" of modern Milanese architecture.[36] From the Piazza Cordusio, the road angled and travelled past the Palace of the Jurisconsult (Giureconsulti) and through the Piazza dei Mercanti, the traditional market centre, before ending in the Piazza del Duomo. In keeping with the city's desire for self-promotion, the sequence enhanced Milan's image as the prosperous, well-ordered commercial capital of Italy.

In the 1880s and 1890s, Milan solidified her position as an industrial and financial centre in the national economy.[37] The expansion of suffrage in 1889 resulted in the greater involvement in local politics of industrialists, shop-keepers, and other members of the "new bourgeoisie."[38] These changes had important consequences for the physical landscape of the city. Following the collapse of the Italian banks in 1893, the city's foremost banking and credit institutions were rebuilt with German capital and expertise and found a new home in central Milan, overtaking the traditional Italian banking cities of Genoa, Rome, and Turin (which had held the leading position since unification) and setting the Lombard capital apart from Italy's industrial triangle.[39] Milan's business leaders pioneered the commercial applications of the telegraph and used this new technology to accelerate communication between Milan and markets in Berlin and Paris. As a result, by the end of the century, Milan's Stock Exchange functioned as the primary link between all Italian and European markets.[40] When the Simplon Tunnel opened in 1906, it further facilitated passage between Milan and northern Europe and propelled trade and business growth forward. To accommodate the city's expanding commercial activity, new banks, financial institutions, and offices proliferated in the centre of the city. The novelist Carlo Linati described the atmosphere of Milan in these years as being "pervaded with a feeling of excitement, of being projected toward the future ... New buildings were being erected, cleaned, and renovated. One lived in the state of intoxication that comes with renovation and risk. You could feel that the city wanted to fulfill its destiny of becoming a metropolis."[41] To escape legislation requiring major industrial concerns to provide more and better services for workers, companies such as Alfa Romeo (1906), Breda (1903), Marelli (1905), and Pirelli (1906) constructed sprawling new factories in the area north of the city towards Sesto San Giovanni in what had once been rural farmland.[42] By 1910, more than 60 per cent of Milan's industrial activity took place beyond the Spanish Bastions.[43] Central Milan increasingly lost its heterogeneous character and became the domain of the city's financial and commercial institutions.

In the 1880s, the urban population rose rapidly, partly as a consequence of failures in the agricultural sector, and had far outpaced projected growth, only to slow briefly and then pick up again at the start of the new century, when it climbed to 491,460.[44] Beyond the city walls, the population doubled between 1881 and 1901.[45] The area appealed to newcomers from smaller cities and towns and migrant factory workers who favoured housing near the industrial complexes where they worked.[46] This settlement pattern gave rise to the first workers' ghettos in Bovisa, Bicocca, Dergano, and other towns to the north of Milan. A significant number of factory workers resided in tenement districts located around the Porta Ticinese and Porta Romana in the southern part of Milan and the Porta Garibaldi in the northern part.[47] Cooperatives such as the Building Society for Worker's Dwellings (Società Edificatrice Abitazione Operaie, 1879) attempted to address the need for salubrious working-class housing by constructing new residential districts outside Porta Vittoria to the east (1883) and Porta Magenta to the west (1890).[48] These communities included a variety of services as well as single-family dwellings modelled on northern European housing experiments. Housing also filled in the former Lazzaretto, a large rectangular complex founded at the end of the thirteenth century to house victims of the plague, which had since been used for a variety of military and religious functions and contributed to the expansion of the city to the north-west. The upper middle class and the nobility occupied large apartments and palazzi along the quiet streets between Corso Venezia and Via Manzoni and in a recently constructed quarter to the east of the Sempione Park and Castello.[49] These residences stood in close proximity to the offices, cultural institutions, social clubs, and commercial enterprises patronized by the city's elite. As was typical of areas that were becoming industrialized during this period in Europe, the influx of new residents encouraged the growth of the city out from its centre, with a concentration of businesses, services, and comfortable residences in the city's centre and the establishment of workers' housing, factories, and ware-houses on the periphery. The policies adopted by the municipal government in subsequent years would reinforce these residential patterns and make this one of the characteristic features of early-twentieth-century Milan.

The process of modernization was not only economic and technological but also social and cultural. Milan's artistic, intellectual, and leisure activities, like its commercial and financial concerns, revealed the local elite's connec-tions to and reliance on English and European models. For example, most of the ruling class spoke French and had a knowledge of German and English, both of which were useful in business.[50] Clubs such as the exclusive Garden Society (Società Giardino) dated to the end of the eighteenth century; how-ever, new social clubs reflected the contemporary tastes, habits, and inter-ests of the bourgeoisie. These clubs included the Philological Circle (Circolo Filologico, 1872), the Lawn Tennis Club (1893), the Touring Club Italiano (1894) – based on those already present in England, France, and Belgium – and the Automobile Club of Milan (1903).[51] Other cultural institutions such as the Museum of Natural History (Museo di Storia Naturale, 1895), the A. Manzoni High School for Girls (Scuola Superiore Femminile A. Manzoni, 1895), and Bocconi University (1901) contributed to the city's progressive image.[52] Publishing – books, periodicals, and newspapers – further enhanced the city's cultural and intellectual sectors. The Milanese newspaper *Corriere della Sera,* founded in 1876, set new standards of journalism based on English examples. From its headquarters on Via Solferino in a building designed by

Luca Beltrami and Luigi Repossi (1903–04), the newspaper disseminated the opinions of the leading voices of business and industry throughout Italy under the capable direction of Luigi Albertini.[53] The headquarters was one of a number of new buildings that abandoned the ornamental excess favoured at the end of the nineteenth century, reflecting the search for a simple but dignified expressive language that could be reconciled with modern construction techniques (viz., reinforced concrete).[54] In the arc of time between unification and the end of the century, Milan had gone from being an important but relatively modest Italian city to a national centre of cultural and economic affairs.

Progressive citizens, in the tradition of the local elite's participation in civic affairs outside the bounds of formal government institutions, created professional schools, established building societies, set up health clinics, and founded other charitable works to improve the conditions of workers, recent immigrants, and the unemployed.[55] In this respect, Milan served as a national example of how private funds could contribute to the greater social good, even if the nation lagged considerably behind the rest of Europe in the provision of housing for the poor and working classes.[56] The Society for the Encouragement of Arts and Crafts in Milan (Società d'Incoraggiamento per arti e mestieri in Milano), a cooperative association of merchants, industrialists, proprietors, and professional men founded in 1838, ran technical schools to train a largely unskilled workforce.[57] Between 1859 and 1881, civic leaders provided capital and organizational support for the formation of more than one hundred mutual help associations and cooperatives. The Building Society for Worker's Dwellings, Public Baths, and Laundries (Società edificatrice di case per gli operai, bagni, e lavatoi pubblici), founded in 1861 and directed by a board composed of aristocrats, industrialists, and prominent professionals, sponsored the construction of the San Fermo Quarter. The block held apartments with sanitary amenities (a private toilet and sink), and residents had access to communal facilities (such as a laundry and kindergarten). The complex was also well connected to major transportation systems and near companies that supplied a variety of working-class jobs.[58] The Humanitarian Society (Società Umanitaria), which was established with a generous bequest from Prospero Moisè Loria in 1893, dedicated itself to the working classes by offering charitable assistance and cultural and educational programming, and by conducting original research into the socioeconomic conditions of workers. These and other organizations provided relief but were incapable of fully addressing the scale of Milan's problems by the end of the century.

Milan projected an image of cosmopolitan sophistication and financial success, but, like its European counterparts, it also grappled with the darker aspects of an emergent capitalist economy and rapid urban growth. The ruling class harbored a fundamental distrust of large cities, despite the material benefits of Milan's economic achievements. Concerns focused on the spread of communicable diseases (tuberculosis was endemic among the urban poor), on the possibility of a revolution led by the urban proletariat, and on the more abstract social ills that they believed were nurtured by the city's impoverished residents.[59] Novels such as Gerolamo Rovetta's *La Baraonda* (*Bedlam*, 1894) captured the social dimension of this urban anxiety by exploring the human implications of industrial and commercial growth fueled by the greedy aspirations of corrupt businessmen and politicians.[60] Factory workers who now came to Milan from provinces throughout the region were angered by poor living conditions, low wages, and the high cost of food. The Socialist Party, one of a number of workers' movements that had gained traction in northern Italy in the last decade of the nineteenth century, found a particularly receptive audience among disenfranchised factory workers in Milan. These workers embraced the tactics of organized strikes and demonstrations as effective means of protest; both became common occurrences in Milan.[61] The reactionary ruling elite and authoritarian national government turned to the police and military to control unrest as civil disturbances reached a peak at the end of the century. In one notorious riot in 1898 protesting the inflation of bread prices, about one hundred civilians were killed when the military stepped in to restore order.[62] As in the European cities Milan sought to emulate, city leaders struggled to manage the range of urban problems – overcrowding, rising death rates, poor sanitary conditions, civil unrest, and so forth – that increasingly defined the modern city.

Events during the first decade of the twentieth century revealed the fissures in Milan's political, economic, and social system. In many ways, Milan's image as the centre of a modern and industrial economy rested on unstable ground. Italy depended on importing coal, especially from Great Britain, to meet her energy needs. Notably poor in raw materials, such as iron, and slow to develop the resources she did possess, Italy could not compete in the production of steel and other materials necessary for industrial expansion. Banking reforms had helped to stabilize the financial sector. However, confidence in Italian banks remained low, and financial institutions were reluctant to fund risky ventures. The nation's transportation network was unreliable and inefficient and crippled the city's economic growth.[63] In an effort to institute reforms at the local level, Mayor Ettore Ponti (1905–09), a political moderate and textile manufacturer, took steps to establish Milan's first subway system (already a feature of Paris and London) and to construct a monumental new train station, part of a larger effort to improve the rail system encircling the city. To address the needs of the immigrant working population, his administration launched a municipal housing program in 1905 (a consequence of the Luzzatti Law of 1903).[64] Universal male suffrage in 1913 resulted in the election of the city's first socialist mayors, Emilio Caldara (1914–20) and Angelo Filippetti (1920–22). The socialist administration shifted focus away from major civic works projects (such as the new train station) and instead directed the city's expenditures towards the expansion of municipal services (specifically, sewer and water lines, which the city had started to lay only in 1887) and the establishment of welfare programs to meet the needs of the proletariat.[65] During this period, the Institute for Public Housing (Istituto per le Case Popolare) experimented with the construction of low-density residential quarters for the lower classes, based on garden city models. Nevertheless, the city remained socially, politically, and economically unstable. A painting by Futurist artist Umberto Boccioni, *Riot in the Galleria* (1910), shows how even the most elegant public spaces – the brawl takes place in the Galleria Vittorio Emanuele II – had become sites of violence.[66] In the months leading up to Italy's entry into the First World War, Milan's streets served as a political forum in which various factions fought over a range of issues, including whether or not Italy should participate in the international conflict that had erupted beyond its border. Immediately following the declaration of war (in May 1915), Milan experienced three days of riots.[67]

The war ended in 1918, with the Versailles Settlement in 1919. Like the rest of Italy, Milan struggled to maintain order, restore civic services, promote economic growth, combat inflation, and provide for soldiers returning from the war. Organized strikes and failing infrastructure regularly brought services and businesses to a grinding halt and impeded economic recovery. Local industries did not always make a smooth transition from a wartime to a peacetime economy. Unemployment rose from 15,000 to 135,000 between 1920 and 1922.[68] By 1921, the city's population had reached 718,523.[69] Aware that existing services were unable to meet the needs of the city's residents, the municipal government attempted to improve and increase public amenities – such as schools, roads, markets, and sewer systems – which, hampered by its beleaguered budget, it had virtually ignored since the first decade of the century. The 1912 master plan by engineers Giovanni Masera and Angelo Pavia did not substantially alter established patterns of growth, and little had been done to carry the project forward. No longer a city defined by bourgeois optimism, Milan had entered the industrial age but had failed to achieve the kind of social and economic harmony of which city leaders had boasted at the National Exhibition of Arts and Industries in 1881.

Fascism had its origins on the streets of Milan, and its early history was intimately tied to the political, social, and economic structure of the city. In

1912 Mussolini (born in the small hamlet of Dovia di Predappio in Emilia-Romagna) assumed leadership of the Socialist Party's national daily *Avanti!*, which had been based in Milan since 1911. He moved there with his wife Raquele and young daughter Edda and resided in a simple flat on Via Castel Morrone. In Milan, Mussolini adopted new modes of dress and social connections to obscure his provincial origins and to increase his chances of fulfilling his political aspirations.[70] Angered by the Socialist Party's refusal to support Italy's participation in the First World War, he broke ties with both the party and the paper in 1914. That same year, he launched his own paper, *Il Popolo d'Italia*. Mussolini announced the founding of the fascist movement (Fasci di Combattimento, which roughly translates to "Fighting Bands") on 23 March 1919 in a meeting held in Palazzo Castani, a Renaissance palazzo overlooking Piazza San Sepolcro in the heart of the city. The fascist leader's early supporters – most of whom were young, disenfranchised men – were drawn to Mussolini's fiery rhetoric and promise of action. Also present at this meeting were what historian Adrian Lyttelton has characterized as an "upwardly mobile 'elite'" that included an assortment of nobles, landowners, and industrialists as well as white-collar professionals and the petty bourgeoisie eager to claim a position within traditional Milanese society.[71] Mussolini, directing his movement and *Il Popolo d'Italia* from rented rooms on Via Paolo da Cannobio in an impoverished residential district near the cathedral (figure 1.7), included in his platform such causes of the left as proportional representation, women's right to vote, a work day of eight hours, and a minimum wage.[72] Financial support from local industrial leaders funded the movement's activities, while public demonstrations (particularly those that took place in the Piazza del Duomo) called attention to fascism's growing number of supporters, and *Il Popolo d'Italia* spelled out Mussolini's platform.[73] In the general elections of November 1919, the movement suffered a crushing defeat. Fascist candidates received only 5,000 of 275,000 votes in Milan, and by the end of the year the movement had fewer than 800 members.[74] Undeterred, Mussolini pushed his politics to the right in search of greater middle-class support and, in the following year, he effectively expanded his base among the urban middle classes and in rural areas of northern Italy, transforming fascism into a mass movement. The success of this strategy bore fruit in the general elections of 1921 when thirty-eight fascists won parliamentary seats, giving them a minority of just over 7 per cent. Mussolini received nearly two hundred thousand votes in Milan.[75] The need to bring order and discipline to the movement, which had become increasingly violent, spurred the formation of the National Fascist Party (Partito Nazionale Fascista) in November 1921.[76] In the following months, fascist groups in Milan established headquarters (*case del fascio*)

Figure 1.7. Via Paolo da Cannobio, Milan, early twentieth century. From Lissone and della Morte, *La Milano voluta dal Duce e la vecchia Milano*.

throughout the city. These outposts gave a new energy and permanence to fascism's presence in the city and anticipated the regime's ability to harness the symbolic potential of the built environment.

In December 1922, Mussolini's Fascist Party helped a fascist sympathizer and prominent doctor, Luigi Mangiagalli, get elected as mayor of Milan (1922–26), a move that gave the newly formed party its first official access to the municipal government.[77] This represented the local manifestation of a trend that spread throughout northern Italy in 1922: municipal governments acceded, typically without force, to fascist control. In Milan, capitalizing on the unrest created by strikes organized by socialist and communist groups all over Italy in the late summer and early fall of 1922, fascist supporters secured the allegiance of voters frustrated by the continued disorder. The turning point in Milan came in the aftermath of a general strike begun on 1 August, to which fascist squads provided an organized opposition. Taking action, they occupied train stations, operated and escorted trains, and protected railway workers who had refused to participate in the strike. The strike collapsed a few days later, and triumphant fascist groups expelled socialists from Milan, attacking and destroying the headquarters of their newspaper on Via San Gregorio, and occupied Palazzo Marino, the seat of municipal government. The local prefect dismissed the socialist administration and called for new elections, with the hope of establishing a stable government.[78] At a national level, the sustained government crisis and fear of civil war resulted in the invitation to Mussolini, issued by King Victor Emmanuel III, to serve as prime minister of Italy in October 1922. Two months later in Milan, Mangiagalli, not a member of the Fascist Party but sympathetic to its platform, presided over a newly formed council composed of fascists, liberals, populists, and nationalists. One of his first tasks was to balance the budget, a primary concern of the local establishment and a reminder of the failures of the preceding socialist administration.[79]

At the same time, Mangiagalli confronted the recently appointed prime minister's ambitious plan to significantly expand Milan and to transform it into a modern Italian city along fascist lines. Recognizing Milan's critical position as a gateway, Mussolini sought to exploit the Lombard capital's function as a principal point of entry into Italy and to remake the city so that it would "be second [only] to Rome in its political importance, and the Athens of Lombardy for its civic grandeur."[80] In September 1923, Mangiagalli extended the boundaries of Milan to include thirteen independent adjacent towns.[81] The decision to annex surrounding territories reflected both the centralizing impulses within the regime and its awareness of planning strategies already adopted in northern Europe. The Greater Berlin Act of 1920, for example, incorporated adjacent suburbs and towns, increasing the city's area more than tenfold and doubling the population to nearly four million. German planners now contended with large-scale regional planning models that used new transportation infrastructure to link old centres with suburban communities rather than small-scale local projects that encouraged the demolition of the urban core.[82] With the incorporation of new territories, the population of Milan rose to 864,790 and the city grew in area from about 76 to 185 square kilometers.[83] Similar expansion, though on a more modest scale, was planned for select Italian cities, including the industrial port city of Genoa, the southern port cities of Naples and Reggio Calabria, and the ancient port city of Venice.[84] To connect Milan to regional centres the government sponsored the construction of high-speed roads, and to position the city within emerging networks made possible by air travel a port for seaplanes was begun in 1928 and for airplanes in 1935. Mussolini's plans for "Great Milan" (*Grande Milano*) also included the comprehensive reworking of the centre of the city to reinforce its value as a political and cultural symbol.[85] Other cities, including Rome (the political and spiritual heart of fascist Italy) and Genoa, were marked for similar renewal. Crafted by Arnaldo Mussolini, the prime minister's brother, adviser, and director of *Il Popolo d'Italia* from 1922 until 1931, this vague initiative projected a population of more than one million for Milan.[86]

To establish criteria for a new master plan, Mangiagalli appointed a twelve-person planning commission led by the politically progressive Cesare Chiodi, the municipal engineer (*assessore all'edilizia*, 1923–25).[87] Chiodi, who was trained at the Milan Polytechnic, which had strong ties to the city's industrial and-bourgeois establishment, was instrumental in founding urban planning as a discipline at that school in the late 1920s.[88] Planning, still an emerging field in Italy, was primarily the domain of engineers in the municipal technical office (*ufficio tecnico*) in this period.[89] Representing the major poles of influence in the shaping of municipal plans, the commission consisted of several engineers, including Cesare Albertini, who would eventually design Milan's new master plan, and several architects, including Paolo Mezzanotte, who later played a role in the design of Milan's new business quarter, as well as a representative from the Board of Monuments (Soprintendenza dei Monumenti), the agency responsible for the artistic patrimony of the city. Chiodi understood planning as a means of improving the moral and physical health of a population through the imposition of order, control, and technological innovation. Alert to English and German planning strategies developed in response to the problems of the industrial city, he advocated the removal of industry and working-class housing from the centre of the city and minor changes to the existing fabric to accommodate additional businesses and governmental and cultural institutions in the report he submitted to the city in 1925.[90] In this report he recommended the expansion of the city's transportation infrastructure to connect the centre with a system of satellite towns, based on garden city models, with the aim of preserving the traditional character of the region's landscape while meeting modern demands.[91] In the context of contemporary Italian planning, the proposal offered an innovative solution to the city's problems.

In 1926, Ernesto Belloni, Milan's first fascist-appointed *podestà* (1926–28) – a position that replaced that of the democratically elected mayor – took control of municipal affairs unchecked by public opinion.[92] To continue the work begun under Mangiagalli, he sponsored a national competition for a new master plan (*piano regolatore e d'ampliamento*), comprising both the city's centre and undeveloped areas beyond the traditional city, to meet the needs of a projected population of two million.[93] Belloni's brief, in keeping with European trends, emphasized improved public services, traffic circulation, and public transportation; although plans were drawn up in the early twentieth century, the city still lacked a subway system. For the urban core, the *podestà* instructed designers to reduce density, to preserve the historic character of the city, and to create new "architectural complexes conceived with aesthetic unity."[94] In addition, he encouraged competition entrants to provide space for much-needed public offices and institutions "necessary to the intellectual and civic life of the city."[95] Belloni's instructions showed that the city welcomed a bold and comprehensive urban solution featuring significant new construction in the centre of the city and the redistribution of the population from the centre to the periphery. The competition reinforced the perception that Mussolini had reformed stagnant government procedures, understood the needs of the community, and was able to produce results.

The competition jury first met in June 1927 to review the entries and to award three prizes. Civic and artistic leaders from Milan and Rome made up nearly half of the twenty-four-member jury, and city functionaries filled the remaining seats.[96] Several of the jurors would play a central role in the architectural and urban development of the city during the following decade. Mussolini's brother, Arnaldo, remained active in local affairs until his untimely death in 1931. Albertini, the head of the municipal technical offices from 1925 and secretary of the commission, assumed leadership of the newly created city planning office (Ufficio Urbanistico) in 1927 and designed the master plan for Milan approved in 1934.[97] The director of the Institute for Public Housing (Istituto per le Case Popolari), Giuseppe Gorla, served as the influential deputy *podestà* under De Capitani d'Arzago (1928–29) and then as the minister of public works (1940–43). The conservative art critic for *Corriere della Sera* and director of the art journal *Dedalo*, Ugo Ojetti, contributed to debates over Milan's urban form in numerous articles and was an outspoken opponent to the

1934 master plan.[98] Finally, the politically powerful Roman architect Marcello Piacentini shaped the city by serving as an adviser to the city's planning office, as a juror for several local architectural projects, and as the architect of the massive Palace of Justice (1932–40). For each of these men, the ideas that were presented in the competition entries and hashed out in the jury deliberations served as a point of reference in the coming decade.

Arnaldo Mussolini's introduction to the jury's report reveals a significant shift in fascism's official attitude to urban centres since the early 1920s, when Mangiagalli had first announced Mussolini's plans for Milan. In the opening paragraph of the report, Arnaldo explained, "Fascism ... does not favour concentrating the population in large cities."[99] Low birthrates, high mortality, growing unemployment, and continued civil unrest in industrial centres justified the regime's distrust of dense urban areas and resulted in new laws intended to stem the growth of cities.[100] However, large cities played a necessary role in the economic life of Italy and augmented its prestige, as they did in Hitler's Germany, where Nazi rhetoric also identified the metropolis as the source of a variety of moral, social, economic, and cultural evils.[101] As evidence of the economic benefit and stature accorded to large cities, the initial pieces of legislation, enacted in 1928 and 1931, did little to alter established patterns of urban expansion. The first proved to be too vague to effect any real change, and the second applied only to Italy's migrant workers, who took seasonal agricultural and construction jobs.[102] In 1939, the government introduced more effective laws that required all newcomers to major cities to demonstrate that they had regular employment in that city before they were permitted to establish residency.[103] Nevertheless, the population of Milan and other large cities, including Rome and Naples, continued to grow. Milan's population increased from approximately 950,000 in 1928 to 992,036 in 1931 and 1,114,111 in 1936.[104] Attempting to address the paradox that this presented for Milan, Arnaldo explained that cities like it "are important for their efficiency and their work" and described the city as "passionate with life, rich with initiative, with impulses, with various and fertile activities in the field of production and in art and culture."[105] The emphasis on Milan as a centre of industrial and cultural production accorded with the image city fathers had cultivated since the nineteenth century. However, Arnaldo directed attention away from cosmopolitan bourgeois associations with words such as "efficiency," "impulses," and "fertile" that framed Milan's energy in fascist terms. In the following decade, the cover of the city's monthly chronicle showed a skyline that seamlessly incorporated factory smokestacks, medieval bell towers, and new construction tied to the regime. Significant urban centres, despite the regime's emphasis on rural values, played a necessary role in the national economy and provided evidence of the regime's commitment to modernization.

The first- and second-place entries proposed radically different approaches to Milan's urban form, and the conflict embodied within these two plans structured the contours of the debate over Milan's urban form in the interwar period.[106] The jury awarded first prize to Milanese architect Piero Portaluppi and engineer Marco Semenza (both members of the Milan Rotary Club) for the efficiency and technical skill of their plan, titled "For the sake of love" ("Ciò per amor").[107] Their plan proposed eliminating much of the congested medieval fabric with broad new streets and creating a system of large piazzas to facilitate the flow of traffic, with new residential quarters filling in the periphery. Second prize went to the Club of Urbanists (also known as the Club degli urbanisti) for "Forma urbis Mediolani," a title that referred to the city's medieval history.[108] The most prominent members of this group were architects associated with the Milan-based Novecento, a loosely defined movement that advocated a return to classical principles in their search for a modern architecture, and with the Milan section of the Artistic Association (Associazione artistica fra i cultori di architettura) established in 1926 to promote architects' involvement in a broad range of cultural affairs, including town planning.[109] Although the Club of Urbanists received praise from the artistic subcommittee for preserving the historical character of the city, the jury decided that their plan failed to provide a blueprint for future growth and thus merited only second place.[110] Third prize went to engineers Cesare Chiodi, Giuseppe Merlo, and Giovanni Brazzola for "Nothing without study" ("Nihil sine studio"). Their project limited the expansion of the centre of the city and, like the second-place project, presented a strategy for growth derived from garden city models in which new settlements preserved the characteristic landscape and monuments of the surrounding countryside and relieved congestion in the centre of Milan. The different visions of Milan's future articulated by the winners defined two major camps. One, voiced by the second- and third-place winners, gave primary importance to the scale and features of the traditional city and advocated a decentralized pattern of growth. The other, formulated by the first-place winner, favoured the efficiencies of engineers and speculators and reinforced the centralized order of the city established by Beruto at the end of the nineteenth century.

After the competition, *Podestà* Belloni charged Albertini with the task of refining the Portaluppi-Semenza plan, which had met with Mussolini's approval.[111] Despite his considerable professional achievements and his role in shaping the direction of Milan's urban growth in the interwar period, Albertini remains a largely unstudied figure. He earned his engineering degree from the Milan Polytechnic in 1896 and since 1898 had worked in the city's technical office.[112] He rose steadily through the ranks of that office and played a key role in shaping the city's approach to planning in the first years of fascist rule, participating in the twelve-person commission led by Chiodi in 1923 and serving on the jury for the master plan competition in 1926. Albertini represented the city at the Housing and Town Planning International Federation's 1929 meeting, which was held in Italy in recognition of the nation's recent contributions to the discipline through the master plan competitions for Milan (which offered a procedural model for developing a master plan) and Rome (which confronted the problem of updating antique urban centres).[113] He regularly presented papers at national and international conferences and published numerous articles, many of which appeared in the city chronicle *Milano* and the journal he directed, *La Casa*, where he promoted urban planning as a distinct discipline within the academy.[114] Albertini's approach to urban planning differed substantially from that of other leading voices guiding the transformation of urban centres in the interwar period. The influential Roman architect and planner Gustavo Giovannoni proposed selective clearance or thinning (*diradamento*) in order to preserve the unique historical character of Italian cities (particularly Rome). Piacentini advocated the establishment of new administrative centres adjacent to existing centres (a strategy employed in his plans for Rome as well as the smaller cities of Bergamo and Brescia). Albertini argued that Milan, despite its ancient origins, had few monuments of artistic merit worthy of preservation and that the city's fundamentally commercial character as well as the demands of modern life (in particular, industrial and economic growth) required the maintenance of the city's monocentric order and the substantial reconfiguration of its historic centre.

Evocative of modernist fantasies of total renewal, Albertini's 1934 plan helped to establish a structure for growth in which the urban core would become the exclusive domain of the middle and upper classes and the institutions they operated and patronized (figure 1.8). The large-scale demolitions planned for the centre of the city, the sale of land owned by the railway, and the relocation of low-prestige institutions such as prisons and army barracks from Milan's centre to the periphery made a significant quantity of land in the city's centre available for redevelopment. Plans for the "business district" in advance of the master plan's approval as well as contemporary efforts to find an appropriate place for major institutions, such as the stock exchange, commodities exchange, several other trading markets, and the law courts, indicated that this newly freed land would be for government agencies, banks, businesses, and other vital engines of the modern (and capitalist) city. The sale of land to speculators eager to build well-appointed residences for middle- and upper-class buyers and to private corporations was intended to help offset the cost inherent in his proposal.[115] As a result, new construction in the city's centre

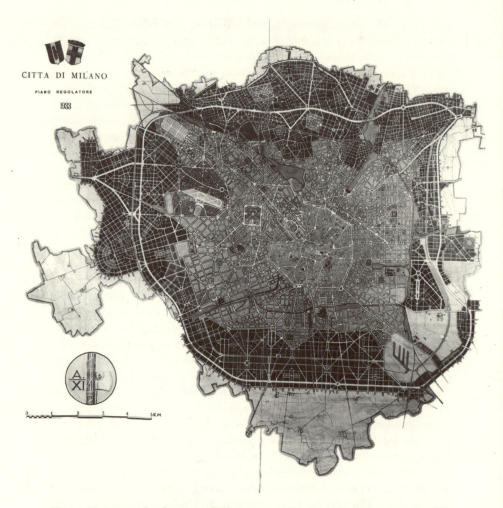

Figure 1.8. Master plan for central Milan, Cesare Albertini,1933. Civica Raccolta delle Stampe Achille Bertarelli, Castello Sforzesco, Milan.

usually consisted of large mixed-used buildings – with shops and services on the ground floor and residences above (for the anticipated wealthy patrons) – and office buildings. This led to the city's centre becoming more compact and further reinforced the division between centre and periphery. Buildings marked for demolition typically housed the urban poor, and the government justified these *sventramenti* (a word that means clearing as well as disemboweling) in terms of hygiene, traffic, and aesthetic improvement. Displaced from the centre, working-class residents and the poor were left to find whatever housing and services they could at the edge of the sprawling city.[116]

Milan continued to function as a city associated with economic progress and cultural innovation in the interwar period, despite the repressive politics associated with Mussolini's fascist government. Particularly in the first decade of fascist rule, local industries experienced growth – notably in the sectors of mechanical industry, electricity, iron and steel, chemicals, and textiles – and the city's tertiary economy expanded.[117] The Italian chapter of Rotary International, founded in 1923 in Milan by the Scots expatriate James Henderson and exclusive in membership, shows that the international orientation and elitist character of the local business establishment persisted into the fascist era.[118] The club, which included Mussolini's brother Arnaldo among its members, remained in operation until 1938, when the Fascist Party forced its closure in the wake of a surge of anti-bourgeois sentiment, despite the many alliances between industry and the regime.[119] Even as the state restricted journalistic freedom, the local press and established social networks served as a platform through which cultural leaders, including Ojetti (the president of the Artistic Association) and Margherita Sarfatti (Mussolini's mistress), organized opposition to Albertini's plan for Milan and other government-sponsored initiatives.[120] The economic limitations of Albertini's scheme and the onset of the Great Depression resulted in the city's rapid accumulation of debt as it constructed massive new public buildings, opened new roads, built schools, and expanded city services. Burdened by a growing deficit, the city was often at the mercy of private interests, who were only too willing to exploit the financial potential of Albertini's plan for their own gain.[121] Echoing frustrations that had their origins in the post-unification period, some residents complained that "Rome eats, Milan pays."[122] The economic, social, and symbolic order of nineteenth-century Milan established a point of departure and a critical point of reference for the fascist regime's efforts to transform the city. In the following chapters, a close look at several civic buildings that are representative of the regime's variable interests and ambitions throughout the *ventennio nero* will provide a better understanding of that project.

CHAPTER TWO

Respectable Fascism:
Fascist Party Headquarters, 1922–1931

The neighbourhood group continues to be a strictly political centre. It must be austere, severe, and active in every aspect of social welfare. Already defined duties include vigilance against residual anti-nationalist sentiments and severe actions against disunity and those who spread discord. In the end, its duty is to popularize fascism. The action of the Duce and the leaders of national and international politics provide the ideas necessary to achieve this goal every day.

– *Il Popolo d'Italia*, 1929[1]

The dramatic reworking of the city included the construction of a variety of buildings and public spaces – schools, hospitals, transportation hubs, recreational facilities, and parks, among others – intended to shape the character, habits, and attitudes of Italian citizens.[2] The strategic placement of Fascist Party headquarters (*case del fascio*) represented the party's first coordinated effort to control the activities of its members and to use architecture to insinuate itself into the urban fabric.[3] In large population centres such as Milan, there was a provincial headquarters in the city's centre in addition to numerous neighbourhood outposts, somewhat like the hierarchy of a Catholic cathedral and the parish churches within its jurisdiction. The provincial headquarters was called a *casa del fascio* in the first decade of fascist rule but later was more often referred to as a *sede federale* or *palazzo del littorio*; it housed the offices of the highest-ranking local officials and a variety of ceremonial spaces, supervised the activities of neighbourhood groups, and served as a direct link to the central administration in Rome. The neighbourhood outposts were called *case del fascio* and also *gruppi rionali*; they occupied the lowest rung of the party's organizational structure and functioned as the primary point of contact among the party, its institutions, and ordinary citizens. (For the sake of clarity, I use

case del fascio as a general term that refers to both provincial and neighbourhood group headquarters.) In the first decade of fascist rule the appearance and
location of *case del fascio*, and the activities held there, were used by party
leaders to communicate the party's legitimacy and stability, to encourage associations with glorious periods in the city's past, and to foster connections with
current centres of power and influence.

Founded on 23 March 1919, during a rally in a rented hall in central Milan,
fascism began as a urban political movement, and its initial supporters were dis-
gruntled war veterans, adventurers, former revolutionaries, students, and disaffected socialists, including Mussolini himself. The Fascio di Combattimento
(the name Mussolini gave to his organization) fostered a rough and revolutionary popular image. Intimidation and violence served as tactics through
which the fascists sought to weaken opposition, particularly that of socialist
and communist forces. Paramilitary action squads (*squadre d'azione*) wearing
their trademark black shirts roved through the city's streets and encouraged
the perception that fascists were "hot headed, unruly, ... with bombs always
in their pockets."[4] In one notorious Milan raid in the spring of 1919, a group
of ex-servicemen (*artidi*) and fascist sympathizers raided the socialist daily
Avanti!, killing three men and burning the journal's offices before retreating.
In the months after the National Fascist Party (Partito Nazionale Fascista) was
founded (1921), members of Mussolini's Fascio di Combattimento, action
squads, and other supporters gathered in neighbourhood restaurants, bars, restaurants, and other customary meeting places throughout Milan to formally
organize groups (*gruppi*) or district circles (*circoli rionale*).[5] The first statute
enacted by the Fascist Party (1921) established the organization's hierarchical
structure and mandated the creation of party-controlled neighbourhood groups
in communities with more than twenty party members.[6] The related establishment of *case del fascio* as fixed meeting places for these groups enabled
Mussolini to better control his base (mostly young men, who had been acting
in the name of the party, but not always in its best interests) and to appease
moderates as he gained power through legitimate channels in the early 1920s.

Neighbourhood groups, a product of Mussolini's need to organize his supporters, were shaped by the habits, customs, and financial resources of each
group's members. Their first headquarters contained offices and meeting halls
for party-sanctioned gatherings, as well as simple athletic facilities for paramilitary training. The 1921 statute, anticipating what would be a long-term
fascination for military-style pageantry and regalia within the party, stipulated
that each fascist group was to have a pennant (*gagliardetto di combattimento*) –
one of the ways in which these groups preserved ties to the movement's paramilitary action squads – but said little about their character and mission.[7] The

first groups adopted the names of heroes from the Italian Risorgimento and of men involved in the conflicts with Austria over the contested territories of Trento and Trieste (which had been under Austrian control for almost the entire nineteenth century but became part of Italy in 1919). Groups established in the mid-1920s were more often named for local party members who died during Mussolini's rise to power. This practice, as well as a variety of ritual activities celebrating national and fascist martyrs, not only preserved the radical legacy of fascism's origins but also underscored the party's goal of replacing Italians' allegiance to the Catholic Church with devotion to the state, which the preceding liberal state had also pursued.[8] Attilio Longoni, an aviation expert, *sansepolcristo* (a founding member of the Fascist Party), and, as the party's, highest-ranking official in Milan, in 1923 underscored the dual character of party headquarters by describing these centres of fascist activity as "churches for our faith and small fortresses for our battles."[9]

Fascist groups also administered programs fostering education, health, and social welfare to build support for the party. In this respect, they drew on the lessons of the Catholic Church's long history of offering public assistance programs and the example set by Catholic Action (Azione Cattolica); that group was founded in 1867 as the Society of Italian Catholic Youth (Società della Gioventù Cattolica Italiana) to oversee a network of youth organizations with the intent of fostering a more Christian society.[10] Neighbourhood groups also represented the fascist interpretation of a larger European social and architectural phenomenon exemplified by socialist People's Houses (*Case del Popolo*) and Soviet workers' clubs, which aimed to bring about social and political change.[11] The types of activities and services sponsored by fascist groups not only mirrored those of established groups but also took place during times traditionally dedicated to leisure activities or religious observance. For example, party leaders typically scheduled important events on Sundays.[12] Such strategies had success in cities and towns throughout the peninsula, but were particularly effective in northern Italy, where a strong tradition of patriotic and agrarian associations provided an organizational foundation for fascism to infiltrate.[13] Nevertheless, officials noted that party-sponsored events failed to attract large numbers in Milan.[14] This suggests that although the party had achieved political support, it had failed to fully penetrate the city's diverse social fabric, which was made up of aristocrats, recently launched industrialists, an established bourgeoisie, middle-class office managers and professionals, and factory workers.

Despite substantial differences in the scale and architectural character of individual headquarters, *case del fascio* were located in prominent positions in the city whenever possible in order to call attention to fascism's presence. In the summer of 1922, the Sciesa Group – named for Amatore (Antonio) Sciesa, a local man who had been executed by the Austrian police for distributing revolutionary material in 1851 – inaugurated its modest new headquarters, one of the first such officially sanctioned party branches. The group, the wealthiest and most powerful party-controlled group in Milan, drew its membership base from the central area of the city, where the local elite resided. Like most groups in this early period, it rented space in an existing building to serve as its base of operations – in this case, on the Via Senato at the corner of a small plaza (figure 2.1). Via Senato, one of the main roads of the city, traces Milan's medieval boundary and was lined by a canal until it and other waterways throughout the city were covered in the early 1930s, as part of the municipal government's effort to improve health conditions and renovate the city's infrastructure.[15] Elegant residences backed up to the canal; Palazzo del Senato, a principal monument of Counter-Reformation Milan, stood further along the street, a location that *Il Popolo d'Italia* described as "optimum" because it was "central and yet not suffocated in tight alleys."[16] The placement of the group's headquarters on a plaza at the intersection of a well-travelled street exemplifies the party's interest in taking advantage of existing urban conditions: it occupied a visible site, and the facing piazza and broad street could be easily commandeered for rallies and demonstrations. In addition, its proximity to prestigious addresses added luster to the status of the Sciesa Group and anticipated Mussolini's goal of courting the local elite and distancing his political party from its revolutionary beginings.

The provincial headquarters served as the symbolic and logistical centre for the party's activities in Milan. Mussolini first directed the movement from his offices at *Il Popolo d'Italia* on Via Paolo da Cannobio, a minor street that ran through a squalid working-class neighbourhood south of the Duomo (see figure 1.7).[17] In response to the movement's growing bureaucracy and ambitions, Mussolini relocated its operations in 1920 to a suite of rented rooms on Via Monte Pietà just north of the Duomo. Two years later, the party set up a significantly larger headquarters on Via San Marco at the corner of the "aristocratic" Via Borgonuovo, near *Il Popolo d'Italia*'s new editorial offices on Via Lovanio.[18] By this point, the headquarters contained offices not only for local officials but also for an expanding number of organizations associated with the party – the Fascist Youth Group (Avanguardia Giovanile), University Group (Circolo Universitario), and others – as well as a reading room, fencing hall, and large meeting hall. Although four neighbourhood groups had established independent branch offices by this point, the provincial headquarters still held the D'Annunzio, Porta Garibaldi, and Porta Nuova neighbourhood groups (Circolo Rionale).[19] Mussolini noted that the move represented fascism's effort

Figure 2.1. Sciesa Group headquarters from 1922 to 1923, Via Senato, Milan. From Lissone and della Morte, *La Milano voluta dal Duce e la vecchia Milano.*

to "construct – in a Roman fashion – stone by stone, its ideal buildings," an early harbinger of his commitment to the symbolic potential of architecture.[20]

In 1923 the Fascist Party significantly augmented its presence in Milan when it purchased a stately eighteenth-century palazzo on Corso Venezia for its provincial headquarters. Political Secretary Longoni capitalized on the party's connections to business and industrial leaders to finance the undertaking, a strategy that would become routine in the following decades. As a result, the Milan Federation, in part because of the wealth concentrated in the region, had better financial resources than the party had in other cities and towns, particularly those in southern Italy. Donations from Mussolini, membership subscriptions, the sale of books, medals, and other memorabilia, contributions from members, and (in this example) rent paid by the organizations housed within the building also helped fund party activities and aquisitions.[21] The palazzo was located on one of the most distinguished streets in the city (figure 2.2), featuring many magnificent palazzi built in the sixteenth century and later. The late-eighteenth-century Palazzo Serbelloni, one of the city's most notable neoclassical buildings (which had once been the temporary residence of luminaries such as Napoleon Bonaparte and Victor Emanuel II), stood a short distance away; and located just two doors down was the early-twentieth-century Liberty-style Palazzo Castiglioni designed by Giuseppe Sommaruga, an example of how wealth produced by recent industrial expansion promoted artistic patronage in Milan. Further along, the broad street opened along its northern edge to the public gardens laid out in the second half of the nineteenth century. By virtue of its location, the headquarters fostered associations with the city's late-eighteenth- and late-nineteenth-century histories, periods of cultural and commercial growth in which Milan benefited from connections to northern European centres of influence. Contemporary accounts noted that the remodelling of the building included plans to create a hall for concerts and lectures, a restaurant with a veranda, a fencing hall, a library, and space for the fascist Institute of High Culture (Istituto di Alta Cultura fascista). Indeed, the 125-room palazzo had ample room for the party's operations as well as auxiliary services for members.[22] Its location and appointments were intended to conform to upper-middle-class taste and compare favourably with the refinement of the clubs frequented by the local bourgeoisie.

The new provincial headquarters provided visual evidence of Mussolini's recent political accomplishments and the expanded responsibilities of the Milan Federation. Mussolini now led the national government as prime minister, and his supporters controlled Palazzo Marino, the seat of Milan's municipal government. The Milan Federation oversaw fifteen neighbourhood groups and a growing list of party-affiliated organizations. It inaugurated its new headquarters on 28 October in honour of the first anniversary of the March on Rome (in 1922), an event that symbolized the fascist conquest of the national government and became an important date on the party's ritual calendar. At the inauguration and in the presence of Mussolini, who made a special trip from government headquarters in Rome, Longoni described the

Figure 2.2. Provincial Fascist Party headquarters from 1923 to 1927, Corso Venezia, Milan. A flag hangs from the building's central balcony and an upper window. *La Rivista Illustrata del Popolo d'Italia* 2, no. 4 (1924), 27. The Wolfsonian-Florida International University, Miami Beach, Florida, The Mitchell Wolfson, Jr. Collection.

building as "beautiful and architecturally aristocratic."[23] His language reinforced the party's effort to appear cultivated and to separate itself from its beginings on Via Paolo da Cannobio, where the first fascists had gathered in a room furnished with only "four old tables, a few rickety chairs, and some ramshackle shelves."[24] In a separate address in which he sought to dissociate the party not only from its beginnings but also from its socialist rivals, Mussolini reinforced the notion that *case del fascio* should be architecturally distinguished "house[s] of beauty" that "evoke emotions of strength, of power, of beauty, and of love."[25] Photographs of the Corso Venezia building show spacious rooms dressed with Corinthian columns, glass chandeliers, and patterned wallpaper. Longoni's office featured furniture in an "antique Venetian" style decorated with bronze swags and upholstered in blue fabric (figure 2.3).[26] The furniture did not follow a consistent aesthetic – some pieces were elegant and decorative while others were more sturdy and utilitarian – but all spoke of fascism's material and political success. One commentator noted, "a great

Figure 2.3. Office of the Secretary of the Provincial Federation, Corso Venezia. *La Rivista Illustrata del Popolo d'Italia* 2, no. 4 (1924), 31. The Wolfsonian-Florida International University, Miami Beach, Florida, The Mitchell Wolfson, Jr. Collection.

party that directs public affairs must have a line of high distinction and refinement [*signorilità*] in its appearance."[27] Photographs of the building show an automobile in the courtyard, perhaps intended as a reminder of fascism's claim to represent a new order that was at home in the modern world, even as it relied on conventional signs of power and prestige.

In 1925 the Baracca Group, another party-controlled neighbourhood group, engaged the services of one of its members, Paolo Mezzanotte, and his brother Vittorio, to design its new headquarters on Via Boninsegna (figure 2.4).[28] Milanese architect and engineer Paolo Mezzanotte, a lecturer at the Milan Polytechnic (where he had Giovanni Muzio as an assistant), participated in numerous professional city and party organizations, and wrote regular pieces on the contemporary and historical architecture of Milan for a leading Italian architectural periodical, *Architettura e Arti Decorative*, which in 1932,

Figure 2.4. Baracca Group headquarters, Paolo Mezzanotte, Via Boninsegna, Milan, 1925–6. Mezzanotte's building is at the far left and was later given an addition. From Lissone and della Morte, *La Milano voluta dal Duce e la vecchia Milano*.

as *Architettura*, became the official voice of the National Fascist Syndicate of Architects (Sindacato Nazionale Fascista degli Architetti).[29] Mezzanotte had collaborated with Enrico Griffini, a prominent local architect and later an important figure in the Rationalist movement, on several projects, including the 1922 competition for the Chicago Tribune.[30] Ferdinando Reggiori, a Milanese critic and architect, aptly described Mezzanotte as "not among the youngest, but for age and production, correctly placed between the old school of the pre-war period and the new school of the post-war period."[31] During the first half of the 1920s, he played a central role in shaping the regime's image in Milan.

The Baracca Group, named after First World War pilot Francesco Baracca, served a significant working-class population for whom a building of this scale would have been difficult to afford: 30 per cent of the Baracca Group members were factory workers. The project was made possible through substantial funding provided by Marquis Alfonso Cornaggia, the president of the group, and contributions from the wealthy bourgeoisie who inhabited the palazzi lining the quiet streets to the west of Sempione Park and from a number of leading political and cultural figures.[32] Moreover, Mezzanotte seems to have designed the building without charge, an extension of the practice of providing professional services to the Catholic Church at no cost, and a benefaction that was made by others in designing Fascist Party buildings throughout the interwar period.[33] The individual who was probably responsible for marshaling these forces was Mussolini's brother and confidant, Arnaldo, who was also a member of the Baracca Group and lived relatively nearby with his family on Via Massena.[34]

Although he never assumed an official role in the party hierarchy or in Mussolini's government, Arnaldo played a critical role in defining the party's presence during the first decade of fascist rule. This was particularly true in Milan. A heavyset man with small round spectacles, Arnaldo worked as an accountant before taking over the direction of *Il Popolo d'Italia* in 1922 when Mussolini relocated to Rome. His Catholic faith and business connections – he was a founding member of the exclusive Milan Rotary Club – helped attract the interest and resources of the upper-middle class.[35] He directed the party's cultural engagement via his involvement, often behind the scenes, in this and other architecture projects in Milan – including the provincial party headquarters on Via Nirone (1926–27) and the Trading Exchange (1928–31), both designed by Mezzanotte – and in the city's 1926 master plan competition, for which he wrote the final report. Arnaldo's artistic sensibilities were undoubtedly formed by his close contact with Mario Sironi, an artist who was also the chief illustrator for *Il Popolo d'Italia* for much of the 1920s, and with Margherita Sarfatti, an influential Milan-based art critic and Benito Mussolini's mistress, who wrote a regular column for the newspaper in the 1920s and later co-edited two of its subsidiary publications, *Ardita* (1919–21) and *Gerarchia* (1922–43). By 1926 Sarfatti had left Milan for Rome to be near Mussolini; however, the party's support of Mezzanotte's "modern architecture in the classical tradition" suggests her lingering influence among Milan's fascist elite.[36]

In contrast to the ornate architectural and decorative flourishes that predominated in the party's provincial headquarters on Corso Venezia, Mezzanotte's building on Via Boninsegna represented a more restrained classicism that recalled northern Italian Renaissance models. This architectural approach, in addition to positioning the party within a local narrative, resonated with Mussolini's instructions that Fascist Party headquarters have "harmonious and strong lines."[37] The modest two-storey building had as its major exterior feature an arched door surmounted by a pediment that led to a central balcony on its second storey. A pair of white marble fasces (the symbol of the Fascist Party), which were unveiled at a ceremony that was held as the building neared completion, identified the new building with the party and helped give the structure an air of civic importance.[38] On the interior, four spare Tuscan Doric columns directed the visitor towards the main hall, which was embellished with simple lighting fixtures and a plaster ceiling ornamented with geometric forms. Large windows unadorned by curtains lined the perimeter. The offices were decorated with sturdy wooden furniture and a few framed pictures. Giuseppe Palanti (1881–1946), a professor at the Accademia di Brera in Milan, donated a fresco he had painted depicting Mussolini on horseback against a backdrop of antique ruins for the Imperial Hall (Salone Imperiale). The fresco reinforced connections between the regime and the glories of ancient Rome – a theme that dominated fascist rhetoric and imagery beginning in the early 1920s – and showed how figurative imagery could augment the didactic role of party buildings. Some of the interior furnishings also called attention to the function of the building as one of the "churches for our faith," from Longoni's 1923 description of it quoted above.[39] The main entrance hall featured a bust of Francesco Baracca – a young pilot from Emiglia-Romagna who became a national hero after he died in combat in 1918 – sculpted by a well-known Milan-based artist of the period, Geminiano Cibau (1893–1969). Upstairs in the library stood a reliquary urn preserving and protecting Baracca's jacket – dramatically emblazoned with the youth's emblem, a prancing horse – and a fragment from an Austrian airplane brought down by him.[40] These images and artefacts introduced a commemorative aspect to the *case del fascio* and reinforced the rhetoric of sacrifice and combat that accompanied fascist rituals.

The building's location, northwest of the city's centre between the fairgrounds and the former Spanish Bastions, took advantage of lower land values and positioned the party in a sector poised for significant residential growth. Like other neighbourhood party outposts throughout the city, the Baracca Group's headquarters housed a wide range of charitable and social activities. The group provided spaces for branches of the after-work leisure organization Opera Nazionale Dopolavoro (OND), founded in 1925; the recreational youth organization Opera Nazionale Balilla (ONB), created in 1926; and other similar organizations through which the regime provided a variety of services.[41] These agencies, which were placed under party control by successive national party secretaries, encouraged allegiance from groups resistant to fascism, replaced established recreational, cultural, and charitable organizations, and helped prevent civil unrest in periods of high unemployment. Officials intended that the headquarters would provide labourers who passed time "loafing or went to misbehave in taverns" with a place to go that was "healthy, pleasurable, with many amusements, drinks, and fraternal assistance."[42] The centre had an "enormous and beautiful gymnasium," a more elaborate version of the facilities provided at the Sciesa Group headquarters on Via Senato.[43] There was also a boxing ring, and an adjacent garden, the site of the later headquarters building designed by Piero Portaluppi (1937–40), was to be used as a playing field.[44] To encourage socializing, drinks were for sale in the lounge, and on the third floor were a billiard table, a library, and other diversions. To attract and indoctrinate members, the group sponsored frequent conferences, lectures, and concerts held in the "magnificent and splendid" Imperial Hall.[45] Completed in 1926, this building was apparently the first purpose-built *casa del fascio* in Milan and served as a model for the more prestigious provincial party headquarters begun later that year to replace the one on Corso Venezia.[46]

The party began to gather resources to construct its first provincial headquarters in the city when Mario Giampaoli – a *sansepolcristo*, participant in the March on Rome, local party official since 1923, and advocate for the working classes – became federal secretary of Milan (1926–28).[47] The party had outgrown its provincial headquarters on Corso Venezia, and Giampaoli wanted to house in one building all the offices and services overseen by him.[48] In addition, plans for a new building reinforced the growing reach and confidence of Mussolini's regime.[49] Mussolini established a dictatorship in 1925 and eliminated local elections in 1926. Although the act significantly diminished Milan's autonomy, the Lombard capital preserved a degree of independence, in contrast to Rome, where Mussolini appointed a governor, and to Naples, where he established a High Commission (Alto Commissariato), both of which reported directly to the central government. Mussolini designated Ernesto Belloni (a wealthy industrialist, founding member of the fascist movement, and former head of the Mussolini Group) *podestà* to secure the party's control over municipal affairs and to strengthen the party's ties to the business community and fortify its relationship with the ruling class.[50] Although Giampaoli served as the local party secretary, Belloni and Arnaldo Mussolini operated as the party's unofficial leaders in Milan, and the project is best understood as an expression of their efforts to direct the public face of fascism. In choosing a designer for the new building, they turned to Mezzanotte, who had recently completed the Baracca Group headquarters and was acquainted with Belloni through his involvement in the city's many social clubs.[51]

As with the earlier headquarters on Corso Venezia, the location of the new provincial headquarters communicated the party's effort to position itself within the symbolic centre of the city. When the party purchased four residential buildings along Via Nirone (later renamed Via Fascio) to make way for the new headquarters, there was little about the site that suggested it would make a fitting location for a symbolic public building.[52] The narrow street faced the rear of the former army barracks (Caserma S. Ambrogio) in a residential district between the Piazza San Ambrogio and the commercial centre. However, in a scheme that suggests behind-the-scenes collaboration between municipal and party leaders, the city planned to construct a new Palace of Justice on the site of the former barracks and introduce two new roads that, had they been built, would have substantially altered the character of the quiet residential street (figure 2.5). The plan for the proposed new roads included a sizable open space in front of the headquarters and placed the *casa del fascio* adjacent to a projected major east-west artery linking two significant areas of central Milan – Piazza Cordusio and Piazza San Ambrogio – and part of a larger redevelopment scheme. Laid out in the late-nineteenth century, Piazza Cordusio was only a short distance from the Duomo and was the location of several of Milan's leading financial institutions, including the Stock Exchange. The large, L-shaped Piazza San Ambrogio had as its principal monument the plain brick Basilica of San Ambrogio, founded in the late-fourth century; this complex grew up around the tomb of Saint Ambrose and was one of the most important sites of early Christian Milan, a period when the city's importance surpassed that of Rome. Behind the basilica, the octagonal marble Monument to the Fallen (Monumento agli Caduti, 1924–28), designed by Milanese architect Giovanni Muzio and others, was under construction.[53] Like other monuments erected throughout Italy during this period, this one conflated First World War memorials with the fascist celebration of heroic sacrifice for the nation, offering the party an easy way to insert itself into the nation's collective memory. Party leaders anticipated that the provincial headquarters would not only claim a prominent position in this redesigned urban fabric but also be viewed within the context of established symbols of cultural, religious, and civic authority. The new building also contributed to the continuing diminution of central Milan's residential character. Indeed, *Il Popolo d'Italia* noted that displaced tenants struggled to find new housing and that one "more obstinate than the others" delayed construction by refusing to vacate a building slated for demolition.[54]

Figure 2.5. Detail of the proposed master plan for central Milan, 1928. Mezzanotte's Casa del Fascio is marked with an open circle. *A*, Piazza San Ambrogio; *B*, Monument for the Fallen; *C*, proposed site for Palace of Justice; *D*, Piazza Cordusio. *Milano*, August 1929, 466.

Mezzanotte's *casa del fascio* (figure 2.6) showed how an updated interpretation of the traditional neoclassical Milanese palazzo might be reworked to serve the needs of the Fascist Party.[55] The overall proportions, as well as details such as engaged composite pilasters, a central balcony, and a crowning pediment, reinforced connections with local adaptations of this architectural type, themselves based on Renaissance models. At the same time, Mezzanotte's project showed the party's desire to create a building that would be distinct from earlier architectural examples. The new building on Via Nirone had a bold and robust character, a consequence of Mezzanotte's handling of the details and materials, brick and travertine. Indeed, Mussolini had criticized an earlier version of the project for not being sufficiently "simple and severe."[56] Mezzanotte's final version of the building accorded with Mussolini's desire to present the party as a forceful and vigorous organization and to make this headquarters a local manifestation of his command. Design decisions also responded to the practical needs of the party. The long central balcony provided a necessary platform from

Figure 2.6. Casa del Fascio, Paolo Mezzanotte, Via Nirone, Milan, 1926–7. *Architettura e Arti Decorative* 2, no. 7 (1928): 321.

which party officials could address crowds gathered in the street below during public rallies. Fasces, placed on each of the obelisks set between the lateral pairs of composite pilasters on the second storey, made explicit the political function of the building; and the bundles of shields and arrows beneath the fasces served as a reminder of the party's militant origins.[57] The adoption of an architectural

vocabulary that borrowed elements from local neoclassical examples reinforced officials' efforts to make the party appear legitimate during a period of
rapid political change; it also emphasized the bourgeois character of the party's
base and buttressed Arnaldo Mussolini's and *Podestà* Belloni's efforts to attract
the local industrial, business, and social elite.[58] Paired with symbols of the new
political order, these architectural associations presented fascism both as part of
a continuous Milanese tradition and as a force for change.[59]

In designing the interior plan, Mezzanotte again turned to the palazzo as
a model, modifying this typical locus of secular authority to serve the particular needs of the party. He organized the first two stories around a double-
height atrium of reinforced concrete (see figures 2.7 and 2.8).[60] The spatial
arrangement recalled the open courtyards of palazzi throughout Milan and
recent commercial adaptations of this architectural type.[61] While the opulent atriums of banking halls and department stores glorified the individual
as a consumer in a capitalist economy, Mezzanotte's atrium drew attention
to the collective nature of fascist participation. A curved apse and a narrow
stage at one end clarified the atrium's purpose as a large meeting hall, a
ubiquitous and important feature of party buildings. On the ground floor,
Mezzanotte also placed the membership office (conveniently located near
the main entrance) and offices for the Association of Mothers and Widows
of Fallen Fascists (Associazione Madri e Vedove dei Caduti Fascisti) and
the Organization of Fascist Women (Fascio Feminile). To the right of the
entrance hall, the stairway to the second floor originally led to the Room of
Honour (Salone d'Onore) and to a memorial space commemorating the first
thirteen fascist martyrs, as well as to administrative offices, including the
office of the local party secretary. Upper floors contained additional offices
for the Milan Federation and space for various other affiliated organizations,
including the federation's newspaper *Il Popolo di Lombardia* and the Institute
of Culture (Istituto di Cultura).[62] Reinforcing the headquarters' administrative and elite status were its lack of informal gathering spaces such as bars
and game rooms.

Mezzanotte's atrium provided an open space for large gatherings and suggested how transparency could be used to convey the symbolic and practical needs of the party. In order to enlarge the hall, initially conceived as a
smaller single-height space, Mezzanotte added galleries along its perimeter,
apparently following a suggestion made by Mussolini.[63] Mezzanotte further
expanded the flexibility of the atrium by using glass to physically separate
but visually connect several distinct spaces within the palazzo. On the ground
floor, glass doors separated the atrium from the vestibule and could be opened
to accommodate larger numbers of people during popular events. On the second floor, similar glass doors divided the upper-gallery level from the Room of

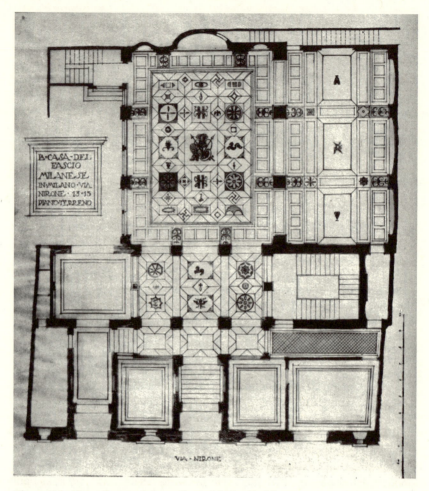

Figure 2.7. Plan of ground floor, Casa del Fascio, Mezzanotte. *Architettura e Arti Decorative* 2, no. 7 (1928): 320.

Honour (figure 2.9), the second most important meeting space within the building. The glass doors leading from the Room of Honour to the balcony on the front façade reinforced the fluid relationship between the interior and exterior of the building and facilitated the pageantry of party gatherings. The extensive use of glass, a material associated with modern architecture, gave the interior

Figure 2.8. View of atrium, Casa del Fascio, Mezzanotte. *Architettura e Arti Decorative* 2, no. 7 (1928): 323.

of the building a contemporary feel and visually united its ceremonial spaces. The spatial arrangement, and perhaps also the interest in transparency, later provided a model for Giuseppe Terragni, whose unabashedly modernist *casa del fascio* in Como (1933–6; see figure 5.1) remains the best-known example of this building type.[64]

Nevertheless, Mezzanotte's reliance on historical models distanced the party from recent calls for a substantially new architectural language in Italy. A series of four articles from December 1926 through 1927 crafted by the Milan-based Gruppo Sette and published in the cultural journal *La Rassegna Italiana* announced the Italian engagement with the European-based Modern Movement in architecture.[65] Inspired by the work and writings of Le Corbusier and others, a group of seven recent graduates from the Milan Polytechnic – including Terragni – argued that Italian architecture needed to embrace the "new spirit" of European architecture and should explore the opportunities made

Figure 2.9. Room of Honour, Casa del Fascio, Mezzanotte. The plaque commemorating the first fascist martyrs (installed in 1927) is visible just beyond the glass doors at the end of room. *Architettura e Arti Decorative* 2, no. 7 (1928): 323.

possible by new construction techniques and materials.[66] The group and its adherents advanced their ideas through exhibitions, most notably the First and Second Exhibitions of Rationalist Architecture held in Rome in 1928 and 1931 and the Triennale, held in Monza in 1930 and thereafter in Milan. Architecture journals, such as the Milan-based *Casabella*, directed by Giuseppe Pagano from 1933, and *Quadrante*, directed by Massimo Bontempelli and Pier Maria Bardi from 1933 to 1936, provided a platform through which architects could present their work, contribute to debate, and argue for modernism's role in the creation of fascist Italy.[67] Mezzanotte's architecture offered an alternative to the more radical implications of Rationalist architecture; in the design of the Casa del Fascio, however, his embrace of a spare classical vocabulary and his use of a reinforced concrete structure and of extensive glass on the interior suggested that the Milan Federation sought to appear modern.

 Since the early 1920s Fascist Party headquarters had served as the setting for ceremonies in honour of deceased party members and displayed a variety of memorials, typically in the form of plaques, photographs, and portrait busts, in remembrance of the nation's and party's lost "heroes." Party leaders also assigned the widows and mothers of the fallen a visible role in party rituals. The appointment of Augusto Turati (1926–30) as national party secretary and his adoption in 1926 of a new party statute that defined fascism as "fundamentally a faith" reinforced the sacred tenor of party life and provided the impetus for the proliferation of ceremonies and altars dedicated to so-called fascist martyrs throughout Italy in that year.[68] Shortly before Mezzanotte completed the party's new provincial headquarters the architect added the memorial space adjacent to the Room of Honour. The few extant photographs of the interior of the building focus on the meeting spaces – the atrium and the Room of Honour – and offer only a glimpse of this memorial room, which held a marble slab honouring soldiers who died in the First World War. The slab – illuminated by a candelabrum – also listed the names of the first thirteen fascist martyrs, conflating sacrifice for the nation with sacrifice for the party.[69] Mezzanotte added the plaque and candelabrum after Arnaldo Mussolini, who toured the project two weeks before its inauguration and had a particular interest in cultivating the spiritual dimension of fascism, specifically requested its addition.[70] It appears to be the first instance in a *casa del fascio* of a memorial chapel (or *sacrario*), a distinguishing feature of this building type by the early 1930s.

The year after the opening of the *casa del fascio* on Via Nirone, the regime's operations in Milan suffered a series of setbacks. To help fund his ambitious public-works program, *Podestà* Belloni had negotiated a loan of thirty million dollars from the American bank Dillon Read & Co. in 1927. The terms of the loan had placed the city at a disadvantage. However, it was not until credible accusations of embezzling city funds were leveled against Belloni that Mussolini dismissed him in September 1928.[71] Three months later Mussolini dismissed Party Secretary Giampaoli for "profiteering." Giampaoli's removal signalled Mussolini's decision to abandon the secretary's campaign to appeal to the working classes and instead to place party leadership firmly in the hands of the local elite.[72] The day after Giampaoli's removal, Mussolini dispatched the national party's vice-secretary, Achille Starace, to Milan under orders to "normalize" the Milan Federation. Starace eliminated numerous mid- and lower-level officials, many of whom were allies of Giampaoli. Arnaldo Mussolini, also tarnished by the scandal, became involved in the Scuola Mistica Fascita (1930–43), a school dedicated to purifying fascism thorugh the formation of a new fascist elite.[73] By spring 1929, the Milan *fascio* had begun to regain stability. The new federal secretary of Milan, Luigi Franco Cottini (1929–30) – a lawyer, son of a general, and the leader or *federale* of the Sciesa Group – affirmed the party's interest in courting the upper-middle class. At the same time, Cottini's status as a fascist since 1919 and his

Figure 2.10. Provincial Fascist Party headquarters from 1931–40. Palazzo Besana, Piazza Belgioioso, Milan, early nineteenth century. From Lissone and della Morte, *La Milano voluta dal Duce e la vecchia Milano*.

participation in the March on Rome appeased Milanese fascists who sought to restore the founding values of fascism, and swayed local party politics.[74] Cottini, a young and not terribly capable leader, promoted fascist squads whose activities irritated local police officials and would eventually lead to his dismissal in the summer of 1930.[75]

Three years after officials inaugurated the *casa del fascio* on Via Nirone, Cottini relocated the provincial headquarters to the neoclassical Napoleonic-era Palazzo Besana (Giovanni Battista Piuri, 1819) in Piazza Belgioioso (figure 2.10). Cottini, like Giampaoli before him, cited the inadequate size of the current headquarters as the reason for the move.[76] Moreover, the Via Nirone site had failed to achieve the kind of urban prominence anticipated by party leaders when they embarked on the project. A number of factors, including fiscal mismanagement in the mayor's office, forced the city to set aside its plans for the new network of roads and a new Palace of Justice in that district. In addition, scandals involving the highest-ranking local party and city officials tainted the project as a reminder of a corrupt administration. The imperial aspect of the Palazzo Besana's massive colonnade conveyed fascism's strength and permanence in the face of significant upheaval. Although the Sciesa Group already occupied the Palazzo Besana and had begun to negotiate its purchase, Cottini, in his role as federal secretary, determined that the building was, "for tradition and majesty," better suited as a provincial headquarters.[77] In a gesture that mirrored the Italian government's practice of renovating and converting palaces for state functions, the federation emblazoned the façade of the Palazzo Besana with a bronze *fascio* crowned with a laurel wreath and "P.N.F. Federazione Provinciale Milano." The architectural setting, tied to the party through symbol and text, presented an image of triumph as the party attempted to repair its image in the Lombard capital.

The new location of the provincial headquarters suggests that the Fascist Party in Milan now sought to reinforce its connections to fascism's origins and to play a more aggresive role in directing local affairs. The building occupied the long side of Piazza Belgioioso, adjacent to the Casa di Manzoni (the residence of late-nineteenth-century Italian author Alessandro Manzoni) and opposite Giuseppe Piermarini's Palazzo Belgioioso (1772), a celebrated example of Milanese neoclassicism. Maintaining the strategy employed in the selection of the Corso Venezia and Via Nirone sites, the party positioned itself in proximity to reminders of late-eighteenth- and late-nineteenth-century Milan. However, the Piazza Belgioioso, in contrast to those earlier sites, carried fascist associations. After the party's electoral defeat in 1919, Mussolini had addressed his supporters from the back of a truck parked in the piazza, and it served as a meeting point for fascist groups participating in political demonstrations throughout the following decade.[78] The new headquarters' location in the piazza also positioned the party alongside existing centres of power. On one end, the piazza opened onto Corso Littorio (1928–30, now Corso Matteoti), an arcaded street that was one of the first important urban projects directed by the fascist government. It connected the recently expanded Piazza San Babila, a key feature of the urban plan for Milan being developed in the same years, with the new Piazza Crespi (now Piazza Meda, opened in 1926), where several local banks as well as luxury office and residential buildings were located. Even more important, the plaza was steps away from the Piazza della Scala, onto which faced the sixteenth-century Palazzo Marino, the seat of the municipal government. The new provincial party headquarters thus provided a visual and spatial demonstration of the party's effort to erode the authority of the municipal government, despite Mussolini's 1927 decree that the party remain subservient to the state.[79] Situated between two poles of local power – the city government and the business and commercial interests that drove Milan's economy – the Palazzo Besana shows fascism's reliance on local systems as a practical route to power and its progressive effort to undermine established power structures.

The Milan Federation restructured the building's interior to meet the needs of the organization. Construction contracts went to party members and local firms, who offered materials and labour at reduced rates.[80] The entrance atrium – the walls of which were faced with donated marble – led to several meeting rooms, an elaborate memorial chapel (Cappella dei Caduti), and a lecture hall capable of accommodating a thousand people. Also included on the ground floor were offices for serving the general public (such as membership and public assistance) and for managing the operations of the federation (including the technical and bursar's offices). The second storey, reached by a "monumental staircase," held the offices and reception rooms for the highest-ranking local officials.[81] Local reports emphasized the grandeur of the interior spaces and appointments and gave particular attention to the memorial chapel, described as "the mystical temple where the spirit of the unforgettable thirteen [first fascist martyrs] will be exalted in silent meditation."[82] This room had as its focal point the marble plaque created for the old Via Nirone headquarters. Above the plaque hung a bronze crucifix and beneath it a marble base, in front of which stood a censer, two roman lamps, and a kneeling stool. Black marble accented by green stripes ornamented the floors, heavy red-and-gold cloth covered the walls, and a luminous gold ceiling completed the ensemble.[83] The incorporation of the marble plaque from the earlier headquarters created a degree of continuity between the buildings, but its location on the ground floor and the material richness and ecclesiastical character of its setting suggested a fundamentally new approach to memorial spaces within party buildings. Mussolini paused here in silent prayer during the inauguration of the building, a demonstration of its particular importance.[84]

The world economic depression caused by the collapse of the American stock market in October 1929 caused a significant strain on the party's finances. The failure of the local real estate market prevented the party from selling its Via Nirone property, which was intended to help finance the purchase of Palazzo Besana.[85] At the same time, the Fascist Party expanded its already considerable network of welfare programs. The party's relief efforts followed the rise and fall of the Italian economy as well as local cycles, and were particularly intense from the end of 1929 to 1934. Public assistance programs, described by Mussolini as "a work of human, national, and fascist solidarity," targeted the unemployed, the displaced, and groups favoured by fascism, such as war veterans.[86] In Milan, the working class felt the brunt of the economic depression, and it exacerbated their distrust of the government's relationship with local industrial concerns. As a fiduciary report from Milan from November 1931 noted, "Factory workers find themselves burdened by the nightmare of unemployment ... they accuse the government of having supported the industrialists at the expense of the working class."[87] Throughout the winters of 1930 and 1931, neighbourhood party headquarters gave out bread, rice, and coal to unemployed factory workers in Milan.[88] To structure the administration and distribution of aid, the party formed the Public Assistance Agency (Ente Opere Assistenziali, EOA) in 1931.[89] The party's limited financial resources combined with the devastating effects of the depression prevented significant investment in new construction until the mid-1930s.

During the first decade of Fascist rule, *case del fascio* provided the party with a critical opportunity to demonstrate its presence, to build support for the regime, and to suppress opposition. In the early 1920s the nascent political party commandeered existing structures and made minor changes to these buildings to signal fascism's arrival as a political force. By the mid-1920s, Milan fascist-controlled neighbourhood groups had established outposts in and around the historic centre of the city (typically near transportation hubs), in formerly independent villages (such as Turro), and in developing residential districts (figure 2.11). The young party had made substantial political gains and, distancing fascism from its beginnings as a radical political movement of the left, now sought to present itself as a legitimate and credible political force within a continuous Milanese tradition. The renovation of prestigious buildings and the construction of new ones went hand in hand with this agenda. The grandeur of the provincial party headquarters on Corso Venezia, the updated neoclassicism of the provincial headquarters on Via Nirone by Mezzanotte, and the austere monumentality of the Palazzo Besana emulated the tastes and habits of the local elite. Each of the three provincial party headquarters exemplify party leaders' efforts to identify with the city's noble heritage and contemporary importance as an economic centre. Their visual and spatial associations with monuments from Milan's venerable past emphasized the city's role from the end of the third through the fourth century as the political and religious centre of the Western Roman Empire and as a political and cultural centre in the late eighteenth century; and their proximity to areas marked for redevelopment and even, in the case of Mezzanotte's provincial headquarters,

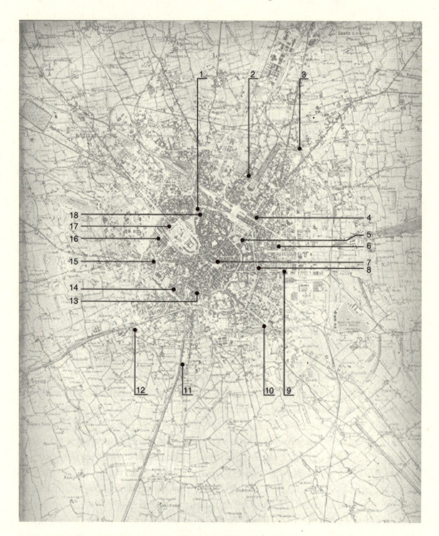

Figure 2.11. Map of Milan from 1932 showing the approximate location of *case del fascio* circa 1925. *1*, Mussolini (Via Volta 20); *2*, Filzi (Via Schiapparelli 2); *3*, Turro (Via Valtorta 2); *4*, Oberdan (Via P. Castaldi 39); *5*, Provincial Headquarters (Corso Venezia 69); *6*, Tonoli (Via G. Uberti 2); *7*, Sciesa (Via S. Pellico 8); *8*, Corridoni (Viale Premuda 17); *9*, Melloni (Viale Piceno 6); *10*, Battisti (Via Mantova 10); *11*, Montegani (Via De Sanctis 11); *12*, Diaz (Via Pestalozzi 16); *13*, Isonzo (Via Mullino Armi 17); *14*, Cantore (Via Ausonio 16); *15*, Baracca (Bastioni Magenta 8); *16*, Delcroix (Via V. Monti 57); *17*, Crespi (Arco della Pace, Casello Levante); *18*, D'Annunzio (Via Moscova 58). Map from Reggiori, Milano, 16. Graphics Blake Coran.

their use of reinforced concrete and interior glass connected them to the spaces and institutions associated with the modern city. The party similarly established headquarters in other cities to position its authority in relation to local narratives of power and prestige. For example, it used the Palazzo Braschi (1927–43), which faced both the Piazza Navona and Corso Vittorio Emanuele, for its provincial headquarters in Rome – a choice that referenced that city's ancient, medieval, Renaissance, and modern history. As the Baracca Group's headquarters on Via Boninsegna suggests, in the coming decade the Fascist Party would favour new construction in developing sections of the city. In this period, the party attempted to gain a foothold in these areas as it sought to play a more active role in the shaping of Milan. This later building campaign provides an opportunity for a more detailed consideration of the ways in which local forces (particularly the city's industrial concerns) influenced the party's activities.

CHAPTER THREE

The Commercial City:
The Trading Exchange and Piazza degli Affari,
1928–1939

The organization of the Stock Exchange presents itself as intimately connected to a broad range of other problems; first among these is the organic and rational organization of the centre of the city.[1]

Organized industry, though wary of the revolutionary potential of fascism, saw Mussolini and the National Fascist Party as the best means to reform outmoded government institutions and policies and to bring order and discipline to Italy. This sector offered funds and tacit support to the regime after Mussolini's March on Rome in 1922 and benefited from many of his new economic initiatives. An air of optimism among local business leaders surrounded a host of new initiatives. The Milan Fair (Fiera di Milano, 1920) established permanent exhibition grounds on the site of the former Piazza d'Armi west of the city's centre in 1923. Speculators took control of property in areas of the city that had not yet been developed, and large industrial concerns (viz. Breda, De Angeli, and Pirelli) continued to expand their factories, which began to resemble small cities outside Milan's central area. Leading banks such as the Banca Commerciale and Banca Popolare constructed grand new headquarters in marble and stone in the centre of Milan, facilitated by their alliances with fascist-controlled city hall.[2] The institution that best represented the financial and commercial sector's image was the city's newly created state-run business association, the Provincial Economic Council (Consiglio Provinciale dell'Economia), which operated as the independent Chamber of Commerce (Camera di Commercio) until 1924. The construction of the new Trading Exchange (Palazzo delle Borse, 1928–31), designed by architect and engineer Paolo Mezzanotte with his brother Vittorio, and the related plan for a new plaza (Piazza degli Affari, 1928–39) within a new business district (*quartiere degli*

Figure 3.1. Exchange (Palazzo delle Borse), Paolo Mezzanotte with Vittorio Mezzanotte, Milan, 1928–31. From Lissone and della Morte, *La Milano voluta dal Duce e la vecchia Milano*.

affari) represented a key element in the regime's effort to assert its authority over the city's economic institutions and to eclipse in importance and prestige the public buildings and spaces associated with the centres of bourgeois power and influence established in the late nineteenth century (figure 3.1).

At the end of 1925, Angelo Salmoiraghi, an industrialist who was president of the Chamber of Commerce (1900–24) and head of the organization's governing body (1924–26) during its restructuring as the Provincial Economic Council, oversaw the purchase of property in central Milan to house a new Stock Exchange (Borsa Valori). Since 1901 the Stock Exchange had occupied an elegant curved building designed by Luigi Broggi in Piazza Cordusio, the commercial and financial heart of the city from the late nineteenth century on (see figure 1.6). Rapid financial growth and technological change meant that the building no longer accommodated the Exchange's needs and, to make matters more pressing, its lease was set to expire in September 1931.[3] Salmoiraghi also intended to consolidate the Stock Exchange, the Commodities Exchange (first Borsa Cereali, later Merci), and the numerous other markets scattered throughout the city in this new building.[4] Pressed to find available land in Milan's dense urban core, the council eventually negotiated the purchase of two

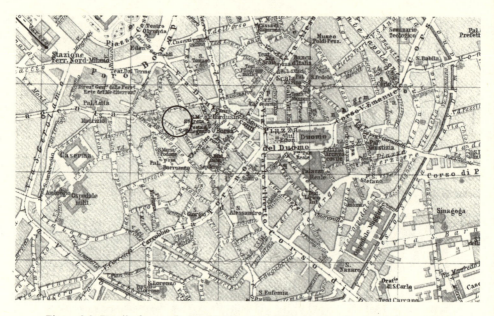

Figure 3.2. Detail of map of central Milan circa 1906 showing the site of the new Exchange. From Karl Baedeker, *Italy: Handbook for Travellers by Karl Baedeker, First Part: Northern Italy*, 13th ed. (Leipzig: Karl Baedeker, 1906), foldout opposite p. 128.

adjacent buildings owned by the Unione Cooperativa, west of Piazza Cordusio: the nineteenth-century Palazzo Turati (designed by Ernesto Pirovano), which fronted Via Meravigli, and a contiguous "building with an industrial character of a more recent construction," which faced one of the many narrow cobblestone streets that ran through the quarter (figure 3.2).[5] The council planned to demolish this industrial building and to incorporate Palazzo Turati's façade and some interiors into the new structure.[6] The site's proximity to the city's leading banks and financial and commercial institutions preserved the Stock Exchange's stature and assured that traders would have easy access to related businesses and financial services.

Salmoiraghi saw the project not as an isolated event but as part of a coordinated effort in which the transformation of one of the "most vital areas of the great Lombard metropolis" would aid in the formation of the new "city."[7] Alert to the municipal government's plans for restructuring the city's centre – Mussolini's fascist government had announced its intent to transform Milan in 1923 – the council's president anticipated that the new Exchange would be the most significant feature of a major urban complex on a new public plaza in the heart of the city and a central component of its "organic and rational development."[8] Indeed, the council envisioned a large piazza facing the Exchange, closed to vehicular traffic and lined by "grand porticos destined to accomodate market-goers."[9] As the plan for the district developed under Mayor Mangiagalli (1922–26), the municipal government agreed to tear down the dilapidated residential Casa Colombo and other adjacent buildings to free up space for two new plazas, Piazza degli Affari and the smaller Piazzetta dei Grani. The two plazas measured approximately three thousand square metres in total and were to provide space for commercial activity as well as a ceremonial front for the new building.[10] Equally important, the plan promised to transform a depressed residential section of the city into a centre of vibrant commercial activity. This strategy of urban improvement shows the legacy of nineteenth-century planning. However, the scale of the task and the government's decision to consolidate previously independent organizations and to cluster related services is an early example of the policies that city planners and government agencies would adopt in the interwar period.

In 1926 Ernesto Belloni replaced Salmoiraghi as head of the council and became Milan's first appointed fascist mayor (*podestà*). It was probably during his brief tenure as head of the council that the agency hired Paolo Mezzanotte (who knew Belloni socially and had recently completed the Casa del Fascio on Via Nirone) to design the new building. Later that same year, Carlo Tarlarini replaced Belloni (first as the council's acting head [1926] and then as its influential vice-president [1927–32]), although the council was supervised by the local prefect after 1927), and the urban dimension of the project began to take shape (see figures 2.5 and 3.3). To link the Exchange to an existing transportation network, to facilitate the flow of cars to and from the new business district, and to bring light and air into a crowded section of the city, municipal engineer and head of the city planning office Cesare Albertini proposed a major new east-west axis connecting Piazza Cordusio and Piazza San Ambrogio and supported the creation of a large piazza in front of the new Exchange. The scale of the project was in keeping with other urban initiatives, such as the restructuring of Piazza San Babila and the opening of Corso Littoria (latter Matteotti), that were begun during Belloni's tenure.

The road linking Piazza Cordusio and Piazza San Ambrogio, although it was never built, provides an early indication of Albertini's plans for the redevelopment of central Milan. It also sheds light on how concerns about traffic and hygiene, which had preoccupied city officials, engineers, and others involved in planning debates in Italy from the late 1880s, could be linked with fascist programs. Beginning at Piazza Cordusio, the road, featured in one of several

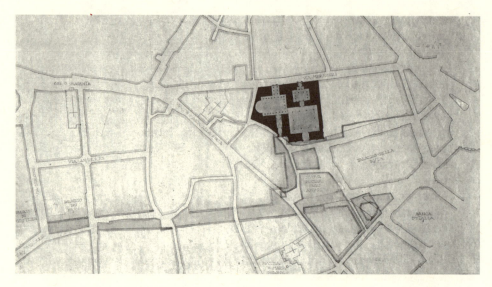

Figure 3.3. Proposed plan for the new business district in central Milan, October 1927. Archivio Storico Camera di Commercio, Milan.

plans for portions of central Milan presented to the public in 1928, would have passed the main post office (Palazzo delle Poste centrali, Paolo Cesa Bianchi, 1905–07, and Giannino Ferrini, 1910–12) and the Banca d'Italia (Luigi Broggi and Cesare Nava, 1907–12), then cut through the proposed new business district, offering a view of the Fascist Party's provincial headquarters on Via Nirone, before ending in Piazza Ambrogio, the site of the Monument to the Fallen (Monumento agli Caduti, 1924–28, designed by Giovanni Muzio and others), the anticipated future location of a new Palace of Justice, and the location of the complex of San Ambrogio – a reminder of Milan's role as a major religious and political centre of the Western Roman Empire. Movement through the city along the new axis would thus have presented a sequence of structures dedicated to the nation's economic, social/political, judicial, and spiritual life, respectively – the Exchange, Fascist Party Headquarters, Palace of Justice, and Monument to the Fallen – and culminated in a reminder of Milan's glorious past. The scale and form of the new street accommodated the fluid nature of automobile traffic coursing through the modern city and a new kind of visual awareness in which monuments were seen as part of a rapidly unfolding sequential display. In contrast to Rome, where new roads reframed ancient monuments, new thoroughfares in Milan incorporated reminders of the past within a spatial composition featuring buildings and sites associated

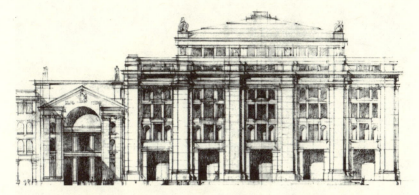

Figure 3.4. Mezzanotte, project for the Exchange, October 1927. Archivio Storico Camera di Commercio, Milan.

with the modern commercial city. More specifically, the new axis offered a fascist alternative to Via Dante, the street that best encapsulated the symbolic concerns and spatial strategies of the post-unification liberal city government, and it directed residents' and visitors' attention towards institutions and monuments that resonated with the ambitions of the new regime.

Inspired by northern European architectural models, in particular those of the Vienna School, Mezzanotte used the building's formal qualities to reinforce the city's image as an international centre of commercial and financial activity in an initial proposal from 1927 (figure 3.4). He emphasized the Stock Exchange, the larger and more important of the two markets, by centring the five-bay façade on Piazza degli Affari and capping it with a low dome. Pilasters extended from the base of the façade to the cornice, and windows and niches filled in the spaces between the pilasters on the upper stories. Set back from and to the left of the entrance to the Stock Exchange, the Commodities Exchange faced the small Piazzetta dei Grani. Mezzanotte defined this secondary entrance by giving it a large central arch framed by Ionic pilasters, which reached nearly the full height of the façade. A pediment supported by pilasters and an attic topped by two sculptures on either side completed the composition. The main façade's simplified classical forms and minimal ornament also echoed Ulisse Stacchini's contemporary proposals for the massive new Central Train Station (1912–31), a symbol of fascism's commitment to modernization and Milan's strategic importance to the national economy.[11] However, despite the financial community's historical connection to northern Europe, Belloni and Tarlarini, the president and vice-president of the council, appear to have

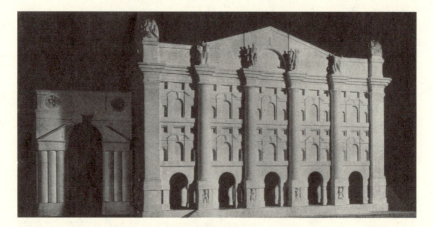

Figure 3.5. Model of the Exchange. *Rassegna di Architettura*, no. 3 (1932): 98.

been reluctant to embrace the international and utilitarian associations of this scheme.

Mezzanotte obsessively revised his project throughout the following year, and the changes he made suggest that the council's most influential members favoured a more obviously monumental neoclassicism (figure 3.5).[12] In subsequent versions, Mezzanotte raised the attic of the Commodities Exchange in order to more clearly evoke antique examples. In addition, he broke the pediment and substituted the pair of Ionic pilasters for three engaged Tuscan Doric columns to make the composition appear more sculptural. For the Stock Exchange, Mezzanotte reinforced associations with the classical temple, a building type commonly employed as precedent for important residential and civic buildings in Milan since the eighteenth century, by removing the low dome – an architectural feature rarely used for Italian civic structures. Instead, he finished the attic with a high entablature and pediment pierced by a thermal window. The primary feature of the main façade became four enormous engaged Doric columns, each of which measured more than six and a half feet in width and eighteen feet in height.[13] He ornamented the base of each column with allegorical sculptures representing the four elements – earth, air, fire, and water – by Gemignano Cibau and Leone Lodi. These high-relief sculptures alluded to the natural forces behind Milan's diverse economy and the range of markets housed within the complex. In contrast, the vignettes of an idealized peasant society sculpted for the top of each column more narrowly exalted the region's agricultural heritage. Although Mezzanotte continued to revise the window treatments and other details, the basic organization of the two façades would remain the same until the final stage of the project, when changes to the urban program resulted in a significant modification to the façade of the Commodities Exchange. Mezzanotte's repetition of classical motifs – the arch, column, and pediment – not only accommodated the financial community's preference for architectural forms that conveyed stability and permanence but also represented a distinctly Milanese interpretation of the monumental classicism favoured by the regime during the mid-1920s.

The fascist regime, like the previous liberal state, employed a style of celebratory neoclassicism in an effort to transcend the nation's deep historical and cultural divisions and foster a sense of national identity and purpose. Projects such as Marcello Piacentini's Monument to Victory in Bolzano (1925–28) showed how the lessons of ancient Rome could be transformed to serve the symbolic needs of the regime; and scholars have viewed the Exchange as an example of the regime's growing control over artistic production and its preference for a neoclassicism based on Roman antiquity.[14] However, the precedents favoured by Mezzanotte emphasized Milan's neoclassical tradition, embodied in the architecture of Luigi Cagnola (1762–1833), who designed the spare Ticinese Gate (Porta Ticinese, 1801–14) and the triumphant Arch of Victories (Arco delle Vittorie, later renamed the Arco della Pace, 1807–38).[15] Carried out during the prosperity and relative independence that Milan had enjoyed as the capital of first the Cisalpine Republic and then the Kingdom of Italy under Napoleon (1796–1814), these projects were elements of a much larger urban initiative that included the city's first Exchange (Borsa di Commercio) as part of a proposal by Giovanni Antonio Antolini (1753–1841) for a grand government centre along the Foro Bonaparte. In a lengthy article written for *Architettura e Arti Decorative* in 1928 (later *Architettura*), Mezzanotte celebrated Cagnola's "correct and severe" architecture and the French government's willingness to invest in the civic infrastructure of the city.[16] At the same time, he pointedly expressed concern that some architects were too constrained by the "superior will of the ruler" and produced bland and derivative projects.[17] Mezzanotte's Exchange embraces the robust monumentality associated with state-sponsored architecture during the first decade of fascist rule. However, his eclectic classicism reinforced connections to Napoleonic Milan, a strategy that strengthened Mussolini's legitimacy but also weakened the authority of Rome as the political centre of fascist Italy.

Mezzanotte's sensitivity to local architectural traditions, which was manifested not only in articles and books on Milanese architecture but also in his personal library, found further expression along the narrow and winding Via delle Orsole and the larger Via Meravigli.[18] The side of the Commodities Exchange along Via delle Orsole is lower than the main façade and preserves the scale, forms, and materials associated with the medieval and Renaissance city.[19] Elements such as the two low-faceted drums (a feature of local churches) and brick (a common building material in Milan for much of the city's history) introduced vernacular forms from this pre-industrial past (figure 3.6), an aspect of the project acknowledged by the local press.[20] In the wake of Italian unification the Milan-based architect and theorist Camillo Boito (1836–1914) had championed the simplicity and functionality of fourteenth-century Lombard architecture as an alternative to the classically derived monumental architecture most often employed by the state as a symbol of national identity. Mezzanotte's shift in palette, scale, and form not only related the building to its context but also showed how the region's medieval traditions, suggesting the legacy of Boito, could be used for contemporary civic buildings. Along the more dignified Via Meravigli, Mezzanotte preserved the nineteenth-century façade of Palazzo Turati. He thus designed the building to show the city three distinct façades: a monumental stone façade along Piazza degli Affari that was sympathetic to local neoclassical traditions and accorded with a growing official preference for classicism, a more modest brick façade along Via delle Orsole that evoked medieval and early Renaissance buildings in the city, and the existing façade along Via Meravigli that affirmed the importance of the nineteenth-century context. Despite its monumental scale and character, Mezzanotte's Exchange showed a sophisticated understanding of the urban and architectural character of the traditional city and remained oriented to Milanese, rather than national, architectural traditions.

During construction, workers uncovered the remains of a first-century CE Roman theatre at the southwest corner of the site. Although the adjacent Via San Vittore al Teatro and the curve of Via delle Orsole preserved the memory and form of the theatre, it had never been excavated. Its unearthing provided an opportunity to relate the Exchange, and by extension modern Milan, to its more remote antique past.[21] Mezzanotte, following orders from the board of antiquities (Soprintendenza alle Antichità), revised the project to preserve the ruins of the theatre and make them accessible to the public through an entrance along Via delle Orsole leading directly to the site.[22] He framed the opening with oversize fasces (the symbol of the Fascist Party and of Roman judicial authority) and planned to place a giant pine cone (*pigna*, the ancient Roman symbol of rebirth) in the niche above the door (see figure 3.6). Together, the fasces and the pine cone conflated Milan's ancient and modern history and served as a visual metaphor for Mussolini's rhetoric of cultural and spiritual renewal. The excavation and display of the ruins fit in with Mussolini's goal of fashioning his regime as the rightful heir of the Roman Empire, a project that was carried out all over Italy and especially in Rome, where such sites as

Figure 3.6. View of the Exchange along Via delle Orsole showing fasces framing the entrance to the Roman ruins. *Rassegna di Architettura*, no. 3 (1932): 105.

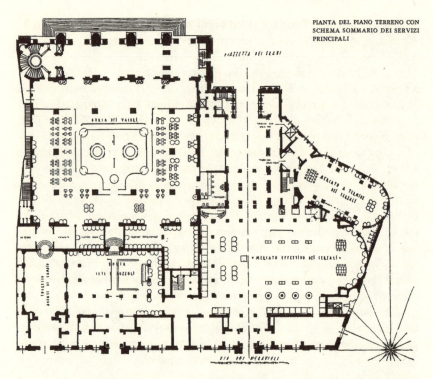

PIANTA DEL PIANO TERRENO CON
SCHEMA SOMMARIO DEI SERVIZI
PRINCIPALI

PALAZZO DELLE BORSE DI MILANO

Figure 3.7. Plan of ground floor, Exchange. *Rassegna di Architettura*, no. 3 (1932): 102.

the Mausoleum of Augustus fostered associations with the Roman emperor and served as a catalyst of urban renewal. In Milan, urban change provided similar opportunities to study the city's antique past – for example, at another dig that was underway along Via Manzoni – but Milan's more modest and less symbolically charged antique ruins never served as a focal point for major new construction.

Mezzanotte's plan for the ground floor of the building, which accommodated the principal markets, not only responded to functional needs by providing large open spaces well suited to commercial activity but also demonstrated a new way of thinking about how the Trading Exchange might engage with the urban and symbolic structure of Milan. To direct traders and the general public to and from the light-filled atriums that served as the main trading halls on the ground floor, Mezzanotte created two parallel colonnaded passageways. One passageway led from Piazza degli Affari to Via Meravigli and brought traders to and from the Stock Exchange (described as "a large covered piazza") as well as the Silk and Silkworm Cocoon Exchange (Borsa Sete e Bozzoli), which were closely tied to the city's textile industry (see figures 3.3 and 3.7).[23] In designing the latter space, Mezzanotte adapted the nineteenth-century Buffoli Gallery (Galleria Buffoli), part of the Palazzo Turati. On the opposite side of the building, a gallery connected the Piazzetta dei Grani and Via Meravigli and provided access to the Grain Market (Mercato dei Grani), which was formerly the Commodities Exchange. The form of these passageways echoed that of the arcade, a building type from the nineteenth century associated with the commercial activity of the modern city. Arcades of modest size were dispersed throughout the central business district – indeed, one already pierced the block – and the very large, centrally located nineteenth-century Galleria Vittorio Emanuele II remained a potent symbol of the city's commercial success.[24] The modified form of the arcade allowed Mezzanotte to address the functional requirements of the Exchange, to situate the new building within a local and even international vocabulary of commercial architecture, and to reframe this tradition within a new political context.

Mezzanotte's proposals for Piazza degli Affari and the adjacent Piazzetta dei Grani also made visible the city's layered history. With encouragement from the Provincial Economic Council, the city had approved "the setting up of a large piazza, closed to vehicular traffic and surrounded by *palazzi* containing porticos and underpasses."[25] Initial ideas for what this might look like appeared in the winning entries of the 1926 master plan competition. The first-place entry by Piero Portaluppi and Marco Semenza included a large arcaded piazza with a major new artery along its western side in front of the site of the Trading Exchange; the second-place entry by the Club of Urbanists (Club degli Urbanisti) also had a large piazza in front of the building, though one that was more modest in scale and open to traffic. Mezzanotte's plan to create two plazas – the larger Piazza degli Affari facing the Stock Exchange and the smaller Piazzetta dei Grani in front of the Commodities Exchange – reinforced the hierarchy of the two markets and helped mediate between the scale of Piazza degli Affari (and related new construction) and the more modest dimensions of the surrounding streets and buildings. Site plans show that he initially intended to preserve the irregular rear façade of the city's main post office (Palazzo delle Poste Centrali) and to construct a portico along the western side of Piazza degli Affari. The idiosyncratic shape of that piazza conveyed a sense of the district's nineteenth-century history, and the portico fulfilled the council's demand to have the piazza function as an open-air trading hall, a feature that evoked the "antique and rational model of the Italic and Mediterranean market."[26] However, the piazza's irregular shape was out of keeping with the plans for central Milan envisioned by the head of the city planning office, Cesare Albertini.[27] In subsequent versions, Mezzanotte masked the rear of the Palazzo delle Poste with new construction to correct geometric and formal irregularities, an urban strategy repeated whenever possible by the planning office in central Milan.

Towards the end of 1928, the city, despite its apparent sympathy with the aims of the national government, quietly dropped its ambitious plan for a new thoroughfare connecting Piazza Cordusio and Piazza San Ambrogio (although this corridor later reappeared in Albertini's 1930 and 1934 plans for Milan). A product of the Belloni administration, the proposed street was set aside or put on hold after Mussolini dismissed Belloni for gross mismanagement of city funds. In his place, Mussolini appointed the well-regarded marquis Giuseppe De Capitani d'Arzago (1928–29), the first of a series of *podestà* from Milan's noble families. An able manager, De Capitani had been president of the Lombard Savings Bank from 1922 to 1924 and an active member of the liberal right before joining the fascist movement. His appointment represented an attempt to bring fiscal responsibility to municipal operations, to stabilize local politics, and to restore confidence in the fascist government, particularly among the ruling classes, whose support of fascism depended on the regime's ability to correct the failures of the preceding liberal and socialist administrations.[28] Although the city had dropped its plan to make the Trading Exchange (and the related piazza) part of a comprehensive reworking of the city's centre, De Capitani decided to maintain the new business district as an important feature of that area of the city and supported the effort to create a large arcaded piazza fronting the Exchange. Indeed, he even helped fund the project.[29] Against this background of mutual agreement, the municipal government approved a plan for the two new piazzas in December 1928 (figure 3.8).[30]

The approved plan featured a portico separating the rectangular Piazza degli Affari from the extension of Via della Posta, which was all that remained of the road connecting Piazza Cordusio and Piazza San Ambrogio. The portico would limit vehicular traffic and provide shelter for traders (as required by the council). It also created an architecturally unified ensemble (as required by Albertini). In keeping with Mezzanotte's sensibilities elsewhere in this project, the columnar screen evoked local urban models. Most notably, it recalled the monumental free-standing Roman colonnade from the second century CE located just inside the medieval Porta Ticinese, Milan's most visually exciting antique monument. In 1935 the city demolished the buildings between the colonnade and San Lorenzo Maggiore, a building whose origins date to the

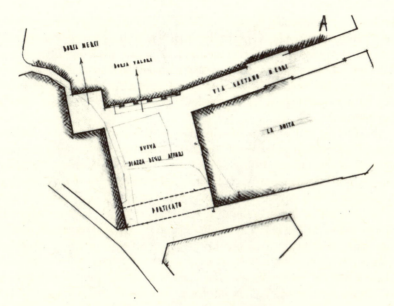

Figure 3.8. Plan for the Piazza degli Affari, December 1928. Archivio Storico
Camera di Commercio, Milan.

imperial Roman period, to create a new piazza for which Mussolini donated
a bronze copy of an antique statue of Emperor Constantine. The columnar
screen employed by Muzio to enclose the octagonal temple – the ceremonial
focus of the Monument to the Fallen in Piazza San Ambrogio – provided a
more contemporary reference. Not unlike this example, the portico for Piazza
degli Affari would have isolated and framed views of the Exchange for visitors
arriving at the complex along Via della Posta.

Despite the city's apparent support, the design of Piazza degli Affari proved
to be problematic from the start. The several versions of the project published
in local newspapers and journals in the following months showed that there
was never any consensus about its form or scale. The newspaper *Corriere
della Sera* published one version on 26 December 1928 (figure 3.9). In contrast to the plan discussed above, this arrangement depicted a much smaller
Piazza degli Affari and a building penetrated at either end by covered passages
(marked A and B) instead of the portico along the southern boundary. This
solution notably reduced the city's financial commitment by freeing up more
land for speculative builders, who held the rights to the properties along the
southern and eastern edge of the piazza. These developers – which included

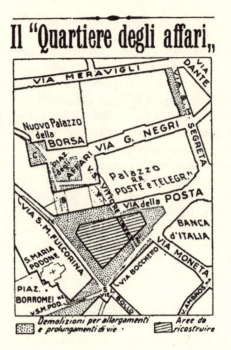

Figure 3.9. Plan for the Piazza degli Affari, 26 December 1928. From *Corriere della Sera*, 26 December 1928.

the Società Feltrinelli, Società Roma, and Società Immobilare Bocchetto – claimed that the proposed plan eliminated any possibility for profit and that it violated contracts.[31] Indicative of the uncertainty surrounding the scheme, the Milan-based architecture journal *Rassegna di Architettura* published another version a month later (figure 3.10). Mezzanotte, in an effort to restore the original scale and intent of the piazza and accommodate the demands of the speculators, enlarged the piazza by extending new construction to the south and inserted a portico around three sides of the piazza. However, neither this nor other similar proposals seemed to be of interest to the municipal government.

In January 1930, Albertini notified Mezzanotte that the city could not proceed with the existing plan.[32] The Ministry of Communications, the government agency responsible for the Palazzo delle Poste, also objected to the city's plan for the project, asserting that Piazza degli Affari and the related new construction eliminated valuable street frontage and limited vehicular access to the post office – both essential to the ministry's operations – and compromised its stature in the district.[33] As the city revised its plans to accommodate the objections

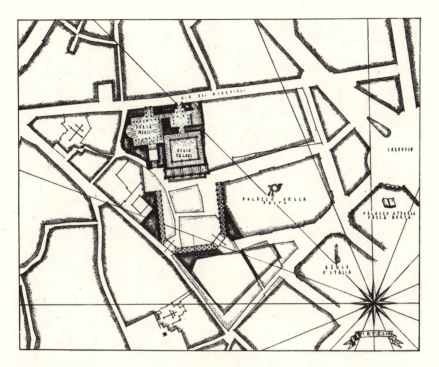

Figure 3.10. Site plan for the Exchange, 1929. *Rassegna di Architettura,* no. 1 (1929): 6.

of the ministry, developers pressured the city to widen Via San Vittore al Teatro and eliminate the secondary piazza in order to allow for taller buildings.[34] The company holding the majority interest – Società Immobilare Bocchetto – even offered to finance the demolition of the existing block of buildings occupying what was to be Piazza degli Affari, provided the city would enlarge the area on which they would be allowed to build. Already deeply in debt and bound by contracts, the city capitulated and drew up new plans.[35] Angry and frustrated, Mezzanotte sent repeated letters to Tarlarini, the vice-president of the council, outlining the history of the project and offering solutions that would maintain the character of the piazza as it had first been conceived and also meet the requirements of speculators.[36] In particular, he objected to the removal of the secondary piazza, the elimination of which created "an unpleasing triangular area with a form that is totally opposed to the norms of urban planning."[37] In the end, the city approved the plan for Piazza degli Affari that limited its financial obligations.[38] Published in the spring of 1931, the new plan significantly reduced the size of that piazza and omitted the porticos around its perimeter,

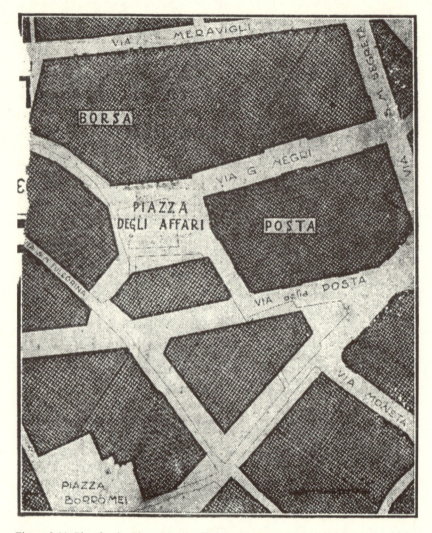

Figure 3.11. Plan for the Piazza degli Affari, spring 1931. From *L'Ambrosiano*, 4 June 1931.

did away with the Piazzetta dei Grani, and required that no changes be made to the post office (figure 3.11). Open to vehicular traffic, the proposed plaza undermined the formal integrity of the original project and limited the piazza's utility as a market and meeting place, but provided ample space for new construction around its southern and western sides.

Municipal support for the creation of a new business district faded follow-ing the dismissal of De Capitani as *podestà* of Milan and the appointment of Duke Marcello Visconti di Modrone (1929–35) to replace him. Visconti di Modrone – a member of one of Milan's most noble families, an industrialist, and the first head of the municipal government to not have a personal relation-ship to Mussolini – continued De Capitani's efforts to restore the city's financial stability.[39] In the first years of his tenure, he set aside prestigious public-works projects in favour of more pragmatic undertakings, including the construc-tion of new roads, sewer lines, schools, and neighbourhood markets.[40] These initiatives contributed to the welfare of the city and provided jobs at a time when unemployment was high, a consequence of the collapse of the American stock market in 1929.[41] They also acknowledged recent legislation intended to limit urban growth (passed in 1928 and 1931) and Mussolini's effort to secure Rome's position as the political, cultural, and symbolic centre of fascist Italy.[42] Nevertheless, in the early 1930s the municipal government's investment in the city began to resume its momentum, and Mussolini again made regular visits to Milan – in May 1930, December 1931, and October 1932 and 1934 – to supervise and inaugurate new construction.[43] New buildings lined Piazza della Vetra and Corso Littorio and began to fill in around Via Larga and between Piazza Fontana and Largo Augusto. Piazza degli Affari, however, remained an open construction site (figure 3.12).

Although the totalitarian ambitions of fascism discouraged public discourse, debate over the appropriate form of Piazza degli Affari entered the public arena during the year after the planning office first announced its plans to significantly alter the piazza. Perhaps prompted by Mezzanotte – who knew Mussolini's brother, the director of *Il Popolo d'Italia* – that newspaper criticized the city for reducing the piazza "to an area of little more than 2,000 square meters," making it a traffic centre rather than a gathering place, and for eliminating the Piazzetta dei Grani, resulting in the loss of the "majestic" arched entrance proposed by Mezzanotte for the Commodities Exchange.[44] The local fascist-controlled paper *L'Ambrosiano* published three articles in which Ferdinando Reggiori, a Milanese critic, architect, and planner and one of the authors of a comprehensive critique of Albertini's plan for the centre of the city published in 1930, faulted the city for backing away from the scale and formal order of the piazza as it had planned from 1928 to 1930.[45] Echoing Mezzanotte's con-cerns, Reggiori argued that the design was governed by the vagaries of specu-lative interest rather than by planning principles, and he described the scheme as "terrible from the point of view of the plan" and lamented that "its setting and aesthetic aspects will be even worse."[46] The controversy also attracted the attention of the head of the National Fascist Syndicate of Architects,

Figure 3.12. View of Exchange showing the Piazza degli Affari before construction.
From Lissone and della Morte, *La Milano voluta dal Duce e la vecchia Milano.*

Alberto Calza-Bini, who, as spokesman for the Council of Public Works, con-
cluded that the current solution failed to meet the needs of either the city or
the Exchange and urged the municipal administration to reconsider the plan.[47]
The conflicting interests of private and public agencies, the entrenched local
opposition, the absence of support from national officials, and the city's inabil-
ity to devote resources to urban improvements continued to delay the project's
resolution.

   While in Milan to celebrate the tenth anniversary of the March on Rome
at the end of October 1932, Mussolini inaugurated the Trading Exchange
in front of crowds squeezed into the streets surrounding the new building.[48]
Although the press celebrated the building for its grandeur and the modernity
of its systems – heating, cooling, communications, and an electronic board
displaying stock quotes – Mezzanotte was faulted by fellow architect Giuseppe
Pagano for his extensive use of stone.[49] Moreover, questions about how the
complex would relate to the surrounding network of streets persisted, and

cartoons lampooned the city's failure to create the new piazza. Under *Podestà* Guido Pesenti (1935–38), who enjoyed personal ties to Mussolini and the status that came from being a *sansepolcrista* (an original member of the Fascist Party), the municipal government began to take serious steps to complete Albertini's master plan, which had been approved in 1934 despite significant local opposition.[50] Shortly after taking office, Pesenti created a commission to address the projects that most substantially altered the form and character of the city's centre.[51] These included the controversial reorganization of Piazza San Babila, where Emilio Lancia's Palazzo del Toro (1935–39) was under construction, and Piazza Diaz, which had begun to take shape with Piero Portaluppi's Palazzo dell'Istituto Nazionale delle Assicurazioni (1933–36), as well as the area surrounding the new Palace of Justice and the Monforte district. The commission did not identify Piazza degli Affari as a major priority, and it was not until 1939, under the administration of *Podestà* Gian Giacomo Gallarati Scotti (1938–43), that the city government began to take an interest in it.[52]

Published in local papers in 1939, the city's new plan showed Piazza degli Affari framed by new construction on all sides and separated from vehicular traffic along Via della Posta (figure 3.13). The building between Piazza degli Affari and Via della Posta, designed by Emilio Lancia, had a portico along its front, and it was joined to adjacent structures by means of arches, a solution that would limit (but not eliminate) vehicular traffic and accommodate traders. The city negotiated with the Ministry of Communication as well as with the telephone company Stipel to resolve the eastern edge of the piazza. In the final agreement, the city agreed to cede the land to be occupied by the new construction, provided that Stipel, whose offices were housed in the portion of the palazzo adjacent to the new piazza, demolish and reconstruct the palazzo in accordance with the master plan at their own expense.[53] Although renderings showed porticos on the eastern and western edges of the piazza, these were never executed, and the utilitarian monumentality of these flat-fronted buildings does little to bring it to life. The plan restored the piazza to its original size of just over thirty-two thousand square feet. Nevertheless, it eliminated the secondary piazza and doubled the width of Via Santa Maria Fulcorina (from twenty-three to forty-six feet), a move that satisfied the developers' concerns about making a profit and the city's desire to improve circulation. The Piazza degli Affari, begun more than a decade after the council and the city first announced their intention to create a new business district centred on the Trading Exchange, represented an uneasy compromise between the various agencies involved in the transformation of the centre of the city.

Il portico dei mercanti - La riforma del palazzo delle Poste - L'allargamento di via Santa Maria Fulcorina

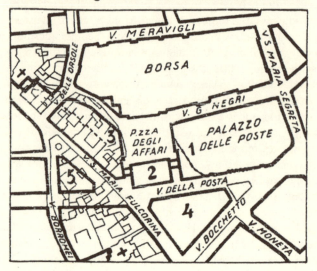

Figure 3.13. Plan for the Piazza degli Affari, 1939. From *Corriere della Sera*, 10 August 1939.

At the end of the 1920s, the president of the Provincial Economic Council had envisioned that the new Exchange and related business district would be a significant element of the municipal government's plans to reconfigure Milan. The new building offered the business community much-needed new facilities and the state a means of presenting the commercial success of Milan in fascist terms. The urban dimension of the project was to provide additional space for trading activities, redevelop a depressed area in the city's centre, and place the Exchange within the symbolic context of the city as a whole. The failure to complete the project along its original lines was the result of numerous factors. Disagreements between the various agencies involved in the project (viz., the council, the city, speculative developers, and the Ministry of Communications), criticism from cultural leaders, the variable direction of the municipal administration, and the absence of a powerful local patron ultimately created an environment in which the project stagnated while the city invested its time and money elsewhere. In the same years that the project for Piazza degli Affari floundered, the municipal government oversaw the completion of Corso Littorio (now Corso Matteotti) and the related Piazza Crespi (now Piazza Meda), which were developed by several major banks and the Crespi family, a local industrial dynasty and the owner of *Corriere della Sera*. Even a bribe from the minister of finance, who oversaw the Stock Exchange, failed to restore the municipal government's interest in Piazza degli Affari.[54]

The example of Piazza degli Affari demonstrates not only that Milan's urban transformation required constant negotiation but also that the new political order had only partial control over existing economic, cultural, and political forces. Even after the rise of fascism, established power structures remained in place and created an environment in which the political objectives of fascism were always conditioned by local interests, sometimes quite dramatically. Anticipating the elimination of the Piazzetta dei Grani from the project, Mezzanotte began to work on a new solution for the entrance to the Commodities Exchange in the fall of 1930. In place of the travertine triumphal arch originally projected, Mezzanotte now proposed a simple brick arch (visible to the left of the Stock Exchange in figure 3.12).[55] Next to the monumental stone façade of the Stock Exchange and intended as a temporary solution, the entrance has the quality of an architectural fragment or ruin and offers a quiet commentary on what was to have been a major feature of the city. The Trading Exchange and the modest Piazza degli Affari are ultimately best understood not as symbols of the authority of the fascist regime, but rather as a record of the competing forces and conflicting interests that controlled Italy's commercial centre in the interwar period.

CHAPTER FOUR

Fascist Authority:
The Palace of Justice, 1932–1940

Justice must preside over men's lives, it must have a universal character.
— Arnaldo Mussolini, 1930[1]

After Mussolini formed a dictatorship in 1925, he aggressively employed established instruments of state control – the police, army, and legislature – to reinforce and secure his command. Force and punishment served as a method to control and direct the population, even if the kinds of terror unleashed in Italy never reached the extremes of Nazi Germany or Stalinist Russia. In the same years that Mussolini approved a series of new legal codes authored by a conservative fascist theorist, Minister of Justice Alfredo Rocco (1925–32), the municipal government began construction of a massive new Palace of Justice (Palazzo di Giustizia, 1932–40) in central Milan (figure 4.1). Designed by the politically powerful Roman architect Marcello Piacentini (1881–1961), this building was not only the largest building constructed in Milan in the interwar period but also the most important of a number of law courts built during the fascist era.[2] The project provided the regime with an unparalleled opportunity to demonstrate the strength of the central government in Milan, which, with its great wealth and influence, threatened the authority of Rome. Indeed the stark and physically overwhelming building remains the most forceful architectural demonstration of state power in that city, where it serves as an imposing setting for legal dramas.

Preliminary planning for the new Palace of Justice began in 1923 with identifying an appropriate site for the project, a task that Mayor Luigi Mangiagalli (1922–26) assigned to the planning commission, which was headed by liberal engineer and city planner Cesare Chiodi. The municipal government was responsible by law for providing adequate accommodations for the judiciary.

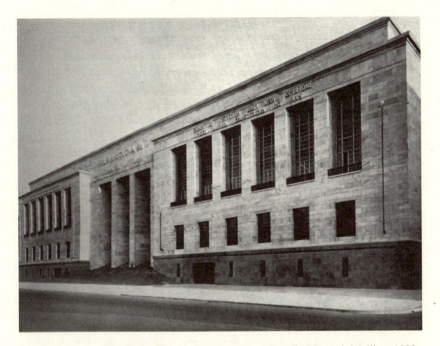

Figure 4.1. Palace of Justice (Palazzo di Giustizia), Marcello Piacentini, Milan, 1932–40. *Architettura*, nos. 1–2 (1942): 1.

Crowded conditions and outdated facilities in the late-sixteenth-century Palazzo del Capitano di Giustizia, the traditional home of the Milan judiciary located behind the cathedral, justified new construction. However, little had come of the city's efforts since officials had begun to discuss the need for new law courts a decade earlier.[3] In keeping with Milan's commitment to the rational reorganization of major civic institutions, Mangiagalli hoped to consolidate all the law courts and offices distributed throughout the city's centre in a single building.[4] For Chiodi, the new building presented an opportunity to relieve congestion there and to revitalize an underutilized area of the city. After the state withdrew its offer to sell a promising site on Via Parini, the commission proposed the site of the former slaughterhouse along Bastione di Porta Magenta (now Viale Papiniano) on the southwestern edge of the city.[5] Chiodi favoured this site because it met several important criteria: it moved the courts away from the dense area around the cathedral; it was one of the few sites within the Spanish Walls large enough to house the law courts; and it was publicly owned, which gave the city a purchasing advantage. In addition, Chiodi

anticipated that the new construction would rehabilitate the quarter by spur-
ring residential and commercial growth there. This would not only improve
the economic and social composition of the surrounding community but also
increase the value of city-owned property nearby.[6] Mussolini and Rocco (president of the Milan Chamber of Deputies, soon to be appointed minister of justice) reviewed the proposal and approved the city's initiative in August 1924.[7]
Despite consensus on this project at the highest levels, local lawyers and magistracy were outraged when they learned of the city's plan.

The law community vigorously attacked the proposal in the press, arguing
that there was little about the site that made it a suitable location for one of
the most important courts in the nation. To begin with, although it was located
along a major ring road, the site was not well connected to the city's centre or
to major transportation hubs. Perhaps more important, it was surrounded by
residential buildings of modest size, a prison stood in the immediate vicinity,
and it was isolated from leading business, cultural, and government centres – in
short, there was little about the location that conveyed the courts' significance
as a prestigious civic institution. The head of the Court of Appeals in Milan,
Piero Alberici, captured the spirit of their objections when he declared that
the proposal would effectively send "justice to the slaughterhouse."[8] It soon
became apparent that the project would not go forward, and hopeful architects
sent alternative proposals directly to the mayor and to Mussolini. Some of the
architects suggested adapting large-scale structures of historical importance,
such as the medieval Castello Sforzesco and the Ospedale Maggiore. Others
advocated new construction.[9] All of them proposed sites within the centre of
the city, and most endeavoured to make a clear link between the new Palace of
Justice and the existing urban hierarchy. Mussolini, either persuaded by their
arguments or concerned about gaining their political support, intervened on
behalf of the lawyers and magistracy and urged the city to find another location
for the Palace of Justice, one that was within the symbolic centre of the city.[10]

In 1926, Mangiagalli (a member of the Italian Liberal Party) was replaced
by Ernesto Belloni, the city's first fascist mayor (*podestà*). Soon after being
appointed to that position, Belloni solicited new ideas for the site of the Palace
of Justice as part of the 1926–27 master plan competition. In response to
Mussolini's recent directive, the city had already begun to consider the former
Infantry Barracks (Caserme di Fanteria Garabaldi) on the Piazza San Ambrogio
as a possible location for the judiciary, but no specific plans had been drawn
up.[11] Piero Portaluppi and Marco Semenza, the team that was awarded first
prize, argued that the site was too cramped.[12] Instead, they made the Palace
of Justice the centrepiece of a monumental complex of gigantic proportions
behind the Renaissance Ospedale Maggiore (established in 1456). The hospital

had already begun to expand into this area and a few years later would begin to construct a vast new complex in the Niguardia (Giulio Marcovigi, Giulio Ulisse Arata, and Alessandro Tibaldi, 1932–39), one of the municipalities absorbed into greater Milan in 1923. Rendered with an architectural uniformity and sense of civic grandeur that was reminiscent of the American City Beautiful movement, the complex envisioned by Portaluppi and Semenza comprised various public buildings and featured an open lawn lined by "grand palaces linked by porticos to the Palace of Justice."[13] The winners of the second-place prize, the Club of Urbanists (Club dei Urbanisti), proposed a similar urban arrangement.[14] The report issued by the artistic subcommittee, the body charged with evaluating the aesthetic merits of the proposals, clarified the perceived strengths and weaknesses of each proposal.

The subcommittee, which included Piacentini, the politically powerful and influential future architect of the Palace of Justice, paid particular attention to the formal and symbolic objectives of each proposal. Although it criticized Portaluppi and Semenza for their intent to radically restructure central Milan, the group praised the team's "monumental nucleus" behind the Ospedale Maggiore. This feature of the plan, like Giovanni Antolini's project for the Foro Bonaparte and Giuseppe Mengoni's Piazza del Duomo, proposed a unified and grand architectural and urban ensemble for the centre of the city.[15] The subcommittee judged the Club of Urbanists' submission to be less successful because of its elongated form, its inclusion of buildings intended for private use, and its prominent placement of a concert hall.[16] Neither proposal appears to have been seriously considered by municipal authorities. However, the idea of redefining an entire section of the city anticipated the scale and reach of the final project and established the city's preference for plans in which important government buildings, rather than cultural institutions, were the focal point of large urban and architectural compositions.

In 1927, Belloni signed an agreement – which became a law the following year – that committed the city to spend more than 250 million lire on the construction of new buildings for the state in exchange for the transfer of a substantial portion of state-owned property.[17] The property listed in the accord included the Artillery Barracks on Corso di P. Vittoria, a site that the city had often considered as a possible home for the Palace of Justice (figure 4.2). The parcel was strategically positioned along one of Milan's principal thoroughfares just beyond the city's innermost ring. Major institutions already established in the quarter included the city's main synagogue (Luca Beltrami and Luigi Tenenti, 1890–192), the Humanitarian Society (Società Umanitaria), and the Ospedale Maggiore. Corso di P. Vittoria, a principal east-west artery, led from the city's centre beyond the Spanish Walls to residential neighbourhoods

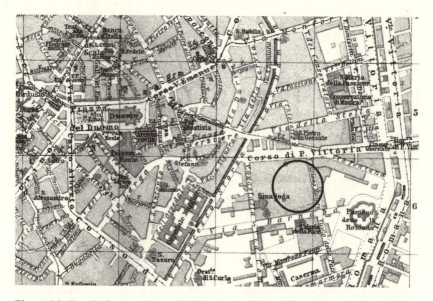

Figure 4.2. Detail of map of central Milan circa 1906 showing the site of the Palace of Justice on Corso di P. Vittoria. From Baedeker, *Italy: Handbook for Travellers.*

developed in the 1920s and out to the future home of the airport in Linate (designed by Gianluigi Giordani in the mid-1930s). The site of the former barracks, approximately one-quarter of a mile (four hundred metres) from the Piazza del Duomo and the Palazzo del Capitano di Giustizia (the traditional centre of the city and home of the law courts, respectively), met the judiciary's expectations and Mussolini's demands for a centrally located building and provided a sufficiently large plot of land on which the city could construct a massive new building.

The sprawling site included private residences, a synagogue, and a convent, and the city planned not only to use it for new construction but also to reconfigure it for redevelopment. In the first plan drawn up by the city, the original block – bound by Corso di P. Vittoria, Via Manara, Via Guastalla, and Via S. Barnaba – was divided into four relatively equal units by introducing two new streets, Via Freguglia and Via Zaccaria, thus imposing a geometric regularity onto what had been a large block accommodating a range of functions. The city designated two blocks for the Palace of Justice, one facing Corso di P. Vittoria and the other behind it. The National Fascist Syndicate of Architects (Sindacato Nazionale Fascista degli Architetti), which was led by Alberto Calza-Bini and included Piacentini as one of its members, criticized the city's

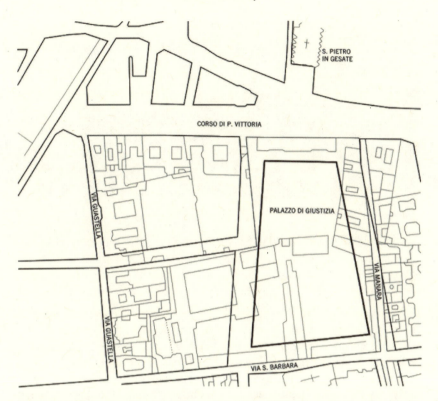

Figure 4.3. Site plan for the Palace of Justice, 1930. From *Il Popolo d'Italia*, 21 August 1930, redrawn by Coran.

decision to house the Palace of Justice in two separate buildings and asked the agency to revise its plan.[18] In response, the city conceded and created a large trapezoidal site slightly set back from Corso di P. Vittoria for a single free-standing new building (figure 4.3). The resulting footprint competed in size with the largest buildings in central Milan: the Ospedale Maggiore, the Castello Sforzesco, and the Duomo. As in the initial version, the plan left the synagogue and residential buildings along Via Guastalla largely untouched but marked for demolition the barracks, numerous residential buildings elsewhere within the block, and a convent, despite the protests of local church officials.[19] At the same time, the city proposed reworking the area that had housed the city's open-air Verziere Market until it was moved in 1911 to an indoor facility further from the city's centre. The redevelopment of this area with broad

Figure 4.4. View along Corso di P. Vittoria from the Palace of Justice. The church of San Pietro in Gessate and adjacent orphanage are in the foreground. Visible on the far right is the crown of the Fascist Syndicate of Industry Headquarters (Casa dei Sindacati Fascisti), Angelo Bordoni, Luigi Maria Caneva, and Antonio Carminati, 1930–2. *Rassegna d'Architettura*, no. 3 (1939): 108.

new roads lined by office and residential buildings was intended to effectively extend the symbolic centre of the city along Corso di P. Vittoria.[20]

The new street pattern signalled the city's intent to use to use the project as a catalyst for change throughout the district. The broad streets framing the Palace of Justice made it possible for new buildings to reach a height of seventy-eight feet (twenty-four metres), approximately twice the height of existing ones, resulting in a 150 per cent increase in the site's building volume, from about 26,500 to 3,980,000 square feet (about 75,000 to 112,680 cubic metres).[21] The city planned to sell lots to private developers and anticipated that a wealthy residential quarter with spacious modern *palazzi* would surround the Palace of Justice. New construction along Corso di P. Vittoria was to take the place of the modest brick and stucco structures that defined the street edge (figure 4.4). Plans were already under way for the construction of the Fascist Syndicate of Industry Headquarters (Casa dei Sindacati Fascisti dell'Industria, and now Camera del Lavoro), a symbol of fascism's new economic model, along Corso di P. Vittoria, a short distance from the new Palace of Justice; and in 1938 work started on a new police headquarters building opposite the Palace of Justice. The arrangement of these buildings resembles that of finance minister Quintino Stella's bureaucratic centre established on Via XX Settembre in Rome after the unification of Italy and of Piacentini's more recent proposals to position government institutions along the major arteries extending out of the national capital.[22] Like the Roman examples, the transformation of Corso di P. Vittoria offered an expedient solution to the persistent problem of reconciling the modern needs of large government institutions with the contraints imposed by the compact centre of the historic city.

On 22 April 1929, the *podestà* of Milan, Giuseppe de Capitani D'Arzago, announced that the city would hold a competition for the Palace of Justice. The competition brief stressed that the new building was to be "simple and severe" and that the architectural design should be worthy not only of justice but also "of Milan and the Fascist age."[23] The terms "simple" and "severe" encouraged architects to reject the lavish ornament of the most important and symbolic court in Italy, Guglielmo Calderini's Palace of Justice (1888–1910) in Rome, and other monuments associated with the bourgeois excess of liberal Italy. Instead, they encouraged participants to adopt an architectural vocabulary appropriate to the militaristic and populist rhetoric of fascism.[24] Competitions, a regular feature of interwar Italian architecture, helped generate public support, provided an illusion of broad involvement, and enabled bureaucratsto generate ideas for projects without being obliged to commit to the results.[25] It was no different. One Milanese architect and city planner, Ferdinando Reggiori, alluded to its exploratory nature when he complained that it was "poorly organized ..., lacked guarantees for the participants," offered only "modest prizes," and did not reveal "the names of the judges in advance."[26]

Capitani D'Arzago's successor as *podestà*, Duke Marcello Visconti di Modrone (1929–35), appointed the jury, which was composed primarily of city officials and representatives of the law courts.[27] The only designers on the jury were Mario Sironi, a prominent artist and the principal illustrator for Mussolini's journal *Il Popolo d'Italia*, and two architects, Ulisse Stacchini and Piacentini. Stacchini, a pupil of Calderini, brought his understanding of Roman monumentality and Beaux Arts planning to the jury discussion; at that time, he was overseeing the completion of his massive Central Station in Milan, which opened with great fanfare in 1931. Piacentini (the son of Roman architect Pio Piacentini) had maintained his contacts in Milan since acting as a juror on the 1926–27 master plan competition; he served as an adviser to the city planning office and designed, with Ernesto Rapisardi, the National Bank for Social Insurance (Cassa Nazionale per le Assicurazione Sociali, 1928–31) in Milan. He had also recently completed the Palace of Justice in Messina, Sicily (1923–29), again with Rapisardi. His working relationship with the Milan planning office and recent work in Messina suggests that he may have participated in the formulation of the site plan and the writing of the competition brief for the new building. Although the jury's deliberations have not been located, the competition results provide a window into the decision-making process of which Piacentini was an integral part and help clarify official expectations for the project.

Not surprisingly, Italy's leading practitioners did not waste their time developing proposals for the project, and the city received only eleven entries, all by relatively unknown architects. After deliberating for nearly six months, the jury announced that none of the projects merited first prize.[28] Second prize went to the most unconventional design in both plan and elevation, Angelo Bordoni, Luigi Maria Caneva, and Antonio Carminati's "White, red, black" ("Bianco, rosso, nero").[29] That team proposed a dramatic projecting curved entrance along the Corso di P. Vittoria, with protruding brick bays reinforced by colossal stone columns capped by statues, an arrangement that recalled Mezzanotte's Exchange in Milan as well as Carlo Broggi's entry in the League of Nations competition of 1927. The jury expressed concern that the project was "perhaps excessively simple" and that the semicircular entrance served to "diminish rather than to augment the impression of grandeur."[30] The jury similarly faulted the other entries for their failure "to achieve the impression of a public building that was desired."[31] The city and the judiciary agreed that the new building needed to be visually arresting and physically imposing in order to convey the authority of the legal system.

A month after announcing the results of the failed competition, *Podestà* Visconti di Modrone formed a commission to determine the best procedure for finding an architect who could carry the project to completion. The commission included members of the Milan judiciary and the city government, several of whom had participated as jurors in the competition.[32] Some members of the commission proposed asking the winners of the second-place prize to revise their project. However, the influential city councilor Cesare Dorici noted that those architects had limited experience and were already engaged in building the nearby Fascist Syndicate of Industry Headquarters (1930–32). He also effectively dissuaded members of the commission who thought the city should hold another competition, on the grounds that this would be costly and time consuming and could not guarantee satisfactory results.[33] Guided by Dorici, the commission determined that the *podestà* should have exclusive authority to appoint an "illustrious" architect. The commission stipulated only that the architect take into consideration the results of the competition and work closely with the city's Office of Technical Services, a move intended to give the city some control over the project, for which they had financial responsibility.[34]

The worldwide depression triggered by the collapse of the American stock market, together with the failure of the housing sector in Milan, created an environment in which the city could not fulfill its obligations to provide new buildings for the state.[35] While the municipal administration stalled, Minister of Justice Alfredo Rocco, the head of the Milan judiciary Piero Alberici, and members of the law community in Milan sent letters to public officials, published essays in the city's leading papers, and otherwise pressured the city to take action.[36] In June 1931, *Podestà* Visconti di Modrone and Dorici, who had served briefly as deputy *podestà*, travelled to Rome to renegotiate the city's financial obligations.[37] Crafted with Rocco, Alberici, and party secretary Giovanni Giurati, the new arrangement included the transfer of the Corso di P. Vittoria site to the city, with the express intent that the site be used for the Palace of Justice and that the building be completed within five years.[38] In August 1931 the *podestà* and the deputy *podestà* met once again with Mussolini and other officials in Rome to discuss construction projects underway in, and planned for, Milan.[39] In early November 1931 the *podestà* of Milan publicly announced that Piacentini would design the new Palace of Justice. The announcement made clear the city's commitment to the new building and placed at the helm the man who had long directed the project from behind closed doors.[40]

Correspondence indicates that Piacentini had been working on plans for the new building since at least the end of 1930.[41] Given Dorici's efforts to place control of the project in the *podestà*'s hands, it seems likely that by the spring of 1930 the decision to appoint Piacentini had already been brokered. Although Piacentini never held an official position within the government, he remains the architect most intimately associated with Mussolini's government. The same year that Piacentini received the Palace of Justice project, Mussolini chose him to design the University City (Città Universitaria, 1932–35) in Rome, and he later directed the massive E'42 Exhibition (later known as EUR, Esposizione Universale di Roma, 1937–43) just south of the capital.[42] Piacentini's stature was enhanced by the friendships and contacts he inherited from his father, facilitated by his ability to manoeuvre within powerful circles, and maintained by his numerous professional appointments. In the case of the Palace of Justice, Piacentini had been involved with the project at nearly every stage of its progress through local and national bureaucratic channels. He served as a juror for both the master plan and the law courts competitions, experiences that afforded him a unique opportunity to shape the contours of the project.[43] His position as a leading member of the National Fascist Syndicate of Architects and his connection to Dorici enabled him to persuade the city to set aside a massive site for the new building. He understood that the judiciary wanted a building that occupied a central position in the city, for practical and symbolic reasons. He also recognized that the planning office, headed by Albertini, favoured efficiency over aesthetics when it came to planning decisions. Finally, his awareness of the project's symbolic value was shaped by

Rocco, who as minister of justice pushed the project forward in its initial stages and then as rector of the "La Sapienza" University of Rome (1932–35) oversaw the completion of Piacentini's new campus there. Piacentini comprehended that the new Palace of Justice should not only be a monument to the authority of the state – a pointed message in a city that was more oriented to commercial than political concerns and had long resisted the influence of Rome – but should also symbolize the unique historical position of the fascist regime.

In Rome on 5 February 1932, approximately six months after having been officially handed the commission, Piacentini presented his design for the Palace of Justice to Mussolini for approval.[44] After reviewing the project, Mussolini pronounced it to be "at once grandiose and rational, and thus worthy of Justice, the Regime, and Milan."[45] Modifications made during the building's lengthy construction – for example, sanctions imposed on Italy after the invasion of Ethiopia in 1936 probably forced Piacentini to restrict the use of glass – had the effect of reinforcing its monumental character.[46] Piacentini concentrated the visual and spatial intensity of the project in the vestibule behind the principal entrance on Corso di P. Vittoria; none of the other entrances are as grand. After passing through an imposing tripartite portal reached by low-rising granite stairs, the visitor stands within a rectangular entrance hall or atrium that fills two levels of the palazzo and extends to the spacious exterior Court of Honour (Cortile d'Onore) (figure 4.5). Diffuse light filters through windows overlooking the court and down from corridors on the second storey. Not unlike the portals on the exterior, gigantic piers contribute to the exaggerated sense of scale, and opulent materials augment the sense of grandeur.[47] At the time of its completion, the building's total area (about 323,000 square feet [30,000 square metres]) was as large as that of the largest building in central Milan, and its height of almost 125 feet (38 metres) overwhelmed surrounding buildings, most dramatically the modest fifteenth-century brick church of S. Pietro in Gessate on the opposite side of Corso di P. Vittoria. Suggesting that scale was a metaphor for progress, some critics viewed its great size as one of its principal accomplishments and noted that its sixty courtrooms and enormous total area would surpass those of the Palace of Justice in Rome, implying both that Milan had outdone Rome and that the fascist state had superseded the preceding liberal government.[48] The horizontal extension of Piacentini's building can also be understood as the Italian response to the American, German, and Russian use of steel (a material in short supply in Italy) to construct buildings of tremendous height. A few urban gestures – such as the tower located at the rear of the building on the corner of Via S. Barnaba and Via Freguglia – further augmented the building's visual prominence and did little to improve its relationship to its surroundings. Perhaps in part because it made so few

Figure 4.5. Entrance atrium, Palace of Justice. *Architettura*, nos. 1–2 (1942): 19.

references to its context, the building served as a model for other law courts built during this period, most notably the Palace of Justice in Palermo (Gaetano and Ernesto Rapisardi, 1938–57), which was intended to function as the symbolic and logistical headquarters of fascism's campaign against the Sicilian Mafia.

The compositional logic and rational organization of the various courts located within the building drew on Beaux-Arts planning models. Each side of the building provides an entrance to one of the courts: the front entrance on Corso di P. Vittoria leads to the Court of Appeals, the highest court in Milan; the side entrances along Via Freguglia and Via Manara lead to the Tribunal Court (*Tribunale*); and the rear entrance facing Via San Barbara leads to the Magistrate's Court (*Preture*). The tower held a library and legal archives (Archivio Notarile). Piacentini organized the various functions of the complex – accommodated largely in offices and courtrooms of varying dimensions – according to a grid broken by eight courtyards, which brought necessary light and air into the block (figure 4.6). He situated courtrooms adjacent to major entrances and at the end of the three major circulation halls or ambulatories. These halls extend across the width of the building to facilitate the movement of and provide space for the general public. To encourage

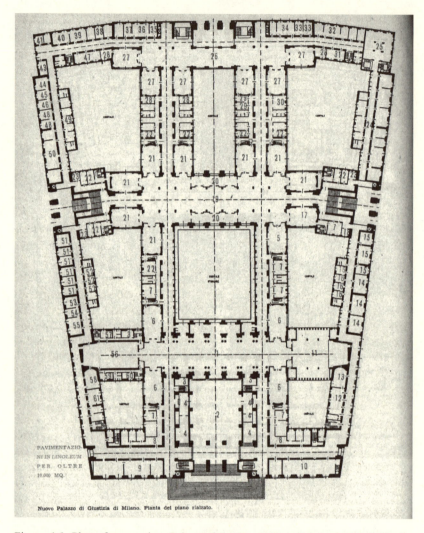

Figure 4.6. Plan of mezzanine, Palace of Justice. *Edilizia Moderna*, 37–9 (April–December 1942): 43.

the rapid and efficient circulation of people who worked in the building and to underscore the modernity of the endeavour, Piacentini made the ground level accessible to automobiles and provided parking for the members of the court near the "numerous elevators." These elevators carried members swiftly to their offices, which lined the extensive system of hallways that circulated throughout the building, without "passing through other offices or travelling a great distance by foot."[49] Following the traditional hierarchy in Italian buildings, Piacentini reserved the second storey for the most prestigious functions of the palazzo. Here he located the offices for the head of the Milan judiciary and the Civil Court of Appeals. By adjusting the size, material richness, and ornamentation of the entrance, vestibule, and ambulatory of each of the courts, he further articulated the relative position of each within the Italian legal system. The emphasis on order, hierarchy, and clarity echoed the rhetoric surrounding the contemporary redevelopment of central Milan, suggesting that the Palace of Justice could be understood as an abstract, idealized representation of a fascist city.

Despite the regime's desire to erect a building uniquely appropriate for its legal structure, the most important conceptual model for this project was Calderini's Palace of Justice in Rome.[50] Piacentini's studio and residence (1929–31) along the Tiber River in Rome provided views of Hadrian's Tomb, his War Veterans headquarters (Casa Madre dei Mutilati, 1925–28, 1936), and Calderini's Palace of Justice. Piacentini criticized Calderini's "mania for sumptuous, rich, and exuberant" decoration.[51] However, he appreciated the older architect's effort to draw from Italian building types. Calderini's horizontal neo-cinquecento façade, heavy rustication, prominent *quadriga*, and use of the term *ambulatorio* for the main waiting hall (rather than the French *sale des pas perdus*) all suggested a distinctively Italian interpretation of this building type.[52] For the exterior of Milan's Palace of Justice, Piacentini maintained Calderini's low horizontal mass and anticipated including a central sculptural element. He also carefully studied Calderini's "very simple and clear" plan.[53] Borrowing directly from the Roman example, he exploited the dramatic potential of a central courtyard and placed the courtrooms at the end of the transverse axis. The similarities between these two projects caught the attention of contemporary commentators, who found Piacentini's Milan building to be little more than a reworking of nineteenth-century examples. In 1936 the periodical *L'Italia Letteraria*, directed by the leading cultural critic and author Massimo Bontempelli and an influential supporter of avant-garde modernism, Pier Maria Bardi, published a simple line drawing of Piacentini's Palace of Justice. A caption emphasized the connection: "The architecture of the Palace of Justice in Rome rehabilitated by the architecture of the Palace of Justice in Milan."[54] Like Mussolini's government, Piacentini's design drew from the established iconography of state power and adjusted this imagery to suit fascist rhetoric.

However, Ugo Ojetti, the outspoken conservative architecture critic for the Milan-based newspaper *Corriere della Sera* and editor of the art journal *Pegaso*, objected to the ways in which the building broke from Italian tradition. In 1933, Ojetti published a scathing letter to Piacentini in *Pegaso* in which he criticized Piacentini's recent buildings and projects, including the Milan Palace of Justice. He complained that Piacentini rejected the arch, vault, and column, "elements that have been for twenty or twenty-five centuries the signs of Rome," and embraced modernism with his "respect for the right angle, for naked and plain walls."[55] In Italy, the controversy over modernism in Italian architecture began when the Gruppo Sette, a group of seven young Milan-based architects, published the first of a series of articles in the architecture periodical *Rassegna Italiana* in 1927. Influenced by avant-garde European architects such as Le Corbusier, the group argued for a new rational approach to architecture that celebrated modern life and conditions. Interwar advocates of modernism as well as post-war scholars have often viewed Piacentini as the great enemy of Italian Rationalism. However, he was not entirely opposed to the architectural reform advocated by the rationalists.[56]

Piacentini's response to Ojetti helps clarify his uncertain relationship to modernist architecture in the early 1930s. Piacentini acknowledged his peculiar status and opined: "Mine is a strange situation. On the one hand, I am categorized with the old, with those who have been replaced by the culturalists ... and on the other hand, my ears are still being pulled reproaching my harmful avant-gardism."[57] To defend his work and his turn away from the iconic forms of Italian architecture, Piacentini argued that "each building period ... has had one or more constructive principles, elements which have constituted the base of every architectonic composition."[58] For Piacentini, concrete, the building material of the modern era, demanded the use of posts and beams. However, he was careful to qualify his support of modern forms. He added: "We will not construct bald façades, consisting of only glass and steel, or of gray and monotonous cement as is used today in northern Europe, in horizontal strips without any symmetry, without porticos and with 'thermometer towers' on the corners."[59] Instead, he urged architects to remain faithful to the principles of Roman building. In the Palace of Justice, for example, the posts and beams expressed the building's concrete frame, while the marble cladding alluded to traditional Italian monumental architecture. To further locate his architecture within Italian history, he pointed to countless examples from Renaissance and Baroque Rome where arches were not used and where columns served a minor role. Piacentini rejected the superficial use of classical and modernist forms and argued for a modern style that respected the architectural principles that had defined the great moments of Italian history. At the same time, plain, classically derived architecture comported with official taste on both sides of the Atlantic during the interwar period.

Piacentini intended for the interior decorative program to convey, in ways that architecture could not, the unique character of fascist law, particularly

Figure 4.7. Ambulatory of the Civil Court of Appeals, Palace of Justice. *Architettura*, nos. 1–2 (1942): 27.

after disappointing competition results and a limited budget undermined plans for the major decorative element, a seated statue of justice, twenty-three feet (seven metres) tall, above the main entrance.[60] It was initiated under the direction of *Podestà* Guido Pesenti (1935–8), who saw the project as a means to strengthen associations between Milan and Imperial Rome after Mussolini's declaration of Empire in 1936.[61] Indeed, the *podestà* hoped that the building and the recently restored San Lorenzo would stand as "two exceptional temples, that of Roman Justice and that of Imperial Religion" during a visit by Hitler scheduled for 1938, which never transpired.[62] The ambulatory of the Civil Court of Appeals contained the most important feature of this program: three low-relief sculpted panels (figure 4.7). Commissioned by Piacentini in 1936, the sculptures are visible from the entrance vestibule. They depict "Roman Justice" (*Giustizia Romana*), "Biblical Justice" (*Giustizia Biblica*), and "Fascist Justice" (*Giustizia Fascista*), by Romano Romanelli, Arturo Dazzi, and Arturo Martini, respectively. Influenced by contemporary currents in fascist thought, Piacentini presented fascist justice as the inheritor of two great traditions in Italian history: ancient Rome and Christianity.[63] The dedication of a panel to biblical themes made reference not only to the legacy of Christian thought in Italian legal traditions and codes, but also to the Lateran Accords of 1929, one of the most significant and popular accomplishments of the fascist state. The accords helped to repair the rift between the Italian state and the Catholic Church that had developed in the wake of Italian unification. Minister of Justice Rocco assisted in crafting this agreement, which included among its precepts the legitimacy of marriage rites performed according to canon law. As architectural historian Terry Kirk shows, one of the principal aims of the architectural and iconographic program for the earlier Palace of Justice in Rome was to distance the legal authority of the Italian Republic from that of the Catholic Church.[64] Piacentini's decision to include biblical themes in this triptych and elsewhere in the building communicated the rapprochement between church and state, even as the fascist regime sought to curtail the church's influence in Italian society and culture.[65]

Piacentini viewed the decorative program as a necessary feature of the building's historical relevance and architectural success, and he commissioned sixty artists to execute more than 140 works of art for the interior.[66] In a letter to Milanese art critic Raffaele Calzini, he explained, "I have always thought that the Town Hall [Palazzo Comunale] in Siena would not look as good if Simone Martini had not painted it, and all of the palaces of the Renaissance from the Schifanoia to the Farnesina would be cold, without feeling, and would not sufficiently speak of their age, if they were stripped of the frescos that cover their walls."[67] For the most prominent works of art decorating the building, Piacentini favoured successful artists with whom he had collaborated on past projects, such as Mario Sironi and Arturo Martini.[68] He also invited a few younger artists, including Lucio Fontana and Fausto Melloti, to participate, in a gesture to avant-garde practitioners and local talent. He instructed these artists to develop subjects that were "closely tied to the theme of Justice," and he suggested, reiterating the topic of the central hall, that their work "could be inspired by biblical or historical subjects."[69] The only restriction that Piacentini placed on the artists was that their work be figurative. Just as Piacentini tied his architectural program to a recognizable architectural tradition, he sought to orient the decorative program to established artistic practices.

As the building neared completion in 1939, the decorative program became the subject of considerable controversy. The head of the Court of Appeals, Tito Preda, sent a letter to the *podestà* of Milan at that time, Giacomo Gallarati Scotti (1938–43), that was scathing in its condemnation of the paintings and sculptures planned for the interior. Preda criticized the art in terms of style and content and demanded that the city remove or cover images that he thought inappropriate or anti-fascist.[70] For example, he thought that all works representing scenes from the Old Testament were Jewish and, in light of the 1938 racial laws, anti-fascist. In contrast to Nazi Germany, fascist Italy never adopted an official policy that controlled artistic freedom. In principle, the state supported all art that embodied the ideals of fascism – from the abstraction of futurism to the realism of the Novecento.[71] This undefined cultural policy became increasingly problematic in the later years of the regime. Piacentini defended the integrity of his project and argued against Preda's naïve and excessive conservatism. It was undoubtedly Piacentini who, in 1942, appealed to Giuseppe Bottai, the minister of education (1936–43) and one of the most influential figures in the formation of official culture during the fascist years, who had long supported artistic pluralism and the use of modern art to advance fascism. In autumn 1940 Bottai intervened, writing a letter to the minister of justice, Dino Grandi, the official who was best able to overturn the decision by the head of the Court of Appeals. Like Bottai, Grandi was also a moderate and had supported fascism from the beginning. In his letter, Bottai appealed to Grandi's "open" and "modern" intelligence and longstanding commitment to the ideals of fascism.[72] Echoing many of Piacentini's earlier concerns, Bottai asserted that Preda's effort to extend the racial laws to the decorative program of the Palace of Justice was a mere pretext and represented an attack on the kind of Italian art that fascism had long promoted. In addition, he proposed that it was a mistake for the state to reject works of art made in its honour. No doubt influenced by Bottai, Grandi ordered all the frescos to be displayed for public view. The involvement of the project architect, artists, magistracy, and local and national government officials shows the often confused and arbitrary process by which important decisions were made. Piacentini's reputation and political clout did not protect him from accusations of departing from fascist orthodoxy. However, his access to powerful and influential figures within the government helped rescue the project.

From the start, the municipal government had envisioned the Palace of Justice as the catalyst for change along Corso di P. Vittoria. As described above, the street was previously defined by modest residential buildings, religious institutions, military barracks, and an orphanage, and was now to accommodate numerous government institutions, of which the law courts were the most visible and the most important. Piacentini played a critical role in this process as architect of two buildings in the immediate vicinity and as adviser to the city planning office.[73] He had in 1935 designed a mixed-use building for the insurance agency and joint-stock company north of the Palace of Justice along Corso di P. Vittoria (Assicurazione Generali di Venezia e Trieste, Anonima Infortuni di Milano, figure 4.8).[74] A nearly identical building, though not credited to Piacentini, stands along the southern side of the law courts. In 1938 the

Figure 4.8. Mixed-use building adjacent to Palace of Justice along Corso di P. Vittoria, Marcello Piacentini, 1935–7. *Rassegna di Architettura*, no. 10 (1938): 99.

provincial government commissioned him to design a new police headquarters (Questura) on a site diagonally opposite the Palace of Justice along Corso di P. Vittoria.[75] Giuseppe De Finetti, a Milanese critic, architect, and urban planner, later noted that "the choice of the location for the construction of the new building was not rational but accidental, and was influenced by interests of the moment, direct and indirect,"[76] an allusion to Piacentini's behind-the-scenes influence. For both projects, Piacentini repeated the scale, materials, and visual vocabulary of the Palace of Justice but adjusted the architectural details to serve the programmatic requirements of each building – for example, the mixed-use building included balconies on the upper stories and floor-to-ceiling windows at street level. As a consultant to the city planning office, Piacentini reviewed the design for the other major institution adjacent to the Palace of Justice, the War Veteran's Centre (Casa del Mutilato, Luigi Lorenzo Secchi, 1937–42) on the corner of Via S. Barnaba and Via Freguglia.[77] As completed, this building's stone base and square central tower echoed the scale and formal language of the Palace of Justice, while its lower profile, brick, and arches related to the brick medieval church of Santa Maria della Pace, part of the complex of buildings that made up the Humanitarian Society on the far side of the street. In each instance, Piacentini made sure that new construction created a plausible context for the law courts but deferred to the Palace of Justice, the symbolic focus of the administrative district.

The nearly twenty-year process of completing the Palace of Justice points to the difficulty the fascist government had in carrying major architectural and urban projects to completion in urban centres. Indeed, the project would probably have taken longer without Piacentini's considerable ability to direct and manage the process: he played a role in determining the site plan, shaped the competition and its results, used his connections to secure the commission, and drew on his relationship with the city planning office and other local centres of power to effect the development of the surrounding urban fabric. Situated within the city walls but on the edge of the ancient urban core, the Palace of Justice presented an austere and unrelenting vision of state control with its grey battered base, blank stone walls, and deeply set ceremonial entrance. In contrast to the Trading Exchange designed by Paolo Mezzanotte, which maintained some continuity with the existing urban fabric, the Palace of Justice stood completely apart from the disorder of the traditional city and would preside over a district of dramatically new proportions configured to accommodate the speed and efficiency of modern mechanized transportation. Piacentini's building not only sought to embody the authority of the central state manifest in Minister of Justice Rocco's legal reforms, but also expressed fascism's desire to alter the character, habits, and mentality of its subjects through the creation of a substantially new kind of Italian city during the second half of the 1930s. In this period, the regime manifested its confidence and optimism in increasingly large-scale urban and architectural projects, and Milan, with its limited cultural patrimony and progressive spirit, presented an ideal testing ground for these ideas.

CHAPTER FIVE

Urban Networks:
Fascist Party Headquarters, 1931–1940

The *casa del fascio* represents the exemplary social organ of fascism. In these "political" houses citizens participate in public life, establish contacts with party leaders, and find a place well suited to meetings and physical exercise. Finally, it is here to which one turns in the least fortunate moments to find help and comfort. An original institution that can resolve the various branches of civic and political life, the *casa del fascio* is one of the most prominent and ubiquitous manifestations of the new climate in Italy. From these premises, the planning and realization of a "*casa del fascio*" derives from the obligation to create an Italian architecture that is the most refined and characteristic of our time.[1]

Located in Como, about an hour north of Milan, Giuseppe Terragni's celebrated glass-and-stone Casa del Fascio (1932–6; figure 5.1) contributed to the growing consensus about the appropriate form and character of *case del fascio* among architects and fascist officials.[2] His design suggested how party buildings could function both as a backdrop for large gatherings – a balcony on the second storey provided an appropriate platform for party leaders addressing crowds below – and as a carefully mediated extension of the urban stage. Terragni's modern design evoked the medieval town hall (*broletto*) – specifically, the one nearby, with its blank surface along the right face of the main façade in place of a tower.[3] The building's atrium, a space used for rallies and other gatherings, is separated from the piazza it faces by a sequence of glass doors. Terragni argued that his project reflected Mussolini's claim that "fascism is a glass house into which all can look."[4] Terragni placed a memorial chapel in the atrium and articulated this space as a series of planar elements inscribed with the names of local martyrs together with the word *presente*, which was the comrades' ritual call.[5] The lessons provided by nearly a decade of experience with this building type (outlined in chapter 2), and particular

Figure 5.1. Casa del Fascio, Giuseppe Terragni, Como, 1932–6. Crowds gathered 5 May 1936. *Quadrante* 35/36 (October 1936): 19.

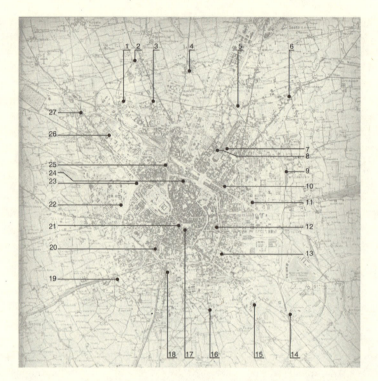

Figure 5.2. Map of Milan from 1932 showing the approximate location of *case del fascio* circa 1940–1. *1,* Bonservizi-Tonoli (Via Mercantini 92); *2,* Gen. Ascelpia Gandolfo (Via Faccio 2); *3,* Paolo Grassigli (Piazza Dergano 9); *4,* Goffredo Mameli (Via Paulucci de Calboli 1); *5,* Piave (Via P. Finzi 10); *6,* Aldo Sette (Via Padova 257); *7,* Eliseo Bernini (Via Soperga 53); *8,* Fabio Filzi (Via F. Filzi); *9,* Franco Baldini (via Conte Rosso 14); *10,* Guglielmo Oberdan (Via Cadamosto 4); *11,* Emilio Tonoli (Via Andrea del Sarto 31); *12,* Filippo Corridoni (Via P. Litta 8); *13,* Cesare Battisti (Via Vasari 15); *14,* Cesare Melloni (Via Rogoredo 13); *15,* Carlo Delcroix (Via del Cinquecento 9); *16,* Ugo Pepe (Via Ripamonti 202); *17,* Sciesa (Via Unione 5); *18,* Lodovico Montegani (Via Tabacchi 6); *19,* Gen. Armando Diaz (Via Andrea Ponti 7); *20,* General Antonio Cantore (Piazza General Cantore 10); *21,* Sede Federale (Piazza S. Sepolcro 9); *22,* Francesco Baracca (Via Privata Duccio di Boninsegna 21); *23,* Edoardo Crispi (Corso Sempione 25); *24,* Gabrielle D'Annunzio (Via della Marcia su Roma 6); *25,* Benito Mussolini (Via Ceresio 12); *26,* Mario Asso (via Jacopino da Tradate 1); *27,* Loris Socrate (Piazzale Santorre Santarosa 10); not on map, Augusto Beretta (Via delle Forze Armate 385, Baggio); Roberto Sarfatti (Via Novara 199). Map from Reggiori, *Milano*, 16. Graphics Coran.

examples such as this *casa del fascio* by Terragni and the top entries from the 1932 competition for a "typical" *casa del fascio* (*Casa del Fascio Tipo*) (discussed in this chapter), served as a point of reference for architects involved in the design of the various party headquarters in Milan in the second half of the 1930s.

In the first ten years of fascist rule, party leaders in Milan were primarily concerned with presenting an image of respectability and legitimacy. *Case del fascio* served as an expedient means of communicating fascism's political success and signalling the party's affinities with the interests of the middle and upper classes. The realignment of fascism's objectives – a consequence of changes in national leadership and in the political and economic life of the nation – resulted in a discernible shift in party-sponsored architectural initiatives during the 1930s. Anticipating some of these changes, in January 1929 Achille Starace, then vice-secretary of Italy's Fascist Party, directed the leaders (*fiduciari*) of neighbourhood groups (*gruppi rionale*) in Milan to build new *case del fascio* "at first on the periphery, where they can effectively carry out – for reasons of their environment – the full scope of their social mission."[5] In the following decade, at least nine of Milan's twenty-eight fascist neighbourhood groups – including the Crespi Group, the Mussolini Group, and the Filzi Group – constructed new headquarters, the majority of which were located in the rapidly developing residential districts north of the city,[6] and the party also sponsored the construction of a new regional party headquarters (*sede federale*), an administrative centre that connected neighbourhood outposts to Rome. (For the location of these new buildings, see map, figure 5.2.) They represent a crucial component of the party's effort to intensify its influence among the general population – especially among the factory workers who populated the city's northern districts and maintained their ties to socialism – and employed a variety of strategies to accomplish these goals. They also show the degree to which city and party leaders had to compete for limited resources of land and money, and they reveal the role of private capital in bankrolling the regime's building activities and the tensions that developed between fascism and local centres of power during the second half of the 1930s.

Starace was appointed national secretary of the party in December 1931. He was the son of a wine and oil merchant in southern Italy, a former lieutenant in the Italian army, and a leader within the fascist movement since the early 1920s. He initiated a variety of new policies that gave the party its overtly militant character and established uniformity in its rituals and symbols – for example, he replaced the "bourgeois" handshake with the Roman salute (*saluto romano*, a gesture in which the right arm is extended straight out and up from the body), encouraged simple and direct language in speech and writing, and specified what medals and regalia could be worn by party members at ceremonies.[7] Although his many critics derided such efforts, he substantially altered the public's perception of the party during his nearly decade-long tenure.[8] A few weeks after Starace's appointment, the sudden death of Mussolini's brother, Arnaldo – an event that represented a significant personal loss for Mussolini and created a temporary power vacuum in the Lombard capital – facilitated the party secretary's efforts to refocus the organization's activities and public image in Milan. The construction of new party buildings and the refurbishment of existing ones were tied to Starace's campaign to turn Italian youth into exemplary fascist citizens (particularly in the wake of fascism's confrontation with Catholic Action youth groups throughout 1931), and to bring fascism to the masses.[9] These buildings served as a backdrop for the party's ritual activities, provided direct access to the many programs it sponsored, and broadcast its presence. Shared architectural features – such as towers and balconies – were a consequence of party leader's efforts to centralize control of the building process and of an emerging agreement about what the architectural character of *case del fascio* should be.

In 1932 the Bologna-based Propaganda Group of the Fascist Youth (Gruppo di Propaganda del Fascio Giovanile) and the influential party newspaper *L'Assalto* sponsored a competition for a "typical" *casa del fascio*. Held in honour of the tenth anniversary of fascism's rise to power, the competition provided the first national platform through which party officials and architects explored the character and form of party headquarters. The competition was open to all architecture students in Italian universities. Pier Maria Bardi, a controversial advocate of modernist architecture and host of the polemical Second Rationalist Exhibition of 1931, was the spokesman for the jury. The jury also included Giuseppe Pagano, a Milan-based supporter of Italian Rationalism and the director, along with Edoardo Persico, of the architectural journal *Casabella*.[10] It was no surprise when the jury awarded two of the three first-place prizes to the unabashedly modern designs by Gian Luigi Banfi and Ludovico Belgiojoso (figure 5.3) and by Enrico Peressutti and Ernesto Rogers, all four of whom attended Milan Polytechnic, the school most closely associated with architectural innovation in Italy.[11] That same year, the four banded together to form the architectural partnership BBPR, which would play a significant role in how Milan would be reconstructed during the post-war period and in shaping post-war architectural debates.[12] Lending some authority to the results were the competition organizer's claim that the party secretary and the minister of education were "well informed of the proceedings," and the

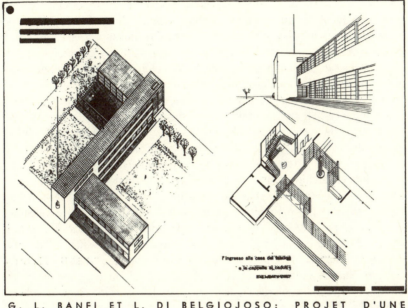

G. L. BANFI ET L. DI BELGIOJOSO: PROJET D'UNE
« MAISON DU PARTI FASCISTE » POUR UNE VILLE DE 30.000 HABITANTS

Figure 5.3. Project for a *casa del fascio* for a town of 30,000, Gian Luigi Banfi and Ludovico Belgiojoso, 1932. The cutaway on the lower right shows the Cappella ai Caduti or *sacrario*. *Casabella* 5 (June 1932): 20.

presence of a member of the national directorate at the opening of the competition exhibition.[13]

The review of the competition published by *L'Assalto* provided a comprehensive study of this emblematic fascist building type, and the winning projects submitted by Banfi and Belgiojoso and by Peressutti and Rogers offered a model for realizing the social and political missions that the party hoped would be fulfilled by their *case del fascio*.[14] Commentators drew attention to the need for familiar and unpretentious buildings to be designed as identifiable civic symbols, as town halls and churches had been in the past. Party leaders believed that such buildings would attract "the factory worker, the student, the farmer, and the office worker" to fascism.[15] The spare vocabulary, low horizontal masses, and details such as floor-to-ceiling glass windows on the ground level of the winning entries met officials' expectations and appealed to the modernist sensibilities of the jurors, who praised Peressutti and Rogers's design for the "intimate simplicity of the exterior."[16] Specific features of the entries by Banfi and Belgiojoso and by Peressutti and Rogers, such as a projecting blocklike tower and balcony (*arengario*), skillfully combined a modernist interest in elemental forms with historical examples of civic authority (viz., northern Italian medieval town halls), and made the buildings a distinct feature of the landscape.[17] The placement of the memorial chapel (*sacrario*) in the entrance hall and the reduction of this space to a single vertical slab positioned in the atrium earned praise from Pagano, who remarked, "[it] is an idea that is not only practical but also corresponds to the fascist religion of 'present-ness.'"[18] The publication of the winning entries in *Casabella* and in the French architectural periodical *L'Architetecture d'aujord'hui*, and a related exhibition (which included plans, sections, and elevations) at the Milan Polytechnic in 1933 – probably organized by assistant professor of architecture Piero Portaluppi (1888–1967) – made the competition results available to a wider audience, especially architects working in and around Milan.[19] The typological consistency advocated by the competition brief resonated with party secretary Starace's effort to create a coherent visual language for the party. Indeed, in 1932 Starace issued a decree that all new *case del fascio* should be equipped with bell towers.[20]

The growing ranks of party members and the wide range of services and activities made available through neighbourhood-based *case del fascio* and administered from the regional headquarters helped to justify new construction. In 1930 the roster of party members in Milan held 13,217 names; by 1933 the number had grown to 39,004; and by 1936 membership had reached 56,117.[21] The increase in membership did not necessarily correspond to a surge of popular support for the party, but was due to the fact that after 1933 party affiliation became a requirement for all public-service officials, including teachers. In addition, membership provided access to numerous benefits and was a practical necessity for many Italians, even after the party disbanded its Public Assistance Agency (Ente Opere Assistenziali, EOA) in 1937.[22] Neighbourhood centres typically included a suite of offices on the ground floor or second floor (where they were accessible to the public) that administered the party's various welfare programs. In April 1938 the city chronicle *Milano*, which published articles about the city (past and present) and current statistics, boasted that the Filzi Group, whose membership was drawn from workers in factory complexes northwest of the city's centre, had "distributed 57,000 kg. of bread, 29,000 liters of milk, 19,000 kg. of rice, 700 kg. of oil, and 24,000 kg. of coal, bonuses for weddings, subsidies to prolific families, and medical assistance to thousands of people" in the past year.[23] Food and fuel provided critical relief for the community, particularly in the winter months when factory jobs were scarce. The distribution of "bonuses for weddings" and "subsidies to prolific families" provided additional economic aid and reinforced Mussolini's initiative to reverse Italy's flagging birthrate. Party officials adjusted these and other programs managed by neighbourhood *case del fascio* to meet the needs of local residents in an effort to prevent unrest (which threatened political and economic stability) and to build support for the party; they also hoped that such programs would supersede the charitable networks forged by the Catholic Church and the city's many philanthropic organizations, and thus weaken the power of those institutions.

With the aim of building consensus through new forms of social interaction, neighbourhood party headquarters provided easy access to modern forms of entertainment and communication. The Filzi Group's new headquarters (Eugenio Faludi, 1936–8; figure 5.4, and see map, figure 5.2, and plan, figure 5.12) was located just one block from Milan's new Central Station.[24] In addition to providing offices for party functionaries, it housed a small library, a bar, a large hall for meetings and games, and a movie theatre, the Teatro Tonale, which was managed by Cinematografico Leoni, an independent cinema company that operated the theatre for most of the week and helped subsidize the construction and maintenance of the new building.[25] The Filzi Group reserved the right to use the space for party events and, in keeping with Starace's focus on youth, required the cinema to show films suited to younger audiences on Thursdays and Sundays.[26] The movie theatre accommodated more than seven hundred people and was the first one built in the district.[27] Party leaders, by supporting the construction of the theatre and linking its services to the *casa del fascio*, brought a very desirable leisure activity and a valuable instrument of propaganda to the neighbourhood.[28] With a similar concern for the dissemination of propaganda through entertainment, radios were often placed in the public rooms of *case del fascio*. A technological advance that was not yet affordable for many Italians, radio was one of the critical tools in Mussolini's campaign to reach the masses: radio broadcasts enabled local populations all over Italy to hear Mussolini's public addresses and to participate in a variety of programming intended to help foster a new sense of national identity.[29] The library, stocked with a carefully curated selection of books, magazines, and newspapers, was an additional resource for the community, and larger libraries served as places for informal gatherings under the auspices of the party.

In several ways, neighbourhood *case del fascio* also reinforced the party's emphasis on Italians' physical strength and athletic ability. After Mussolini's

Figure 5.4. Fabio Filzi headquarters, Eugenio Faludi, Via Filzi, Milan, 1936–8. *Edilizia Moderna* 29 (October–December 1938): 26.

invasion of Ethiopia (in October 1935) and Declaration of Empire (in May 1936), a new rhetoric and imagery of conquest and militarism flooded the nation. Accordingly, new party headquarters devoted substantial space to gymnasiums and other facilities intended to prepare Italian youth for military action. At the Filzi Group headquarters, the party dedicated the majority of its program to facilities for the fascist youth organization, the Opera Nazionale Balilla (ONB) – which in 1937 was restructured and renamed Gioventù Italiana del Littorio (GIL). Athletic facilities – a gymnasium and terrace – occupied much of the top storey of the building in order to insure "the maintenance of physical strength and the exaltation of athletic virtue" among party members.[30] Mussolini, in one of his many addresses to the nation, made clear the paramilitary function of these spaces, telling all citizens to "prepare yourselves to serve her [fascist Italy] at any time with your heart, mind, and arms."[31] The preparation of Italian youth for armed combat intensified after Italy and Germany

signed a military pact on the eve of the Second World War in 1939. Indicative
of this shift, party leaders created or expanded training facilities. For example, the Crespi Group (1937–39) devoted most of their new headquarters to
the GIL, eliminating such features as a library and bar for socializing. In the
same period, the party approved the construction of a new building for the GIL
adjacent to the Baracca Group's headquarters (Piero Portaluppi, 1937–40) and
a new facility next to the Filzi Group's headquarters (in 1939).

The effort to revitalize the party's image in Milan included the construction
of a new provincial party headquarters, which served as the administrative
link between party headquarters dispersed throughout greater Milan and the
national headquarters in Rome. Luigi Ravasco, the administrative secretary of
Milan and the official responsible for managing the new construction, initially
hoped to secure city-owned property on Piazza Verziere or Via Bocchetto, both
highly desirable locations in the city's centre slated for redevelopment.[32] By
the fall of 1935 the Milan Federation had shifted its sights to Palazzo Castani, a
modest Renaissance building on Piazza San Sepolcro owned by the Provincial
Union of Shopkeepers (Unione Provinciale dei Commercianti), and the adjacent residential properties (see figures 5.5 and 5.6). The federation hoped to
broker a deal in which it would exchange the Palazzo Besana, the current
home of its headquarters, for the Palazzo Castani, and party leaders anticipated that the municipal government would help underwrite the purchase of
the adjoining buildings.[33] The city proved reluctant. It was only after continued
pressure from party officials, including Starace, that the mayor authorized the
expropriation of the property abutting Palazzo Castani.[34] Indicative of the way
in which personal relationships helped to shape public projects, Count Carlo
Radice-Fossati, Milan's deputy mayor, whose cousin owned one of the buildings marked for demolition, consented to undertake the negotiations.[35] The
municipal government justified the expropriation by using some of the land
to widen adjacent roads in order to ease movement through this area, which
preserved a medieval street pattern. However, the city ceded the majority of the
property to the federation.

Similar strategies governed the acquisition of property for new neighbourhood party headquarters. In a letter to Rino Parenti, the federal secretary of
Milan (1933–39) – one of the few fascist leaders in Milan whom Starace
had not dismissed following the Giampaoli scandal of 1928, and the highest-
ranking local party official – the party's administrative secretary in Rome,
Giovanni Marinelli, directed Parenti to ensure "that every neighborhood group
has ... a decent headquarters, however modest, in relation to their needs."[36]
Marinelli explained that the federation, not local groups, would now manage

La futura Casa del Fascio

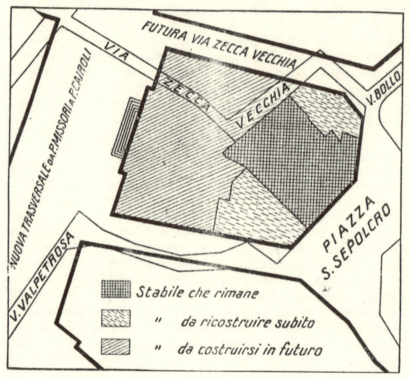

Figure 5.5. Site plan for the Sede Federale, Piazza S. Sepolcro, Milan, published in July 1936. The Palazzo Castani is the "stabile che rimane" or "building that remains" indicated on the plan. From *Corriere della Sera*, 3 July 1936.

all contact between the party and the municipal government. This increased the party's ability to exert its influence and gave it greater oversight of the financial affairs of local groups, many of which were notoriously corrupt. The working-class Mussolini Group, for example, which had been unable to build a new neighbourhood centre for its headquarters because of inadequate funds and mismanagement, occupied the basement of a local school and other unused spaces in public buildings.[37] In addition, Marinelli stipulated that the city purchase property from any group that could no longer afford to manage its holdings. He then required the city to rent the property to the group and assume all maintenance costs until it had sufficient funds to resume ownership.[38] This policy added a significant burden to the city's limited resources and enabled the party to take control of desirable real estate at a minimal cost.

Throughout the second half of the 1930s, the municipal government made city-owned property available to neighbourhood fascist groups at below-market rates and offered numerous other concessions in order to strengthen the party's holdings.[39] The Fabio Filzi Group used its leverage to acquire land northwest of the recently completed massive Central Station for its new headquarters (see map, figure 5.2). The site stood at the intersection of two principal streets in that area, Via Tonale and Via Ponte Seveso (later renamed Via F. Filzi), near the group's former outpost on Via Schiapparelli. The group purchased the land for 350,000 lire per square metre, less than half of the 750,000-lire market price.[40] In a similar fashion, the Crespi Group purchased land for its new headquarters along Corso Sempione, a major north-south artery in a rapidly developing residential area just beyond Sempione Park, paying a very favourable rate of 375,000 lire per square metre, less than half the declared value.[41] In 1938 Guido Pesenti prepared a summary of the city's concessions, which included selling more than six thousand cubic metres at less than half their market value for the construction of new headquarters for six neighbourhood groups, building a headquarters for the D'Annunzio Group (Renzo Gerla, 1937–38), and renting property below market value to nine neighbourhood groups.[42] *Podestà* Gian Giacomo Gallarati Scotti later explained that such special privileges were merely an extension of the "general collaboration between the city and all of the institutions of the regime" and a reasonable response to the limited incomes and growing needs of groups as they performed a wider range of welfare services.[43] However, correspondence between city and party leaders reveals that municipal officials were reluctant to subsidize the party's building program and that allowances were made only after local party administrators and Secretary Starace applied significant political pressure.

The Milan Federation's acquisition of Palazzo Castani and several adjacent properties for the Sede Federale, the new regional party headquarters, gave the party full control of the southwestern side of Piazza San Sepolcro and coincided with the appointment of *Podestà* Pesenti, a founding member of the Fascist Party who had personal ties to both Mussolini and Secretary Starace.[44] The project represented not only an opportunity to reclaim one of the principal sites associated with Mussolini's rise to power but also repositioned the headquarters within the city as it was being transformed by the new master plan. One of the rooms in the Palazzo Castani, where Mussolini had gathered his base of support and founded the fascist movement in 1919, was known among fascists as the Room of the Sansepolcristi (Sala dei Sansepolcristi). This room and Mussolini's offices on Via Paolo da Cannobio and Piazza Belgioioso were regularly evoked in recollections of fascism's early years in Milan; a simple marble plaque surrounded by electric lights adjacent to the entrance recorded the building's pivotal role in the party's history, and the party occasionally used Piazza San Sepolcro for commemorative rallies. On the opposite side of the plaza were the venerable Ambrosian Library (Biblioteca Ambrosiana) and the medieval brick church of San Sepolcro. The square also marked the location of the city's ancient Roman forum, but the antique origin of the plaza seems to have held little interest for party leaders in Milan. In contrast to Rome, where associations with Roman antiquity played a central role in constructing fascism's identity, fascist imagery in Milan favoured references to the conditions of modern urban life out of which fascism emerged. Indeed, the district was to be radically transformed by an expansive new cross street (*trasversale*) proposed in the city's master plan.

However, the city's laws for historic preservation, modelled on the guidelines established by the influential *Carta del Restauro* (part of CIAM's [Congrès internationaux d'architecture modern] Athens Charter [1931]), mandated the preservation not only of individual monuments but also of their architectural and urban context.[45] The scope of the Sede Federale project was thus limited to the restructuring of the Palazzo Castani and the construction of two modest additions flanking it.[46] To avoid the complication of holding a competition, the Milan Federation's Technical Office appointed as the project architect Piero Portaluppi, a politically savvy designer who had already designed several buildings for the party. Portaluppi, who taught at the Milan Polytechnic and was a member of the influential Rotary Club, had a successful practice in Milan designing new buildings and restoring existing buildings for leading industrial families,[47] and was capable both of creating a fresh image for the party and of responding to the historic nature of the site. In April 1936, Portaluppi submitted five versions of the Sede Federale to the federation for review,[48] several of which are on a scale large enough to suggest that the federation had already begun to work with the city to expand the project significantly.[49] In the most ambitious proposal, the two "modest" additions flanking the main mass of Palazzo Castani facing Piazza San Sepolcro were to be six stories tall, detailed with strip windows and porthole windows, and a tower with an open loggia at its top was to rise above the building's main mass from its rear corner on Via Valpetrosa. In the late spring and early summer, local newspapers published a plan of the building site showing that it would extend

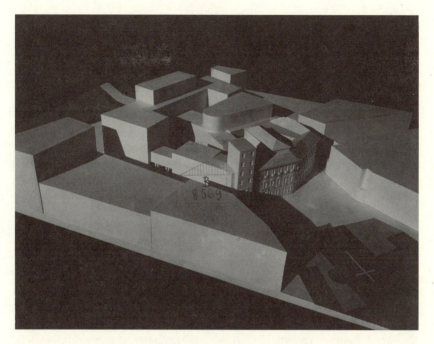

Figure 5.6. Model for Sede Federale, Piero Portaluppi, Piazza S. Sepolcro, Milan, 1936. New construction extends from and surrounds the curved Palazzo Castani. Fondazione Piero Portaluppi, Milan.

from Piazza San Sepolcro to a new thoroughfare connecting Largo Cairoli and Piazza Missori (see figure 5.5).[50]

In November 1936 Portaluppi presented Mussolini with final plans and a model of the Sede Federale (figure 5.6). The building's curved front along Piazza San Sepolcro included the eighteenth-century façade of the three-storey Palazzo Castani and one modern, six-storey tower with a balcony on its eastern side. The spare geometry of the tower signalled a shift in the party's image away from the eclectic neoclassicism promoted by Arnaldo Mussolini in the mid-1920s towards a more abstract visual sensibility. After reviewing the model, Mussolini pointed to the blocklike central pavilion flanked by two lower wings facing the new artery at the building's rear (the proposed Trasversale Missori-Cairoli) and demanded, "All of this is good but when do we begin? Because this is the most important."[51] Despite Mussolini's desire that it be built rapidly, the Milan Federation planned to carry out work for the project in two distinct phases. As indicated in the plans published in July, the first stage of the project called for the adaptation of the Palazzo Castani, with new construction added on both sides of it. The second stage involved the city's gradual expropriation of properties on the site that would be torn down to build the extension towards the new artery.[52] Amassing sufficient funding for the project also took time. Mussolini offered occasional donations to support the project; however, most of the modest contributions for the new building came from individuals, many of whom were affiliated with local industries.[53]

Private capital played an essential role in the party's building campaign throughout the city. The Filzi Group, to finance the construction of their new headquarters, relied on local industries, including the Pirelli Company (Società Italiana Pirelli), the Breda Company (Società Italiana Ernesto Breda), the Officine Meccaniche Stigler, and the Chini Company (Società Italiana Chini), companies that, respectively, manufactured rubber and tires, made mechanical parts for trains and a variety of heavy machinery, produced and serviced elevators and escalators, and manufactured cement.[54] Alberto Pirelli, the director of the Pirelli Company, donated 1,450,000 lire for the Filzi Group's building, and the Pirelli Office of Technical Services (Ufficio Tecnico Pirelli) oversaw its construction.[55] Giovanni Battista Pirelli, the company's founder, served as a director of the Filzi Group in 1923, and the manufacturing company's first headquarters (now the location of the Pirelli Tower) stood a few blocks from the site of the new headquarters.[56] That company's participation can therefore be understood as a continuation of an established relationship with the community and demonstrated businesses' involvement with fascist operations in the area. The collaboration between industrial concerns and party officials in the establishment of *case del fascio* points to their shared concern, also evident in the programming administered by the party, to create an obedient and healthy working class and to limit the influence of socialism among labourers.

Party officials appreciated the substantial benefits of the Pirelli Company's largesse. Indeed, Ravasco, the local party official in charge of the building projects, encouraged other groups to follow a similar financial model.[57] However, the dependence on private sources of capital forced party officials to make concessions. In 1937 Secretary Starace decreed that new construction could use only a limited quantity of iron (*ferro*), because that material was needed for military campaigns in Africa and Spain that had been initiated in the previous two years. Although the reinforced concrete structure of the Filzi headquarters required considerable amounts of this material, the building's architect and the Pirelli Technical Office refused to conceive an alternative design, even after local and national party leaders applied pressure.[58] A few years later, when Alberto and Pietro Pirelli decided to construct, at their own expense and with Pirelli Company expertise, a facility for the GIL (the fascist youth organization) adjacent to the group headquarters, party officials once

Figure 5.7. View of the proposed tower for the Sede Federale, photomontage, 1936. Fondazione Piero Portaluppi, Milan.

again found themselves in the position of having to defer to the company.[59] As Ravasco counselled Marinelli, the party's administrative secretary in Rome, one must use "tact" when making suggestions to the Pirelli Technical Office.[60] The relationship between the Filzi Group and the Pirelli Company exemplifies the tensions in such groups' alliances with centres of economic power, which offered substantial benefits but challenged the party's authority.

Although Mussolini was enthusiastic about Portaluppi's Sede Federale, local opposition to the proposed tower at the intersection of Via Valpetrosa and Piazza San Sepolcro delayed construction (figure 5.7). Portaluppi, employing a traditional urban strategy already associated with party buildings, planned to use the tower to enhance the building's stature in the quarter. New party buildings in Milan similarly used towers, or the suggestion of towers, to augment their visual presence and to convey the party's authority. Most aggressively, Mario Bacciocchi's solid brick tower for the Mussolini Group's headquarters (1936–37), with its height of 131 feet (40 metres), visually anchored the party's activities in the developing area around the Porta Nuova Station (now Garibaldi Station) north of the city's centre (figure 5.8). This tower, requested by Mussolini for the building that would house the group bearing his name (and of which he was a member), was built in the shape of the Roman fasces – the symbol he had chosen for the Fascist Party – and, when completed, was the tallest tower on any of the party's buildings in the city.[61] The large travertine bas-relief panel placed at the corner of the Filzi Group headquarters on Via Tonale conferred a sense of weight and importance on the building's otherwise plain brick-and-glass façade and provided a strong vertical counterpoint to the horizontal fenestration, akin to the traditional role of the tower (see figure 5.4). Recalling the lessons of Austrian architect and city planner Camillo Sitte, Portaluppi positioned the tower of the Sede Federale so that it was framed by the narrow, winding Via Valpetrosa, the primary route for visitors approaching from the city's centre. Within the context of Piazza San Sepolcro, the tower confronted the modest bell towers of the brick church of San Sepolcro, recalling the juxtaposition of sacred and secular authority present in medieval towns throughout Italy, and served as a backdrop for rallies and other demonstrations held in the plaza. Even though many such towers were not designed to be occupied, their location on main thoroughfares and in public plazas suggests that they might have been intended for surveillance and control, a function that would become increasingly prevalent in these buildings as Italy advanced towards war in the late 1930s.

The Sede Federale tower represented a compromise between Portaluppi's original intentions and the architectural and urban approach of the architecture establishment in Rome. In Milan, as in the rest of Italy, the regional superintendent oversaw restoration projects and new construction adjacent to historic

Figure 5.8. Mussolini Group headquarters, Mario Bacciocchi, Via Ceresio, Milan, 1936–7. *Rassegna di Architettura*, no. 9 (1938): 386.

sites and reported to the Office of Antiquities and Fine Arts (Ufficio delle Antichità e Belle Arti) in Rome, under the administrative control of Giuseppe Bottai, the minister of education (1936–43). Alarmed by the modernism of Portaluppi's project, Gino Chierici, the recently appointed director of the Board of Monuments in Lombardy (Sovraintendenza ai Monumenti della Lombardia, 1935–39), alerted the ministry about the Milan Federation's plans for the façade facing Piazza San Sepolcro. In contrast to his predecessors, who established their reputations locally, Chierici came to Milan after earning his professional credentials in central and southern Italy and becoming acquainted with leading professionals in Rome, where he regularly served on the advisory board to the High Council for Fine Arts (the Consiglio Superiore per le Belle Arti).[62] In his letter to the ministry, Chierici expressed concern about the Sede Federale's "frankly modern" character and noted that it had a "violent" relationship to the square.[63] He objected, in particular, to the "form and dimension" of the balcony and the materials: black marble for the base and balcony of the tower (*torre Littoria*).[64] Following protocol, Bottai created a special commission to review the proposal, appointing Marcello Piacentini, Gustavo Giovannoni (a leading figure in professional and academic cultural debates in the interwar period), and Alberto Calza-Bini (the head of the National Syndicate of Fascist Architects) to serve on it.[65] Summarizing the group's position, Bottai explained that the project failed to resolve "the problem of context presented by the particular character of the historic piazza."[66] The assessment was entirely in keeping with the concern for context outlined in Gustavo Giovannoni's *Vecchie città ed edilizia nuova* (1913) and the influential *Carta del Restauro*.[67] To comply with Rome's demands, Portaluppi decreased the height of the tower and changed some of the materials – replacing the dark stone that was originally planned with a warm-toned stone, for example – but refused to reveal similar details for the parts of the building that did not fall under the jurisdiction of the superintendent of monuments.[68] In the spring of 1938, frustrated by the delay caused by the review, Pesenti, Ravasco, and Marinelli all sent letters to Bottai urging a rapid resolution of the situation.[69] Apparently unmoved by their concerns, the minister did not approve the project until the end of August.[70]

Case del fascio constructed beyond the city walls were less constrained by history but no less attuned to context. The Mussolini Group headquarters (see map, figures 5.2 and 5.8) stood at the intersection of the broad tree-lined Via Ceresio and Via M. Quadrio in the working-class quarter from which the organization drew its constituents, near the Monumental Cemetery and the Porta Nuova Station. The area had remained largely rural in character until the late nineteenth and early twentieth centuries, when residential and industrial development began to take hold. These new buildings captured the spirit of the modern city with their brick fronts, reinforced-concrete construction, and simplified architectural details.[71] The cubic four-storey brick building that forms the principal mass of the Mussolini Group headquarters evokes the formal language of this turn-of-the-century industrial and civic architecture and shows the influence of the Milanese architect Giovanni Muzio, who drew from a wide range of references to create a contemporary Milanese architecture.[72] Like Bacciocchi's Mussolini Group headquarters (begun the same year but completed a year earlier), Faludi's design for the Filzi Group headquarters suggests the urban industrial landscape on the edge of Milan during that period, but by means of its blocky horizontal mass, planar façade, and industrial-style strip windows. Travertine details and sculpted ornament – most notably, the bas-relief travertine panel that reached the full height of the building – distinguished the edifice from its utilitarian counterparts while signalling its civic importance (and the benefits of Pirelli patronage). Originally, Faludi had proposed a more dynamic composition, in which the theatre and gymnasium projected out from the façade.[73] However, that solution did not appeal to conservative officials in Rome who requested that the architect revise the design in order to "give it a greater Italian (*Italianità*) character."[74] Despite such restraints, the architects of these buildings, many of whom were from a younger generation influenced by Italian Rationalism, took the opportunity to explore how Milan's image as a centre of modern life and fascism's claim to be a force of modernization might be reconciled with Italy's architectural traditions.

The enormous bas-relief panel on the Filzi Group headquarters building and the smaller ones on the front and sides of the balcony (projecting from the wall perpendicular to the panel), all designed by Leoni Lodi,[75] exemplify how ornament made manifest the party's symbolic goals and, in this example, positioned fascism within the context of working-class concerns (see these panels in figure 5.4). The large panel uses heroic figurative imagery, like much other realist monumental sculpture of the period, to communicate the party's aspirations for an ordered and prosperous society. A quote from Mussolini intended for that panel's lowest register reinforces the work's symbolic intent: "Fascism establishes true and profound equality between all citizens of the nation ... The objective of our march in the economic sector is the realization of a greater social justice for all Italian people."[76] Using the language of revolution and conquest to promote fascism's promise to break down established class boundaries and inequalities, party leaders undoubtedly hoped to appeal to workers in the district and to disrupt their socialist affiliations, which persisted throughout the interwar period. Lodi directed the gaze and movement of the figures on the large panel towards the main entrance of the party headquarters. The front panel of the balcony, above the entrance, pairs symbols associated with the fascist empire (the imperial eagle and fasces) with images of tools used for industrial and agricultural labour, and the side panels feature images of architects' tools and musicians' instruments. From the ceremonial space of the balcony, party officials and radio broadcasts would have conveyed the latest directives from Mussolini to crowds gathered below. Seen by party members assembled around the building, Lodi's bas-reliefs implied that fascism's mission to conquer the chaos of injustice could be fulfilled through the work of the group.

The local elite and middle class, key elements of fascism's base of support in Milan, invested in the party headquarters that were built in their districts (or housed in existing buildings) during this period. Like the working-class groups' headquarters, these other *case del fascio* were intended to solidify fascism's presence in the city, but they were far more luxurious. For example, instead of building a new headquarters, the wealthy and socially prominent Sciesa Group purchased notable *palazzi* in the city's centre and modified the interiors according to their needs;[77] to attract the district's elite residents, they hosted cultural activities there, such as a lecture by architect Giuseppe Pagano.[78] The Crespi Group, whose members came from the bourgeois district west of Sempione Park, constructed a new headquarters (Gianni Angelini, Giuseppe Calderara, and Tito B. Varisco, 1937–9; figure 5.9) on Corso Sempione at the intersection of Via Riva Villasanta after the city failed to approve an earlier proposal to build the new headquarters in the park.[79] Corso Sempione extended north from Sempione Park and had begun to fill in with new development during the late-nineteenth and early-twentieth centuries. To its west were military barracks and abandoned rail lines awaiting redevelopment.[80] The spare grid organizing the Crespi Group headquarters' façade suggested an affinity with the avant-garde currents visible in Terragni and Piero Lingieri's innovative Casa Rustici (1934) just over a block away on the opposite side of the street, and gave the complex a cosmopolitan quality, as did its proximity to Gio Ponti's headquarters for the national radio corporation (Ente Italiano per le Audizioni Radiofoniche [EIAR], 1939) on the opposite side of Via Riva Villasanta. The Crespi Group clad their building with marble and stone, costly materials that tied the structure to the most prestigious edifices in the city. At the same time, the presence of a tower and a balcony clearly associated the new building with neighbourhood groups throughout the city as well as Portaluppi's Sede Federale, which was also faced with stone.

In 1939 the party announced its commitment to completing the Sede Federale in full and released a new plan showing the general outlines of the enlarged building as it reached towards Via San Maurilio, the new artery that now absorbed the narrow and irregular street of the same name south of the Palazzo Castani block (figure 5.10). In this new extension, Portaluppi proposed a remarkably innovative solution in order to relate the building to its urban environment: a new street, Via del Sacrario (today Via Ardeatine), broke through the expanded site to create two distinct building blocks, the Palazzo Castani block fronting Piazza San Sepolcro and the new block fronting Via San Maurilio.[81] Portaluppi united the two independent structures through a spatial sequence that culminated in a mortuary chapel (*sacrario*) at the rear of the Palazzo Castani block.[82] He treated the austere main façade along Via San Maurilio as a uniform wall punctured by regular square windows and a central tripartite entrance. Plans showed that this entrance continued directly into the courtyard beyond and functioned as a covered loggia, open to the life of the

Figure 5.9. P.E. Crespi headquarters, Gianni Angelini, Giuseppe Calderara, and Tito B. Varisco, Corso Sempione, Milan, 1937–9. *Costruzioni-Casabella* 149 (May 1940): 17.

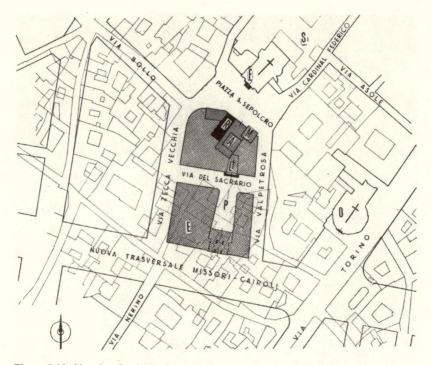

Figure 5.10. Site plan for the Sede Federale, 1940. The plan is labelled to show: *P*, the open courtyard; *E*, the theatre; *L*, the *sacrario*; *R*, the Room of the San *Sepolcristi* (Sala San Sepolcristi); and *M*, the tower. *Rassegna di Architettura*, no. 10 (1940): 296.

street. The arrangement recalled two residential buildings in Milan, Muzio's Ca'Brutta (1919–22) and Portaluppi's Palazzo della società Buonarroti-Carpaccio-Giotto (1926–30). In both examples, an oversize arch spans the street to join two buildings and create a cohesive urban architectural composition. For the Sede Federale, Portaluppi used this architectural element to signal the public aspect of the inner court. From the loggia, the court tapered to direct the viewer's attention to the glass-fronted mortuary chapel, the focus of this calibrated visual and spatial path. To reinforce its sacred associations, Portaluppi framed the entrance to the chapel with four personifications of victory, an arrangement that recalled the Roman triumphal arch and the portals of Christian churches.[83]

Portaluppi's use of glass to expose the ritual functions held within each block also visually united the buildings along the newly constructed Via del Sacrario – at least it would have had the project been completed. Never begun,

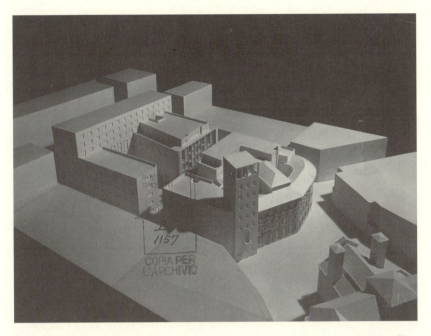

Figure 5.11. Model of the Sede Federale, 1939–40. Fondazione Piero Portaluppi, Milan.

the block facing Via San Maurilio was to hold a theatre for an audience of as many as five thousand people diagonally opposite the chapel along the Via del Sacrario (figure 5.11).[84] Theatres, as well as halls and atriums, served the practical function of providing a large gathering space as well as the symbolic role of emphasizing collective participation. As one journalist noted, "the new [fascist] conception of the individual and of the state is manifest in large assemblies of a diverse mass of citizens."[85] Portaluppi's design placed a glass wall at the rear of the theater to expose a system of stairs that would have served members of the party as they hurried to and from meetings and rallies. The use of glass to suggest and reveal movement within buildings repeated an established motif in modernist architecture. In Italy, Luigi Figini and Gino Pollini, trained at the Milan Polytechnic where Portaluppi was a professor, also used glass to expose the stairways in their addition to the Olivetti Factory (1934–5, Ivrea). However, Portaluppi directed this modernist interest in circulation, transparency, and efficiency to the fascist commitment to service. Specifically, the theatre and the chapel would have reinforced the shared struggle of the living and dead members of the party, connecting the two visually by their proximity and the use of similar materials. Thus the narrow Via del Sacrario physically separated the two blocks of the party headquarters but was designed to symbolically join them and to draw the ritual performance of the party into the public space of the city.

The effort to integrate the ritual activities of the party with the public space of the city evident in Portaluppi's project is found to varying degrees in other of the party's buildings constructed in Milan in the same period. Whenever possible, party leaders purchased property on a corner site facing a broad street or square in order to allow the building to be used as a backdrop for rallies, ceremonies, and other public events. For example, the Filzi Group headquarters stood at the intersection of two major arteries, and the Crespi and Mussolini Group headquarters occupied corner sites along major avenues. In addition to site placement, architects employed a variety of strategies to relate the party's buildings to the adjacent spaces that were used for ritual purposes. In order to emphasize the connection between the Mussolini Group's headquarters and Via Ceresio, Bacciocchi extended the low risers of the granite stairs slightly beyond the façade and oriented the stairs towards both Via Ceresio and Via M. Quadrio, the intersecting street. From the stairs, a low platform extended nearly the full length of the façade. Analogous in function to a balcony, the platform served as a speaking podium and as a place to display the group's pennants, important symbols of the group's solidarity carried in parades and held high during rallies.[86] The group of architects responsible for the design of the Crespi Group headquarters encouraged the movement of crowds and people from Corso Sempione into a light-filled atrium through a wall of glass doors placed along the main façade. The interior atrium or "agora" functioned as a setting for "ceremonies and celebrations" and served as an extension of the public space in front of the building.[87] Terragni's Casa del Fascio in Como, where a series of glass doors had created a nearly seamless relationship between the central atrium and the fronting piazza, was undoubtedly the model.

In most of the party's new headquarters, the mortuary chapel served as the primary focus of the entrance sequence, reinforcing the party's effort to craft what Giovanni Gentile has described as a "cult of the nation." This fusing of religious and political values had its origins in the Risorgimento and was manipulated to potent advantage by the fascist regime, especially during Starace's tenure.[88] Faludi positioned the group's memorial chapel in a shallow marble-clad niche in the vestibule of the main entrance to the headquarters (figure 5.12). The architect's design shows the influence of contemporary examples – including the *casa del fascio* competition of 1932, Adalberto Libera's Sacrario at the Exhibition of the Fascist Revolution (Mostra della Rivoluzione Fascsita) of 1932, Terragni's Casa del Fascio in Como, and BBPR's memorial chapel for the 1934 Palazzo del Littorio competition – as well as the party's overt

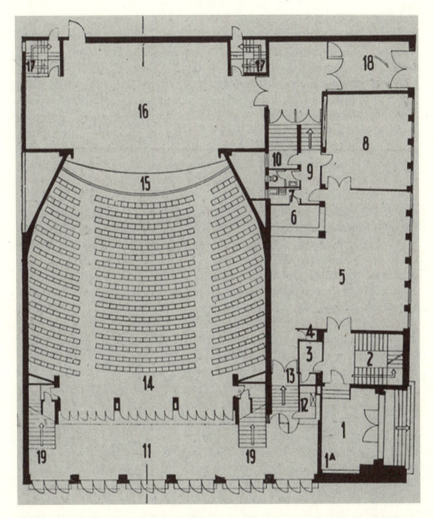

Figure 5.12. Plan of ground floor, Filzi Group headquarters. *1*, atrium; *1*ᴬ, *sacrario*; *5*, game room; *6*, bar; *8*, library. *Rassegna di Architettura*, no. 9 (1938): 390.

attempts to bring uniformity to the its various headquarters. Indicative of the central administration's interest in the details of construction, administrative secretary Marinelli required the Sarfatti Group to revise their plans in order to position the chapel near the entrance (rather than on the second floor) so that it would be "clearly visible to all."[89] In keeping with the planar vocabulary, spare geometry, and use of text found in earlier examples, Faludi inscribed the frequently evoked ritual call "*presente*" into a low black stone band that ran along the rear face of the niche. To the left of the niche, he listed the names of the first thirteen fascist martyrs in simple black type. The low-relief sculpture *The Hero* (*L'Eroe*), a muscular male figure partially covered by a flowing cloth clenching a *fascio* in his right hand, ornamented the ceiling and provided a figurative counterpoint to the abstraction below.

The mortuary chapel (1939–40) at the Sede Federale repeated many of the formal elements of earlier examples and of the Room of Victory (Sala della Vittoria) at the Milan Triennale of 1936 designed by Marcello Nizzoli, Giancarlo Palanti, and Edoardo Persico with the young Milanese artist Lucio Fontana. Portaluppi, recently appointed dean of the School of Architecture at the Milan Polytechnic, left the design of the chapel at the Sede Federale to a group of his students, described in a contemporary review as "the generation born and raised in the wake left and marked by the lost heroes."[90] The group was chosen by competition, and party secretary Starace participated in the selection process.[91] For the chapel, the group placed tall free-standing white marble slabs along the length or nave of the rectangular room to focus the viewer's attention on a votive flame, a crucifix, and a plaque commemorating fascist martyrs at the end of the horizontal axis (figure 5.13). Polished marble slabs, one of which repeated the word *presente* in a broad, bold font, served as the primary compositional elements. A bas-relief entitled *Flight of Victories* (*Volo di Vittorie*, 1938–39) by Fontana filled the ceiling, with five ethereal personifications of victory complementing the weightless slabs below and reinforcing the theme of victory presented on the exterior.[92] The designs for these memorial spaces shared the impulse to reduce the iconography of loss to form, material, and text. They also found in architectural abstraction a means of creating a memorial devoid of nostalgia. This sensibility opposed the excess sentimentality of nineteenth-century monuments and provided a strategy for integrating fascism's mystical "religion" with the rhythm of modern life.

Throughout the nearly twenty years of fascist rule, *case del fascio* served as an essential tool through which the regime sought to establish its hegemony. The Sede Federale designed by Portaluppi functioned as the symbolic and administrative centre for this activity and, not unlike earlier regional headquarters, took advantage of the substantial reworking of the area that was planned. The prominently placed tower and balcony made the building an instantly recognizable centre of the party's power and visually reinforced associations with other neighbourhood party headquarters in greater Milan. Portaluppi's effort to reconcile the complexities of the building site – a product of negotiations with

Figure 5.13. Memorial Chapel (*sacrario*), Gianni Albricci, Mario Tevarotto, Marco Zanuso, Luigi Mattoni, Gianluigi Reggio, and Mario Salvedè, Sede Federale, Milan, 1938–40. *Rassegna di Architettura*, no. 10 (1940): 300.

individual property owners and municipal authorities, changes to the master plan, and limited funds – offered an innovative strategy for integrating fascist ritual with the city at a time of rapid change, and an alternative to the bombastic monumentality associated with the state (as in projects such as Piacentini's Palace of Justice, discussed in chapter 4). To the extent that Portaluppi's project eschewed a single style and hierarchy and echoed the often-haphazard growth of the city and its institutions, the project can be seen as a critique of the strictures of the totalitarian regime as well as of the municipal government's redevelopment of the city centre. During the post-war period, many of the party's headquarters, particularly those whose histories predated fascism, were reabsorbed into the urban fabric. However, a majority of these buildings in Milan, and elsewhere, were transformed into military or police headquarters.[93] In spite of the ways that officials retooled the iconography of these buildings to fit new political circumstances, their architectural character and function as symbols of state authority remain more or less unaltered, posing unresolved questions about the legacy of fascist-era architecture in contemporary Italy.

CHAPTER SIX

Museum, Monument, and Memorial: The Palazzo del *Popolo d'Italia*, 1938–1942

In a totalitarian regime ... the press is an element of the regime, a forceful tool at the service of the regime. In a unitary regime, the press cannot be distinct from this unity.
— Benito Mussolini, 1928[1]

On 15 November 1938, the twenty-fourth anniversary of the founding in Milan of *Il Popolo d'Italia*, Mussolini's mouthpiece, the newspaper's publishers triumphantly announced that they would soon have new headquarters.[2] Its front page exuberantly praised the proposed *modernissima* building designed by Milanese architect Giovanni Muzio,[3] and directly below the headline it included a perspective drawing of a commanding six-storey structure on the eastern side of Piazza Cavour (figure 6.1). Together, the image and text made clear the newspaper's intent to create a modern home for the press, to establish a permanent memorial to the "paper of the Fascist revolution,"[4] and, in visual terms, to dominate Piazza Cavour, a strategically and historically important urban plaza just outside the traditional centre of the city, less than a mile northeast of Piazza del Duomo. The project mirrored the regime's contemporary efforts to expand the influence of the Fascist Party by constructing new party headquarters in various neighbourhoods and to celebrate the sites and institutions most closely associated with the movement's origins. A year later, *Il Popolo d'Italia*'s old offices on Via Paolo da Cannobio – where Mussolini founded the paper and from where he directed his appeal for Italy's entry into the First World War in 1915 – were declared a national monument.[5] Although a renewed interest in commemorating fascism's origins was evident throughout Italy, it resonated most deeply in Milan, the city of fascism's birth.[6] The initiative for a new home for *Il Popolo d'Italia*, which, unlike most fascist institutions, always maintained its primary headquarters in Milan, also coincided

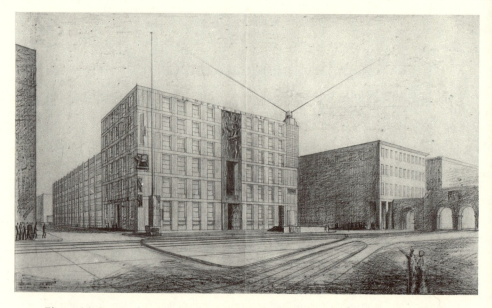

Figure 6.1. Perspective drawing for the Palazzo del *Popolo d'Italia*, Giovanni Muzio, 1938. Published in *Il Popolo d'Italia*, 15 November 1938. Archivio Giovanni Muzio, Milan.

with the municipal government's plans to reorganize Piazza Cavour, creating an opportunity for the press to locate its headquarters on what was anticipated to be a monumental piazza between the city's centre and the Central Station.

The politics of fascism and the mission of Mussolini's paper were closely intertwined. Mussolini founded the Milan-based daily in Novermber 1914, one month after he resigned as editor of the Italian Socialist Party's house organ, *Avanti!*, over political differences concerning his pro-war position.[7] Shortly thereafter he was expelled from the Socialist Party. *Il Popolo d'Italia*'s first offices were on the ground floor of a modest building on Via Paolo da Cannobio, a small street in a disreputable section of the city between the Duomo and the Ospedale Maggiore (see figure 1.7). Armed supporters guarded the doors. The venture received financial backing from the radical left, social reformers, and (because Mussolini ardently supported the war) major industrial concerns – namely, the Turin-based automobile manufacturer Fiat and the Genoa-based shipbuilding company Ansaldo.[8] In its early years, the paper, whose first issue carried on its masthead the slogans "Whoever has iron has bread" (quoting Louis Auguste Blanqui) and "The Revolution is an idea which has found its bayonets" (quoting Napoleon), sought to appeal to the disaffected proletariat and most of its writers were former socialists or syndicalists, although Giuseppe Prezzolini and others associated with the journal *La Voce* in Florence were a notable exception and gave the paper an avant-garde edge.[9] Contributions from Mussolini's mistress, Margheritta Sarfatti – who had been an art critic at *Avanti!* and now oversaw *Il Popolo d'Italia's* weekly column "Cronache d'Arte" (from 1918) – plus local news items from small towns throughout Italy, lists of soldiers who died on the front, and a few serial novels gave the paper a broader appeal.[10] In the early 1920s *Il Popolo d'Italia* served as a way of uniting Italy's autonomous fascist groups throughout the peninsula.[11] It also provided an expedient means to attract potential political allies and financial backers as well as to communicate Mussolini's political breadth to larger audiences.[12] When Mussolini relocated to Rome to lead the national government in 1922, he maintained control of the newspaper by communicating regularly with the editors-in-chief and appointing as director his younger brother Arnaldo, who had formerly worked on the accounting side of operations.

Mussolini's growing political fortunes resulted in progressively better-situated and better-appointed headquarters for *Il Popolo d'Italia*. Even though the paper remained nominally independent of both the Fascist Party and the state, funds from both (as well as continued support from the private sector) facilitated Mussolini's decision to move its editorial offices to a more gracious quarters in a building on Via Lovanio north of the city centre in 1921. The move gave the editorial staff more comfortable offices and located the paper's management near *Il Corriere della Sera* (Milan's leading daily) and the Palazzo di Brera, which housed several of the city's leading cultural institutions. In 1923, the same year that the party bought a palazzo on Corso Venezia for its headquarters, Arnaldo consolidated the paper's operations with the purchase of a recently completed four-storey palazzo at the corner of Via Lovanio and Via Moscova (figure 6.2), adjacent to the Via Lovanio offices it had occupied for the past two years, significantly enhancing *Il Popolo d'Italia*'s stature in the district.[13] The fact that Mussolini's office remained as he had left it after moving to Rome in 1922 reinforced its symbolic aspect.[14]

As editor, Arnaldo used the paper and its subsidiary publications – the most important of which were the monthly journal of political theory *Gerarchia* (1922–43), directed by Sarfatti, and the large-format, well-illustrated weekly *La Rivista Illustrata* (1923–43) – to build support for his brother's regime. The front page of *Il Popolo d'Italia*, embellished with photographs and drawings by artist Mario Sironi throughout the 1920s, served as a platform from which to celebrate the accomplishments of the fascist government.[15] Regular pieces on business, art, sports, and other leisure pursuits moderated the paper's tone and were intended to appease (or at least not offend) the Catholic Church and appeal to the business community, whose backing Arnaldo actively

Figure 6.2. Inauguration of *Popolo d'Italia*'s headquarters on the corner of Via Lovanio and Via Moscova on 23 December 1923. *La Rivista Illustrata del Popolo d'Italia* 2, no. 1 (1924): 7. The Wolfsonian-Florida International University, Miami Beach, Florida, The Mitchell Wolfson, Jr. Collection.

cultivated.[16] Circulation hovered around eighty thousand.[17] Arnaldo's premature death in December 1931 came as quite a blow to Mussolini, who had relied on his brother as a confidant and advisor. To carry on *Il Popolo d'Italia*'s mission, Mussolini named as the new director his "shy and reserved" nephew Vittorio, and as editor-in-chief his old friend Sandro Giuliani.[18] They took advantage of new printing technologies by using photographs in place of Sironi's expressive political cartoons (which he had hand-drawn), but otherwise did very little to respond to new trends in layouts, graphics, and content or the more modern modes of production adopted by other Italian newspapers.[19] To build consensus and limit opposition, Mussolini turned instead to other forms of mass persuasion, such as radio, mass rituals, and cinema, and expanded his control of news and information – first through the Press Office (Ufficio Stampa) and then the Undersecretariat for Press and Propaganda (Sottosegretario per la Stampa e Propaganda).[20] Although *Il Popolo d'Italia* continued to function as the official paper of the regime, it assumed a secondary role in the construction of fascism's image during the early 1930s.

In December 1936 Mussolini appointed a young journalist from Bologna, Giorgio Pini, as editor-in-chief of the paper and charged him with the task of revitalizing it and updating its image.[21] Mussolini wanted not only to infuse the paper with new energy and ideas in order to expand its influence but also to mitigate the effects of recent political, social, and economic upheaval. Although support for the regime remained strong, the invasion of Ethiopia (in 1935), the Declaration of Empire (1936), sanctions imposed on Italy by the League of Nations (1936), and Italy's involvement in the Spanish Civil War (1936–39) placed new pressures on existing resources and required the regime to adopt new tactics to maintain popular approval. Indicative of the revised role Mussolini saw for the paper, he instructed Pini to "get rid of emphatic and rhetorical drawings in order to make room for those that have a satirical and persuasive content (solicit drawings from Sironi)."[22] In the following months, the paper once again featured Sironi's striking illustrations on its front pages. The editorial tone of the paper also shifted, and a number of articles attacked industrial concerns (such as the chemicals manufacturer Montecatini) in response to popular, rather than bourgeois, interests.[23] Moreover, Mussolini sought to expand the paper's readership. In order to compete with Italy's leading papers, he directed Pini to "make *il Popolo d'Italia* a newspaper that gives the reader basic political direction along with all of the information and images of daily life."[24] Pini simplified headlines, made the graphic presentation of the journal's content bolder, added short articles (*corsivi*) on the front page on topics of popular interest, gave greater attention to local and regional news, and increased sports coverage.[25] Sales increased from 150,000 copies in January to 164,000 in February, then to 170,000 in March, and reached 205,000 in April 1937. Although circulation continued to rise – in part due to pressure placed on fascist groups to purchase subscriptions – the paper never outperformed *Corriere della Sera*, Italy's most widely circulating daily, and was never a financial success.[26]

As an extension of his campaign to augment the paper's stature, Pini oversaw the construction of a new headquarters large enough to accommodate its offices and production facilities on Piazza Cavour.[27] In the nineteenth century, the capacious and irregularly shaped Piazza Cavour served as the pivotal link between the urban core and the city's first passenger rail station in what is now Piazza della Repubblica (figure 6.3). To facilitate the flow of traffic to Piazza della Repubblica, the city opened Via Principe Umberto (now Via Filippo Turati) on the western edge of Piazza Cavour. Connecting Piazza Cavour to the city's centre is Via Alessandro Manzoni, at the other end of which are La Scala Theater and Palazzo Marino (the seat of the municipal government), and all along which are many distinguished neoclassical residences. The Arches of the Porta Nuova defined the southern boundary of the piazza and had once permitted access through the medieval walls of the city (see figures 6.1, 6.5, and 6.6). Seventy years later, the city inaugurated a massive new Central Station in Piazza A. Doria (now Piazza Duca d'Aosta). The new building stood further from the urban core but along the same axis as the nineteenth-century station. Via Manzoni, Piazza Cavour, and Via Filippo Turati thus continued to operate as the city's principal transportation hub, especially for businesses, residents, and institutions located in the city centre. Bounded by an eclectic jumble of buildings, and pierced at irregular angles by six streets, Piazza Cavour proved incapable of accommodating the demands of the modern city in the first decades of the twentieth century.

During the 1920s and 1930s, the reconfiguration of Piazza Cavour became a key component of the city's effort to improve the movement of people, automobiles, and trams into and out of the city's centre. Not only were the irregular boundaries of Piazza Cavour out of keeping with contemporary planning principles, but the Arches of the Porta Nuova restricted the flow of traffic through the plaza, despite the passages opened in the brick towers to either side of the arches in the late nineteenth century.[28] All the winning entries for the 1926–27 master plan competition proposed solutions. Portaluppi and Semenza, winners of the first-place prize, transformed Piazza Cavour into a large oval piazza with the medieval arches at its centre and introduced two major new arteries: one that carried traffic from the city's centre directly to the station and another that efficiently connected the plaza to central Milan. The winners of the second-place prize, the Club of Urbanists (Club degli urbanisti) – of which Muzio, the future architect of the Palazzo del *Popolo d'Italia* (now Palazzo dell'Informazione), was a member – also deflected traffic away from the historic Via Manzoni and the arches. To achieve this, the Club also proposed two new streets: the broad Via Trionfale, which would curve through the city towards the new station, and Via dei Giardini, which was to siphon off traffic from Via Manzoni and introduce much-needed green into the city centre by exposing to public view some of the few remaining private gardens in the city centre. Unlike the

Portaluppi-Semenza proposal, their plan left the area around Piazza Cavour untouched except for the isolation of the arches, a solution that was meant to preserve the monument and alleviate the traffic problems produced by its narrow openings. Despite the arches' continued value as a reminder of Milan's history, their scale and location placed them at odds with the modern city's requirements for the efficient and rapid transport of goods, services, and people.

The head of Milan's planning office, Cesare Albertini, adopting and extending ideas in Portaluppi and Semenza's winning project, intended to significantly increase the size of Piazza Cavour. He planned to clear the buildings surrounding the Arches of the Porta Nuova and to add additional openings to the already congested square (figure 6.4). The isolation (*isolamento*) of the arches paralleled the municipal government's treatment of select monuments in Milan, including the Roman columns of San Lorenzo on Corso di Porta Ticinese and the small votive chapel adjacent to the church of San Satiro just south of the Duomo. Similar strategies were employed in other Italian cities, most notably Rome, as part of Italy's ongoing effort to reconcile the nation's cultural heritage with modern needs. Albertini left the western edge of the square largely untouched. However, a major new road (*trasversale*) was proposed that would link the southern edge of Piazza Cavour to Piazza San Babila, a key focus of the city's redevelopment plans. Piercing the eastern side of Piazza Cavour was a smaller street, Via del Vecchio Politecnico, which separated the compound that had long housed the polytechnic and had more recently accommodated municipal offices from what was then the Hotel Cavour immediately to the north.[29] To Albertini's great frustration, *Il Popolo d'Italia* had purchased the site from the city and was planning to use it for its new headquarters, making it impossible for the city to carry out the "best and most obvious" reorganization of the piazza.[30]

Objections to Albertini's initial proposals for Piazza Cavour came from several camps. Muzio was among those who voiced their concerns in conferences, newspaper articles, pamphlets, and letters sent to government officials. Trained as an architect at the Polytechnic in Milan, Muzio in 1926 helped establish the Milan section of the Artistic Association (Associazione artistica fra i cultori di architettura), an organization devoted to advancing architecture within the public realm, and later taught town planning at the School of Architecture at the Polytecnic. The association's activities included the preservation of the built environment and the promotion of artistic and cultural debates as well as exhibitions, competitions, and other opportunities for professional development.[31] In his built works and essays, Muzio championed a contemporary architecture rooted in Lombard neoclassical traditions and

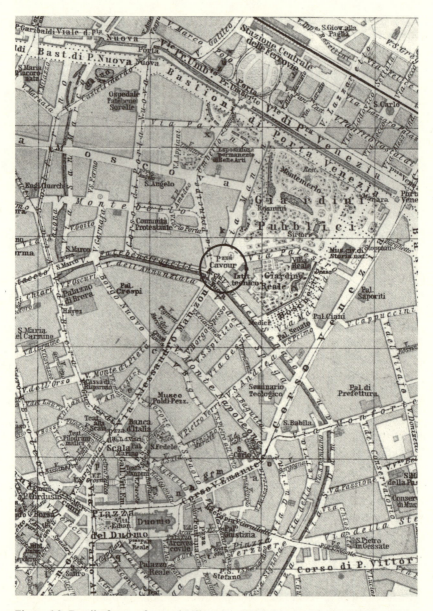

Figure 6.3. Detail of map of central Milan circa 1906 showing Piazza Cavour and the site of the Palazzo del *Popolo d'Italia*. From Baedeker, *Italy: Handbook for Travelers*.

Figure 6.4. Detail of proposed plan for central Milan showing the proposed reconfiguration of Piazza Cavour, 1930. Reggiori, *Milano*, 65.

capable of contributing to a "harmonic and uniform" urban whole.[32] Projects such as his Monument to the Fallen (1924–28) exemplified his engagement with history – one notably different from the archaeological character of that espoused by the Roman Piacentini – and also embraced the urban dimension of architecture. Accordingly, he criticized the municipal government for the fragmentary nature of its urban initiatives and for its acquiescence to speculative interests, a bureaucratic shortsightedness that damaged the old city and failed to provide a solid foundation for future growth.[33] As an alternative, Muzio advocated limiting changes to the city's antique centre and proposed expansion to the northwest, where modern efficiencies could be easily accommodated, a key idea of the Club of Urbanists' entry for the 1926–27 master plan competition. He also criticized the city's arbitrary placement of important institutions and the planning of new neighbourhoods without any public squares,[34] anchors for the establishment of coherent communities. In 1930 Muzio signed his name to a pamphlet offering a detailed critique of Piazza Cavour that he co-authored with Giuseppe De Finetti and Alberto Alpago Novello, both of whom were members of the Club of Urbanists. The group explained that the square "appeared shamelessly trimmed along its southern edges and became a diluted and distorted series of crossings and blunted and blundering corners where the city attempts in vain with planters and street furnishings to create symmetry."[35] The group also objected to the proposed addition of a major artery connecting Piazza Cavour with Piazza San Babila, arguing that it would do little to relieve existing congestion, and would instead exacerbate the visual disorder of the piazza and inhibit pedestrian traffic.

In 1931, Ettore Modigliani, the superintendent of medieval and modern art (Sovrintendente all'Arte Medioevale e Moderna) and advocate for the preservation of the historic fabric of central Milan, wrote to the Ministry of Education expressing his concern about the impact on the Arches of the Porta Nuova of the city's plan for the reorganization of Piazza Cavour.[36] He regarded Albertini's proposal as a prelude to the total destruction of "the oldest bulwark of the city of Milan and reminder of the greatest glory of the city."[37] Indeed, in a period of rapid change, the arches – constructed predominantly with stone blocks pilfered from Roman buildings – served as an important symbol of the city's ancient history. The arches also recalled Milan's resilience against foreign aggression: they had functioned as a part of the city's defence against Austria in 1848.[38] Modigliani recommended that the city designate the central openings in the gate to be used only for public transportation, modify the nineteenth-century arches to accommodate automobiles, and create galleries in the ground level of the adjacent buildings for pedestrian traffic – the same strategy that had been adopted by Camillo Boito for the Porta Ticinese at the end of the nineteenth century.[39] The Ministry of Education, led by Giuliano Balbino, a former Fascist Party deputy (1929–32), decreed that the need to accommodate vehicular traffic did not justify the isolation of the monument and advised the city to develop an alternate strategy in line with Modigliani's recommendations.[40] In addition, Ugo Ojetti, an influential conservative art critic and essayist, collected the signatures of twenty academicians opposed to the city's plan and sent them to the appointed mayor (*podestà*).[41] Despite these efforts, when the city unveiled Albertini's Master Plan in 1934, Piazza Cavour appeared as a large rectangular opening into which seven streets flowed, and the arches served as an aesthetic focal point for the largely reconceived square. Fortunately, though, the artery that had been proposed to connect Piazza San Babila and Piazza Cavour was missing from the plan, suggesting that the campaign launched by Muzio, DeFinetti, and others had met with some success.

In the late 1930s the *podestà*'s office established a series of commissions to resolve some of the more contentious features of the master plan, including Piazza Cavour, and to transform Milan in keeping with Mussolini's new imperial rhetoric.[42] In 1937 Guido Pesenti, who at that time was Milan's *podestà* (1935–38), invited Muzio to participate (shortly before he became involved with the design of *Il Popolo d'Italia*'s new headquarters).[43] A year later the *podestà* further eroded Albertini's influence by creating a new division (*divisione urbanisistica*) headed by Luigi Lorenzo Secchi, which was charged with revising Albertini's 1934 plan. Guided by new forces, the municipal government now proposed preserving the arches in their current location and explained that the central arched openings would serve as passages for trolley cars, the arches at the base of the brick towers would accommodate cars, and adjacent buildings would incorporate openings for pedestrians. To illustrate the municipal government's intentions, an evocative drawing published in the journal *Rassegna di Architettura* entitled "as it is" showed slightly dilapidated modest and irregular two- and five-storey buildings along the eastern and southern edges of the square and a smokestack in the distance (figure 6.5). Below it, the journal republished the rendering of Muzio's project for the new headquarters that had been featured in the newspaper in November 1938 (see figure 6.1). Entitled "as it will be," the latter drawing shows the arches with their broad central medieval vaults, the slightly narrower nineteenth-century arches to either side, and a trabeated gallery along the ground floor of the adjacent buildings.[44] Muzio's building stands as the primary feature of the square framed by new five-storey buildings. Figures roughly drawn in charcoal gesture and move towards the palazzo along the shadowy edges of the otherwise

Figure 6.5. Piazza Cavour "as it is." *Rassegna di Architettura*, no. 11 (1938): 471.

empty and expansive piazza. Located in its new urban context, the Palazzo del *Popolo d'Italia* functioned as a potent reminder of fascism's claim to be a regenerative and modernizing force.

Despite apparent agreement by that time, the city vacillated on its plans to reconfigure Piazza Cavour. In May 1939 *Il Popolo d'Italia* published another rendering of its new headquarters showing modifications to the building's design and to the Arches of the Porta Nuova. The original light pencil drawing from which the cropped image that appeared in *Il Popolo d'Italia* derives shows the arches stripped of their side towers and pulled from their context (figure 6.6). The decidedly ambivalent depiction of the medieval monument includes a tram lumbering through one of the arches and cars speeding around the broken remains. The only figure to pause is a single portly gentleman in the foreground at the left, perhaps the architect himself, who stands there looking vaguely towards the traffic-filled square. In early December of the same year, Gino Chierici, the superintendent of monuments in Milan, wrote an impassioned letter to the Ministry of Education arguing against the city's plan to isolate the arches. Chierici recommended a plan similar to that proposed a decade earlier by Modigliani and explained that it alone offered an economical solution, resolved the immediate traffic problem, and did not impede later revisions.[45] Chierici had successfully forced Portaluppi to redesign his addition to the Palazzo Castani for the Sede Federale a few years earlier. His office now pressured the city to adopt a more moderate solution for the Arches of the Porta Nuova.[46] Nevertheless, the municipal government continued to debate the appropriate form and character of the square until the outbreak of the Second World War.[47]

Figure 6.6. Perspective drawing of the Palazzo del *Popolo d'Italia* from Via Manzoni. Archivio Giovanni Muzio, Milan.

The new building in Piazza Cavour gave the newspaper an unprecedented opportunity not only to create a modern production facility and headquarters but also to redefine its symbolic role as the party's mouthpiece.[48] The choice of Muzio to design the building was made by Giulio Barella, the influential managing editor (*direttore amministrativo*). Barella also played an active role in the cultural life of Milan; as the president of the Milan Triennale, he oversaw the construction of the Palazzo dell'Arte (1932–33) designed by Muzio and funded by the industrialist Antonio Bernocchi.[49] Muzio used his intimate knowledge of Milanese architecture and of the paper, for which he had worked on numerous occasions, to create a building that both accommodated the functional needs of the paper and served as a museum, monument, and memorial to fascism.[50] Unencumbered by buildings on three of its four sides, the site allowed Muzio to design a building that appears as a free-standing structure when viewed from four of the seven streets that lead into the piazza (figure 6.7). Muzio took advantage of this to focus attention on the

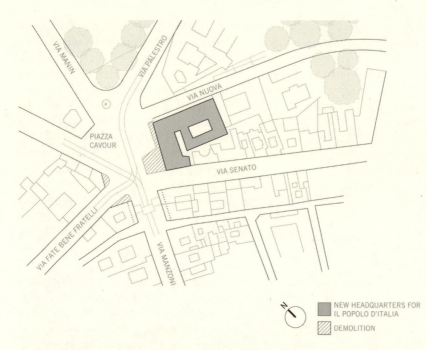

Figure 6.7. Site plan for the Palazzo del *Popolo d'Italia*, 1938. From *Il Popolo d'Italia*, 15 November 1938, redrawn by Coran.

principal façade facing Piazza Cavour, where the building's public and cere-monial spaces were located; the printing presses and staff offices, hidden from view, occupied the building's rear, along Via del Vecchio Polytecnico. For the principal façade, covered in stone, he reinterpreted the antique associations of the neoclassical Milanese palazzo in the building's low base and the horizon-tal rhythm of vertical supports. The building's rear façade would be covered with white glazed brick (*mattoni vetrificati*) and feature broad horizontal win-dows, both of which evoked a factory aesthetic.

The decorative program for the main façade (see figure 6.1) – carried out with Sironi, who had worked as an illustrator for the newspaper and had col-laborated with Muzio on several of its exhibitions and on other projects – reinforced the paper's Milanese origins and its unique status within fascism.[51] Sironi intended the most striking feature of the façade to be a six-storey-high bas-relief in the central entrance bay, encrusted with sculpture and cut by two deep openings (one for the entrance and the other for the ceremonial space behind and above the projecting balcony); and the dark, polished stone of the bay would have contrasted with the colour and material of the light stone facade. Muzio had already employed this technique in such buildings as the Catholic University (Università Cattolica, 1929–49) and the Palazzo dell'Arte, both in Milan. For the large relief, he planned to depict "the origins and the development of the paper of the Revolution."[52] The scale and visual impact of the relief displaced the piazza's focal point, a statue of Cavour (1865), a seminal figure in the Italian struggle for unification and Italy's first prime minister. Sironi had intended the façade to feature other sculptures, too, all of which were later eliminated, including a two-storey *fascio*, a relief of a horse and rider (presumably Mussolini), and two smaller reliefs. At the same time that Sironi's work muted the square's nineteenth-century history, the artist's crude forms and rough handling of stone reinforced associations with the worn Roman plaques and bas-reliefs embedded in the medieval Arches of the Porta Nuova.[53]

While Sironi's sculptures evoked fascism's obsession with Italian history, other aspects of the façade emphasized fascism's commitment to modernization. The façade's severe rectilinear composition (initial sketches show that Muzio had considered an arcuated façade) was a visual correlative of the rational and mechanical production processes contained within the complex. Muzio had also planned to crown the façade's southwest corner with a faceted, rotating beacon and a siren to serve as a "daily reminder to the Milanese that in the Duce's newspaper, the spirit of the Fascist Revolution is always ardent and vigilant."[54] Directly below the crystalline form of the beacon, Muzio would have included a three-storey panel featuring a kinetic display of "illuminated text that announced political events, sports events, etc."[55] Seen from the approach along Via Manzoni, which led from the city's centre to the piazza, or along Via Principe Umberto, which connected the piazza to the new Central Station, this was the most visible corner of the palazzo. Had they been completed, the radiant beacon and scrolling text would have broadcast the newspaper's image as a dynamic source of news and information throughout the city. Other architects, such as Alexander and Victor Vesnin, whose slender tower with an attached searchlight, moving parts, and changeable surfaces defined the exterior of their scheme for the Leningrad Pravda Building (1927), had already proposed the use of mechanized displays of news and information to embody social and political change. However, Muzio sought to reconcile images of modernity with established traditions by means of evocative visual references.[56] For example, the vertical emphasis of the beacon indicated that this corner could be read as a visual counterpoint to the spire of the medieval church of San Marco at the end of Via Fatebenefratelli, which served as the principal entrance to the piazza from the west. Any viewer standing in the piazza would have seen the ephemeral message of the light-filled corner and paired it with Sironi's telluric sculptures – together, dual images that summarized the persistent dialectic between the modern and the ancient in fascist rhetoric and representation.

Muzio's design suggests that the paper intended the main façade to serve as a backdrop for rallies held in the piazza as well as for smaller ceremonies performed on the plinth from which the building rose. *Il Popolo d'Italia*'s headquarters on Via Lovanio already served a ceremonial function. It was used for receptions for party and state leaders during their official visits to Milan and for the annual celebration honouring Arnaldo Mussolini.[57] Muzio's design made such events an explicit part of the new building's architectural program and incorporated the piazza into these festivities. The plinth recalled the low base supporting a classical temple as well as informal seating areas in Italian town squares – for example, stairs in front of a church or encircling a fountain – and reinforced the political aims embodied by the palazzo (see figures 6.1 and 6.8).[58] The raised area included a flagpole at the corner of the main façade's north end and terraced seating ornamented with low-relief sculptures at its south end, although these sculptures were never made. The diminutive grandstand faced the balcony (*arengario*)[59] on the main façade of the palazzo, directly above the entrance. Intended principally for Mussolini's use, this central balcony called forth associations with the balcony on Palazzo Venezia – the headquarters of Mussolini's government in Rome – from which the dictator gave rousing public speeches, and with the more modest rostrums of *case del fascio* throughout Italy. Sironi's bas-relief depicting the history of the paper stood directly above the balcony. When addressing the city, Mussolini would have been seen by crowds gathered in the square in a familiar architectural setting framed by an iconographic program that reinforced his dual role as the leader of fascist Italy and the creator of *Il Popolo d'Italia*. The tiered seating area also faced the screen planned for the southwest corner of the palazzo. Although never installed, the glowing panels would have been used to dramatic effect during mass gatherings broadcasting words and images. In Mussolini's absence, the display would have helped to convey his disembodied message to crowds in the piazza. Paired with the balcony, the rotating beacon with its vertical thrust strengthened associations with the towers of contemporary *case del fascio*. The communicative nature of the façade, the provisions made for organized gatherings, and the incorporation of architectural forms common to the party's centres all affirmed the paper's ties to the party.

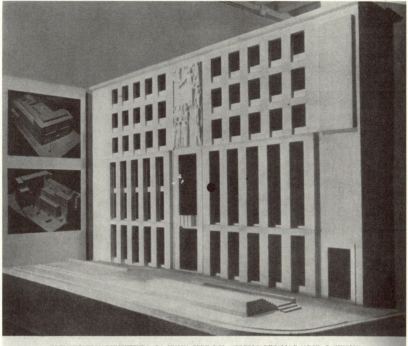

SEZIONE DELL'ARCHITETTURA: LA NUOVA SEDE DEL "POPOLO D'ITALIA" (ARCH. G. MUZIO)
(MILANO. VII TRIENNALE)

Figure 6.8. Model of the Palazzo del *Popolo d'Italia* exhibited at the VII Triennale, Milan, 1940. *Emporium* 5 (May 1940): 212.

   Although the rhetoric surrounding the project and the formal aspects of the initial design reinforced fascism's revolutionary claims, final proposals for the building adhered more closely to neoclassical traditions; for example, Muzio abandoned the strictly planar grid of the 1938 design, projecting the façade's lower section several inches forward to give the building a more legible vertical hierarchy, and eliminated the corner beacon to reinforce its bilateral symmetry (figure 6.8). The decorative program was also reduced, probably because of concerns about cost. Even as Muzio's project became more conventional in its appearance, contemporary accounts sought to emphasize its modernity, drawing attention to the paper's technological sophistication. *La Rivista Illustrata del'Popolo d'Italia*, the well-illustrated monthly companion to the newspaper, outlined the mechanical details of the printing press and the efficient organization of the building's interior, fostering an analogy between the productive efficiency of the press and of the modern factory.[60] In his journal Pini boasted, even before the details of the project were complete, that *Il Popolo d'Italia* would be technically better equipped than any newspaper in Europe. He also claimed that a correspondent from the *New York Times* considered the new building to be superior to that paper's offices in New York City, the city that most fully represented American technological achievement in the European imagination.[61] The fascist regime, self-conscious about Italy's late arrival to the industrial age, used the new building as evidence of the nation's industrial and technological progress. Nevertheless, the modernity of the building remained confined largely to the mechanical and organizational aspects of the press rooms and it never contributed in a substantial way to the symbolic role of the palazzo.

Instead, the symbolic features of the project celebrated the paper's intimate relationship with fascism and were concentrated on the main façade and on the interior spaces in the front of the building, the part facing Piazza Cavour. These spaces included offices for upper management, a memorial chapel (*sacrario*), a museum "illustrat[ing] the principal events of the life of the paper and preserv[ing] its most precious memories," re-creations of several rooms associated with key moments in fascist history, offices for the Fascist Group of *Il Popolo d'Italia* and for the paper's party-run leisure-time organization (*dopolavoro*), and a theatre capable of accommodating five hundred people.[62] To distinguish between the spaces devoted to the routine operations of the paper and those concerned with the history of *Il Popolo d'Italia*, Muzio established a ceremonial route through the building that began with a memorial chapel located directly opposite the main entrance on the first floor (figure 6.9).[63] From there, visitors travelled up a staircase to reach the museum on the second floor, featuring the "Room of October 28" commemorating the March on Rome, "Bonservizi Hall" (named for the fascist martyr Nicola Bonservizi), and the "Room of Arnaldo" (dedicated to Mussolini's brother, the former director of the paper).[64] The Gallery or Museum of the People (Galleria/Museo del Popolo) overlooked the piazza.[65] In his final plan, Muzio presented a unified space to house the various exhibits: two large rectangular rooms fronted Via Senato, and a single large hall with regular vertical supports along its inner edge faced Piazza Cavour (figure 6.10). From this hall one could continue into an antechamber that led to the thirty-two-by-thirty-two-foot (ten-by-ten-metre) Room of the Duce (Sala del Duce) and to the ceremonial balcony. The broad outline of the program reiterated that of the national party headquarters in Rome, the Palazzo del Littorio, for which a competition was held in 1934. In addition to providing offices for party officials, meeting spaces,

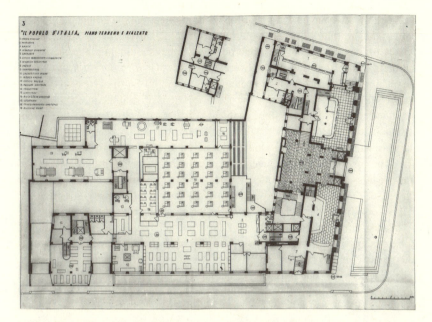

Figure 6.9. Plan of the ground floor and mezzanine, Palazzo del *Popolo d'Italia,* 1938–40. Piazza Cavour is to the right. Archivio Giovanni Muzio, Milan.

and a mortuary chapel, the Palazzo del Littorio was to include a permanent setting for the *Exhibition of the Fascist Revolution* (*Mostra della Rivoluzione Fascista*), the event that served as the conceptual model for the commemorative and symbolic spaces of the Palazzo del *Popolo d'Italia.*

The *Exhibition of the Fascist Revolution,* held in Rome in 1932 to celebrate the tenth anniversary of the March on Rome (27–28 October 1922), was designed by a group of artists and architects, including Mario Sironi, Adalberto Libera, Mario De Renzi, Mino Maccari, Achille Funi, Leo Longanesi, and Giuseppe Terragni. It documented the role of *Il Popolo d'Italia* as a force of social change and cemented the connection between the newspaper and the rise of fascism.[66] As the accompanying catalogue explained, the exhibition served "to demonstrate how a paper [*Popolo d'Italia*] directed by a man [Mussolini] of genius, of sharp will, and of burning passion, can truly construct history."[67] Dino Alfieri (president of the Milanese Institute of Fascist Culture), Antonio Monti (curator and director of the Museum of the Risorgimento in Milan), and journalist Luigi Freddi organized the exhibition, and originally intended to present it in Milan.[68] Although it was ultimately held in Rome, the exhibition

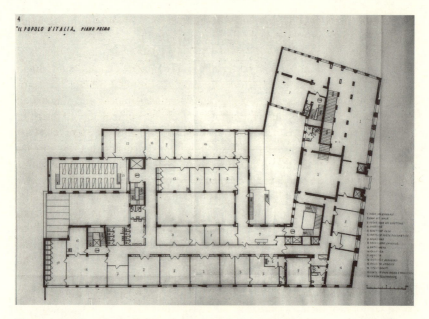

Figure 6.10. Plan of second floor, Palazzo del *Popolo d'Italia*, 1938–40. Piazza Cavour is to the right. *1*, Gallery or Museum of the People; *2*, Sala del Duce. Archivio Giovanni Muzio, Milan.

preserved *Il Popolo d'Italia*'s position at the centre of the visual and narrative story line. The organizers devoted the first room to an exhibit describing the start of the First World War and the founding of *Il Popolo d'Italia*; reproductions of the newspaper, often fragments of text or headlines, were placed throughout the show; and towards the end, the exhibit included recreations of Mussolini's offices in Milan.[69] Most dramatically, Mussolini's office on Via Paolo da Cannobio was placed within what Emily Braun has aptly termed a "cubic tabernacle" in a small rectangular room with thick, canted walls designed by Mario Sironi.[70] From the "grave and silent" Room of Honour, visitors next passed through Sironi's Gallery of the Fasces, a long, rectangular hall featuring a series of oversize fasces at regular intervals along its entire length, resembling a colonnade, and on into the next room, the Shrine of the Martyrs (Sacrario dei Martiri), designed by Adalberto Libera and Antonio Valente.[71] This sequential display illustrated Mussolini's political maturation from revolutionary leader to head of state and established his offices as hallowed spaces in the public imagination. Sironi used several visual techniques from this exhibition in the design of the Palazzo del *Popolo d'Italia*.

In the Palazzo del *Popolo d'Italia*, the T-shaped entrance atrium with a mortuary chapel planned at its far end offers the most complete expression of Muzio and Sironi's program for the interior of the palazzo. From the piazza, the visitor passed though a vestibule into a hall faced with marble blocks and punctuated by three sets of piers with archaic palmette-capitals. Immediately to the right and left, doors opened to a bank and the newspaper's offices, respectively. Past the second set of piers, the hall widened slightly, an expansion that was emphasized on both sides by the corner placement of marble bas-relief sculptures derived from Roman standards. Designed by Sironi, each standard featured six medallions inscribed with primitive glyphs and was surmounted by an eagle, a symbol of Italy's imperial ambitions. Sironi set the standards into the depth of the wall and flush with the smooth blocks of the stone revetment, which were separated by deep vertical joints. The juxtaposition of these two elements suggested the transformation of raw stone into sculpture or architecture. The weighty marble walls and measured rhythm of the piers effectively maintained the monumentality and architectural order of the building's exterior and prepared visitors for their ascent to the gallery spaces above.

Muzio used a shift in material and architectural form to separate the mortuary chapel from the circulation space of the atrium. He placed a single dark stone column with small cushion capitals at either end of the transverse axis and dressed the walls of the mortuary chapel with flush stone blocks; the side walls were later given the same revetment as the rest of the atrium (figure 6.11). The change from pier to column and from rusticated to flush stone slabs corresponded to Muzio's interest in the primary components of architecture already established with his treatment of the wall surface. Plans and elevations from April 1941 show that Muzio and Sironi intended the mortuary chapel to include a large statue of Arnaldo Mussolini set on a low base to the right of the central axis, and that Muzio planned to face the rear wall with large trapezoidal stone slabs and an inscription reading "Arnaldo" in commanding block letters.[72] Apart from the statue, he gave the mortuary chapel minimal decorative embellishment; a blank stone panel occupied each side wall, and two windows at either end of the back wall permitted light to enter from the inner courtyard. Whether because of its high cost or for other reasons, Muzio removed the statue of Arnaldo in favour of a sculpted rectangular panel in the summer of 1941. After this date, plans show various alternatives sketched in pencil and then erased, suggesting that Muzio and Sironi never arrived at a satisfactory solution.[73] The walls, piers, and columns were the only part of the program

Figure 6.11. View showing the rear of the entrance atrium and the stairs leading up to exhibition space on the second floor of the Palazzo del *Popolo d'Italia*. Archivio Giovanni Muzio, Milan.

to be completed. The paper's decision to give the palazzo a mortuary chapel programmatically linked the project to the party's headquarters throughout the city and affirmed the building's role as a siginificant feature of the ritual topography of the city.

The atrium and the mortuary chapel prepared the viewer for the Room of the Duce, "which dominated the centre of the entire building" on the second floor directly above the entrance atrium and on axis with the central balcony.[74] The square shape of this room recalled Mussolini's office as it had been reconstructed for the *Exhibition of the Fascist Revolution*, drawing attention to some of the formal and conceptual parallels between the exhibition and the palazzo. Although several artists were involved in the interior décor, Sironi played a major role.[75] Muzio and Sironi focused on the rear wall (in front of which Mussolini's desk would have been placed) and the opposite wall, which led to the antechamber between the Room of the Duce and the balcony facing Piazza Cavour. The remaining sketches and plans for these elevations show that the back wall was to be treated as an architectural backdrop and the front wall was to be given a didactic role. In one version, a large square panel occupies the space above the entrance to the balcony and features heavy block text reading: "This Century of Fascism is for you and those that come after you."[76] Embedded in the wall below the panel were a *fascio* and the Roman numeral *XX*, a reminder of the twentieth anniversary of the March on Rome. The arrangement replicated Sironi's treatment of the rear wall of Room Q in the *Exhibition of the Fascist Revolution*. Elevations show the wall surface to either side decorated with regular rectangular geometric patterns, striated bands, and arches. These compositions correspond to his dramatic undated charcoal rendering of the wall behind Mussolini's desk (figure 6.12). Its primitive force continued themes first presented in the cryptlike space of the mortuary chapel and suggests that the remainder of the decorative program would have been conceived in similar terms.

The next major element of the ceremonial sequence was the projecting balcony on the front of the main façade, which returned the focus of the project to the public life of the piazza. In contrast to the abstract architectural forms intended for the Room of the Duce, figurative sculptures predominated on the balcony and central bay. Sironi framed the balcony with low-relief carvings of the *fascio* and standard in polished porphyry, two reminders of Roman authority from antiquity.[77] The front face of the porphyry balcony featured a low-relief sculpture, *The People of Italy* (*Il Popolo d'Italia*), designed by Sironi and executed by Carlo Sessa.[78] The sturdy forms and deep shadows of the roughly carved farmers, workers, and soldiers marching towards the central figure of Italia reinforced the ritualized procession suggested by the piers of

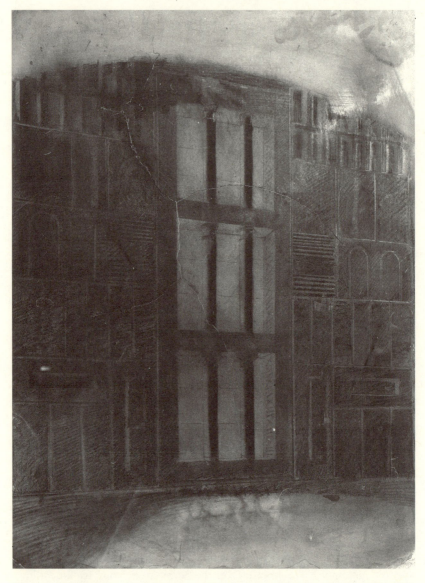

Figure 6.12. Charcoal study for the rear wall of the Room of the Duce (Sala del Duce) in the Palazzo del *Popolo d'Italia*, Mario Sironi. Archivio Giovanni Muzio, Milan.

the façade and entrance hall. Together, these spaces created a scripted path that led from the atrium through the museum to the Room of the Duce. Above the porphyry balcony gleamed Sironi's white low-relief panel in Carrara marble, also entitled *The People of Italy* and carried out by Sessa. Sironi made the imperial eagle and the female personification of Italy holding a Roman sword the focus of this composition and framed the two figures with blank expanses of rough marble and dense groupings of male and female figures representing national attributes and the Italian people. The eagle and warrior Italia were an extension of the late regime's aggressive and militaristic language, and the clustered figures reminded viewers of one of the founding myths of fascism – that the paper and the movement were a manifestation of the will of the people. Directed towards the piazza, where the masses would have converged to hear the words of the Duce, the balcony and decorative program found its ultimate meaning in the piazza, a symbol and site of collective experience and action.

Muzio's Palazzo del *Popolo d'Italia* was the final manifestation of the newspaper's important role in the history of the fascist movement and one of the last expressions of the regime's authority in Milan. Italy entered the Second World War on the side of Germany in the spring of 1940 and, in keeping with the austerity required by the war effort, the opening of the paper's new offices occurred "without useless ceremonies, without fanfare" in 1942.[79] *Il Popolo d'Italia* occupied the palazzo for only eighteen months before the enterprise expired; its final day of publication was 26 July 1943, the day after King Victor Emmanuel III placed Mussolini under military arrest. The building was one of several new structures that were begun in the final years of the regime – perhaps most notably the Arengario (now Palazzo del Turismo, 1935–43), also by Muzio – intended to make fascism a major feature of the city's symbolic landscape. The building, planned to function as a speaking rostrum, was part of the anticipated transformation of Piazza del Duomo and Piazza Diaz (the controversial piazza adjacent to Piazza del Duomo and directly opposite the Gallery of Victor Emanuel II), which was also to include a new regional party headquarters.[80] The Palazzo del *Popolo d'Italia* as well as the Arengario used architecture in addition to new urban patterns to reorient the city away from the institutions and environments associated with the nineteenth-century bourgeois city and towards those that most effectively communicated fascism's presence and command. In the aftermath of the collapse of the regime, the buildings most intimately associated with fascism – including the Palazzo del *Popolo d'Italia* and the Fascist Party headquarters – served as targets of anti-fascist attacks.[81] Throughout the city, ordinary citizens, former fascists, and members of the Resistance participated in parades and demonstrations through which they sought to repossess the public spaces of the city. As has often been noted by scholars, the most arresting example of Italians' effort to use the spaces of the city to announce the demise of the regime was the display of the corpses of Mussolini, his mistress, and other fascist officials in Piazzale Loreto in Milan on 29 April 1945. The spontaneous nature and public spectacle of much of this process of reclaiming the city served as a visceral means of rejecting nearly twenty years of fascist rule and signalling the start of a new era. Yet despite such efforts to signal a rupture with the immediate past, Milan's architectural and urban character remain indebted to the monuments and buildings erected by the regime and to the processes of change set in place during the interwar years.

Epilogue

Speaking at the First National Urban Planning Conference (I Congresso Nazionale di Urbanistica) held in Rome in the spring of 1937, Giuseppe Bottai, the former governor of Rome and recently appointed minister of education, asserted that public buildings functioned as the generative force in the formation of cities and of urban centres in Italy. Bottai declared that "the modern Italian city, the fascist city," would be created from two kinds of urban planning elements: new fascist institutions, such as *case del fascio*, and traditional public buildings, such as the Town Hall and Palace of Justice.[1] The dedication of the regime's resources to a broad range of symbolic edifices – from large-scale monumental buildings to more modest civic structures – was intended to accomplish several goals: to relieve unemployment during the worldwide economic crisis, to appropriate traditional institutions for fascist purposes, to establish new institutions to promote fascist values, and to turn Italian cities into fascist ones. My aim in investigating Milan's interwar transformation, through the public buildings central to Mussolini's effort to develop and maintain support for his regime, has been to clarify the fascist engagement with the Lombard capital. It shows that Milan played a critical though variable role in shaping fascism's national image throughout the *ventennio nero* and that, at least for the majority of government and party officials, the city's identity as a centre of commercial and economic operations and its status as the birthplace of the movement drove symbolic concerns. At the same time, despite fascism's palpable influence in Milan's development during that period, the buildings discussed in detail point to the limits of Mussolini's ability to advance his initiatives in an environment that remained loyal to its own traditions and fundamentally resented Rome's authority. This has been made evident through the action (or inaction) of a large cast of characters – including speculative builders, industrial leaders, municipal officials, and members of the local cultural elite – who remained committed to their own set of priorities. The case of interwar Milan complicates the current understanding of the relationship between architecture and politics in fascist Italy and serves as a point of departure for assessing the Italian situation in relation to that of other totalitarian regimes (and liberal democracies) in the first half of the twentieth century. It also sheds light on this northern Italian city's reconstruction and expansion after the Second World War.

Scholars have devoted significant attention to analysing the ways in which governments with revolutionary claims have used large-scale demolitions, monumental public buildings, and grandiose urban gestures to glorify the state and obscure the complexities caused by social, political, cultural, and economic change. In studies of interwar Europe, much of this research has focused on the ways in which the leaders of totalitarian regimes applied these strategies to capital cities – namely, Berlin, Madrid, Moscow, and Rome – in order to make them more effective and responsive political centres.[2] Metropolitan areas that possessed a personal, symbolic, or strategic value, including Barcelona in Spain, St Petersberg in Russia, and Munich in Germany, were also marked for significant redevelopment, although scholars have focused less on these examples. In the case of Germany (the situation that most closely approximates the Italian one), Hitler assigned secondary urban centres an explicit role within the national hierarchy. For example, Linz, Austria, the city where he spent his youth, was designated for new cultural attractions and industrial expansion (the Hermann Goering Steel Works were established there in 1938). Nuremberg, in part because of its political importance during the Holy Roman Empire, became the "City of Party Rallies." Hamburg, a long-established port city, was to be the "City of Foreign Trade." Munich, the city that, after Berlin, received most of Hitler's attention, took on the dual identity of "Capital of the Movement" and "Capital of German Art." Hitler located the Nazi Party's national headquarters there in a private house appropriated by the government in 1931, until he had Paul Ludwig Troost construct a new headquarters in the same city in 1936. He also approved an urban plan that would have reorganized Munich around intersecting axes anchored by transportation nodes, modelled on Albert Speer's plan for central Berlin. This grand scheme called attention to the city's cultural institutions (including a new opera house and the recently completed House of German Art), and required the destruction of much of the old town to make way for administration buildings and residential neighbourhoods – but only a fraction of it was constructed.[3]

Despite Hitler's efforts to control local affairs, the transformation of Munich and other cities was not always straightforward. As scholars have begun to reveal through new research, the process of adapting the built environment to incorporate architectural and urban forms commensurate with Hitler's ambitions took time; and local personnel, as well as those who sought to benefit from the Nazi program of secularization and industrialization, often wielded more political power than state officials from Berlin.[4] A more complete understanding of central authorities' efforts to position such urban centres (often cities with their own well-established economic, cultural, and political traditions) within the new order, and of local responses to these pressures, would help clarify the way politics has shaped the built environment more broadly and the limits of any central authority to act locally.

Milan's interwar urban development must also be examined in terms of international architectural and planning debates. Albertini's vision of fascist Milan remained closely tied to the great urban plans of the late nineteenth century and that tradition's more recent interpretation in the American City Beautiful movement. As in Daniel Burnham's lavishly illustrated plan for Chicago (1909), Albertini sought to create a well-ordered, scenographically composed city centre in which monumental civic buildings provided a decorous backdrop for urban activities. It paid little attention to the city's growing housing crisis and the concerns of the working classes. Modernity was promulgated in a concern for the rational organization of services, the efficient movement of people and goods, the redevelopment of depressed areas, the construction of new buildings of impressive size, and the belief that commercial and industrial activity would define the modern city and resolve its problems. Cultural institutions played a role in the life of the city but were always secondary to economic and political concerns. The municipal government did little to regulate development on the periphery, a practice that encouraged private developers to construct mid-rise residential buildings without considering their proximity to services and that led to undifferentiated sprawl. Although Novecento architects drew attention to the problems created by this lack of planning, this group also benefited from their involvement in the design of office, residential, and government buildings, particularly in the city centre. The residential communities proposed by Rationalist architects in the 1930s, inspired by the Garden City Movement, German experimental housing projects of the 1920s, and the planning proposals of CIAM (Congrès internationaux d'architecture moderne), critiqued the settlement patterns and priorities established by the Albertini Plan. Projects by Rationalists, including Milano Verde (1938) and Quattro Città Satelliti (1939–40), received substantial critical acclaim; however, they had little influence on the city's interwar development.[5] Their utopian spirit and cosmopolitan values failed to offer the kind of community that appealed most to a population in the midst of upheaval; and the outbreak of the Second World War required authorities to support the war effort and provide basic services to the men, women, and children who did not go to the front.

The Italians entered the Second World War in June 1940. The effects on Milan were immediate, as the municipal government restricted access to public places, limited the circulation of trams, and covered monuments and buildings with scaffolding and sandbags to protect against inevitable aerial bombardment.[6] The Allied bombing of the city began in October 1942 and, over the course of the war, resulted in the damage or destruction of between 16 and 25 per cent of the city's building stock. Factories and infrastructure (major roads, rail networks, and the like) were the primary targets, but the campaign also compromised residential buildings, schools, monuments, and public buildings, many of which were in the historic centre.[7] Following the war the state began to repair buildings damaged in aerial campaigns, including Piacentini's Palace of Justice. It commandeered party-owned property, including former party headquarters, and removed or modified fascist imagery before adapting these buildings to serve new purposes. However, the scale of destruction demanded comprehensive action (particularly in the housing sector) and created an opportunity in Milan – as in other Italian cities – to consider how architects might contribute to the rebuilding of Italy.[8]

In November 1945 the Allied-controlled municipal government (since May of that year) announced a "competition of ideas" for a new master plan. Among the submissions was the AR Plan (Piano AR, or *architetti riuniti*) developed by a group of young Milanese architects who had been active just before the war: Franco Albini, Ludovico Belgiojoso, Piero Bottoni, Ezio Cerutti, Ignazio Gardella, Gabriele Mucchi, Giancarlo Palanti, Enrico Peressutti, Mario Pucci, Aldo Putelli, and Ernesto Rogers. Their proposal sought to dismantle the city's monocentric character and radial form, and responded to the concerns for regional planning spelled out in the Town Planning Act of 1942, legislation passed just before the collapse of the regime and indebted to the lessons of fascist-era master plans. The AR Plan emphasized the development of new transportation networks (including a subway system), decentralized industrial complexes linked to self-sufficient residential communities, abundant green space in and around the city, and a new district to accommodate business, commercial, and financial services.[9]

The city's new master plan, finally approved in 1953, carried the imprint of the AR Plan. However, key aspects of the plan – including the development of a new business district and decentralized residential communities – were either dropped or substantially altered under pressure from business interests.[10]

Perhaps most important of all, the city proved unable to override the contracts between developers and the municipality drawn up in the interwar period and became entangled in private interests that found limited merit in the enlargement of the city's green spaces and social services.[11] The optimism of the "economic miracle" and a renewed interest in Milan's role as a centre of art and culture spurred projects such as the expansion of the Galleria d'Arte Moderna with a new pavilion designed by Ignazio Gardella (in 1949 and 1951–53), and the restructuring of the museums at the Castello by BBPR (in 1956–63). The Torre Velasca plan (BBPR, 1956–58) filled in areas of the city damaged during the war, introduced the skyscraper to Milan, and positioned its architects at the centre of national and international architectural debates. Despite the rhetoric of change and reform, Milan's urban form and architectural character remains deeply indebted to the decisions made and compromises reached by those involved in the building process in the first half of the last century. Their legacy can be found at nearly every scale, from monumental architectural ensembles in the centre of the city to the more modest party headquarters constructed on the periphery, as well as in the challenges that persist in Milan today, such as high density of the centre of the city, lack of green space, and sprawling growth along the city's edge.

Notes

Introduction

1 "[D]eve, …, avere nella grandezza della Metropoli Lombarda l'immagine anticipata della grandezza dell'Italia. Essa deve essere seconda Roma per grandezza
politica, insubre Atene per grandezza civile." "La Milano di domani," *Il Popolo
d'Italia*, 30 September 1923. Unless otherwise indicated, all translations are
my own.

2 In comparison to other Italian cities, the bibliography for Rome during the
interwar period is vast – see, for example, Spiro Kostof, *The Third Rome,
1870–1950: Traffic and Glory,* exhibition catalogue (Berkeley: UC Berkeley
Art Museum, 1973); Antonio Cederna, *Mussolini urbanista: Lo sventramento di
Roma negli anni del consenso* (Laterza: Bari, 1979); Valter Vannelli, *Economia
dell'architettura in Roma fascista* (Rome: Kappa, 1981); Italo Insolera, *Roma
moderna: Un secolo di storia urbanistica, 1870–1970* (Turin: Einaudi, 1993);
Giorgio Ciucci's annotated bibliography "Gli studi sulla città e l'architettura a
Roma durante il fascismo una proposta di bibliografia ragionata," *Roma Moderna
e Contemporanea* 2, no. 3 (1994): 587–604; Vittorio Vidotto, "Roma Fascista,"
in *Roma Contemporanea* (Laterza: Bari, 2001), 172–223; and more recently,
Paul Baxa, *Roads and Ruins: The Symbolic Landscape of Fascist Rome* (Toronto:
University of Toronto Press, 2010). Significant scholarly attention has also been
devoted to the new towns founded under Mussolini in, for example, Riccardo
Mariani, *Fascismo e città nuove* (Milan: Feltrinelli 1976); Henry Millon, "Some
New Towns in Italy in the 1930s," in *Art and Architecture in the Service of
Politics*, ed. Henry Millon and Linda Nochlin (Cambridge, MA: MIT Press,
1978), 326–41; Riccardo Mariani, *Città e campagna in Italia, 1917–1943* (Milan:
Edizioni di Comunità, 1986); Diane Ghirardo, *Building New Communities: New*

Deal America and Fascist Italy (Princeton: Princeton University Press, 1989);
Giorgio Muratore, Daniela Carfagna, and Mario Tieghi, eds., *Sabaudia, 1934:
Il sogno di una città nuova e l'archittura razionalista* (Sabaudia: Comune di
Sabaudia, 1999); and Renato Besana et al., eds., *Metafisica costruita: Le città
di fondazione degli anni Trenta dall'Italia al Oltramare* (Milan: Touring Club
Italiano, 2002). See also Jean-Françoise Lejeune, "Futurismo e città di fondazione:
Da Littoria a Guidonia, città aerofuturista," in *Angiolo Mazzoni e l'architettura
futurista* (Rome: Fondazione CE.S.A.R. Roma, 2010), 59–74. Recent work focus-
ing on provincial expressions of interwar Italian architecture include D. Medina
Lasansky, *The Renaissance Perfected: Architecture, Spectacle and Tourism
in Fascist Italy* (University Park, PA: Penn State University Press, 2004); and
Diane Ghirardo, "Inventing the Palazzo del Corte in Ferrara," in *Donatello
Among the Blackshirts: History and Modernity in the Visual Culture of Fascist
Italy*, ed. Claudia Lazzaro and Roger J. Crum (Ithaca: Cornell University Press,
2005). There is also a significant body of work focusing on Italy's building cam-
paigns in north and east Africa; see Marida Talamona, "Libya: An Architectural
Workshop," *Rassegna* 14, no. 51 (1992): 62–79; Krystyna von Henneberg,
"Imperial Uncertainties: Architectural Syncretism and Improvisation in Fascist
Colonial Libya," *Journal of Contemporary History* 31, no. 2 (1996): 373–95;
Edward Denison, Guang Yu Ren, and Naigzy Gebremedhin, *Asmara: Africa's
Secret Modernist City* (London: Merrell, 2003); Brian McLaren, *Architecture and
Tourism in Italian Colonial Libya: An Ambivalent Modernism* (Seattle: University
of Washington Press, 2006); Mia Fuller, *Moderns Abroad: Architecture, Cities
and Italian Imperialism* (New York: Routledge, 2007); David Rifkind, "Gondar:
Architecture and Urbanism for Italy's Fascist Empire," *Journal of the Society of
Architectural Historians* 70, no. 4 (2011): 492–511.

3 Giorgio Ciucci, *Gli architetti e il fascismo: Architettura e città* (Turin: Einaudi,
   1989), 57.

4 B.R. Mitchell, *European Historical Statistics, 1750–1975*, 2nd rev. ed. (New York:
   Facts on File, 1980), 87.

5 Mitchell, *European Historical Statistics,* 87.

6 "[L]a città italiana più segnata, in termini assoluti e relativi, dal bisturi fascista."
   Giancarlo Consonni and Graziella Tonon, "Milano: Classe e metropoli tra
   due economie di guerra," in *Annali (Fondazione Giangiacomo Feltrinelli)*
   (1979/80): 486.

7 Giancarlo Consonni and Graziella Tonon, "La terra degli ossimori," *Storia d'Italia*
   (Turin: Einaudi, 2001), 143.

8 Luciano Patetta, "Cultura urbanistica e architettura nella Milano degli anni' 30,"
   Milano: Città piano progetti, special issue, *Casabella* 451/452 (October/November
   1979): 47.

9   Emilio Gentile, *The Sacrilization of Politics in Fascist Italy*, trans. Keith
    Botsford (Rome: Laterza, 1993) (originally published as *Il culto del littorio: La
    Sacralizzazione della politica nell'Italia Fascista*).

10 Paolo Nicoloso, *Mussolini architetto: Propaganda e paesaggio urbano nell'Italia
    fascista* (Turin: Einaudi, 2008), 34–81.

11 The rhetoric of empire, as in the rest of Italy, became increasingly important after
    1936. Nicoloso, *Mussolini architetto*, 251–4.

12 Diane Ghirardo, "Inventing the Palazzo del Corte in Ferrara," 97–112.

13 Victoria de Grazia, *The Culture of Consent: Mass Organization of Leisure in
    Fascist Italy* (New York: Cambridge University Press, 1981).

14 Lasansky, *The Renaissance Perfected*, 107–43.

15 Scholars have shown particular interest in housing. See, for example, Giancarlo
    Consonni and Graziella Tonon, "Casa e lavoro nell'area Milanese: Dalla fine
    dell'Ottocento al fascismo," *Classe* 9, no. 14 (1977): 165–259; and Maurizio
    Boriani, "La costruzione della Milano moderna," in *La costruzione della Milano
    moderna: Casa e servizi in un secolo di storia cittadina*, by Maurizio Boriani et al.
    (Milan: Clup, 1982), 51–97.

16 "[C]ovandolo e cocendolo." Ferdinando Reggiori, *Milano, 1800–1943* (Milan:
    Edizioni del Milano, 1947), 58.

17 Dario Franchi and Rosa Chiumeo, *Urbanistica a Milano in regime fascista*
    (Florence: La Nuova Italia Editrice, 1972), 7.

18 Franchi and Chiumeo, *Urbanistica a Milano,* 111.

19 Andrea Bona, "Il Club degli architetti urbanisti: Una battaglia per Milano," in
    *Città immaginata e città costruita: Forma, empirismo e tecnica in Italia tra Otto e
    Novecento*, ed. Cristina Bianchetti (Milan: F. Angelli, 1992), 91–111.

20 Paolo Muraldi, "La stampa quotidiana del regime fascista," in *La stampa Italiana
    nell'età fascista*, ed. Nicola Tranfaglia, Massimo Legnani, and Paolo Murialdi
    (Bari: Laterza, 1980), 248–9.

21 For a review of the theoretical foundations of this research, its primary
    currents, and some of its possibilities see Nancy Stieber, "Microhistory of
    the Modern City: Urban Space, Its Use and Representation," *Journal of the
    Society of Architectural Historians* 58, n. 3 (1999): 382–91. The following were
    particularly useful at various stages of this project: Brian Ladd, *Urban Planning
    and Civic Order in Germany, 1860–1914* (Cambridge, MA: Harvard University
    Press, 1990); Nancy Stieber, *Housing Design and Society in Amsterdam:
    Reconfiguring Urban Order and Identity, 1900–1920* (Chicago: University of
    Chicago Press, 1998); Eve Blau, *The Architecture of Red Vienna, 1919–1934*
    (Cambridge, MA: MIT Press, 1999); Sheila Crane, *Mediterranean Crossroads:
    Marseille and Modern Architecture* (Minneapolis: University of Minnesota
    Press, 2011).

1. Milan in Context

1 "Quest'ultimo è il caso di Milano, fervida di vita, ricca di iniziativa, di impulsi, di attività molteplici e feconde nel campo della produzione come in quello della cultura e dell'arte. Di simili città è necessario seguire punto per punto il ritmo e l'ascensione." Proemio di Arnaldo Mussolini per la relazione del concorso, Archivio Storico Civico, Milan (ASCM), Ornato Fabbriche (OF), c. 141.

2 Aurora Scotti, "Architettura in Lombardia tra fasto, funzionalità e profitto," in Aldo Castellano et al., *La Lombardia delle riforme* (Milan: Electa, 1987), 178. See also Ferdinando Reggiori, *Milano, 1800–1943* (Milan: Edizioni del Milano, 1947), 19–22.

3 See Marco Meriggi, "Lo 'Stato di Milano' nell'Italia unita: Miti e strategie politiche di una società civile (1860–1945)," in *La Lombardia*. ed. Duccio Bigazzi and Marco Meriggi (Turin: Einaudi, 2001), 7–49.

4 The term "liberal" can refer to the Liberal Party, but it is most often used with a lower case to indicate several different political parties that shared related political philosophies in the period following Italian unification.

5 Giancarlo Consonni and Graziella Tonon, "Casa e lavoro nell'area Milanese: Dalla fine dell'ottocento al fascismo," *Classe* 9, no. 14 (1977): 168.

6 B.R. Mitchell, *European Historical Statistics, 1750–1975,* 2nd rev. ed. (New York: Facts on File, 1980), 86–8.

7 Maurizio Boriani provides a very useful overview of Milan's urban and architectural history from unification to the First World War: "Sviluppo urbano, cultura, architettonica e trasformazioni del costruito (1861–1918)," in *Milano contemporanea: Itinerari di architettura e urbanistica*, ed. Maurizio Boriani, Corinna Morandi, and Augusto Rossari (Milan: Maggioli, 2007), 11–36.

8 Maurizio Boriani and Corinna Morandi, "La formazione del sistema urbano e territoriale in Italia," in *La costruzione della Milano moderna: Casa e servizi in un secolo di storia cittadina,* by Maurizio Boriani et al. (Milan: Clup, 1982), 15.

9 For a portrait of the social and economic complexion of the city council in this period, see Marco Meriggi and Louise A. Tilly, "Notables, Bourgeoisie, Popular Classes, and Politics: The Case of Milan at the End of the Nineteenth Century," *Social Science History* 19, no. 2 (1995), 277–80; Boriani, "La costruzione della Milano moderna," in Maurizio Boriani et al., *La costruzione della Milano moderna: Casa e servizi in un secolo di storia cittadina* (Milan: Clup, 1982), 54; Davide Del Curto and Angelo Landi, "Gas-Light in Italy between 1770s & 1880s: A History of Lighting," in *The Culture of Energy*, ed. Mogens Rüdigen (Newcastle: Cambridge Scholars Publishing, 2008), 19–23.

10 Boriani, "La costruzione della Milano moderna," 53.

11 Rail lines connected Milan to Como (1840), Treviglio (1846), and shortly thereafter Genova, Piacenza, and Torino. Luigi Dodi, "L'urbanistica Milanese dal 1860 al
   1945," Special issue, *Urbanistica* 25, nos.18–19 (1956): 24.

12 Reggiori, *Milano, 25.*

13 Ornella Selvafolta, "Housing the Urban Industrial Work Force: Milan, Italy, 1860–
   1914," *Journal for the Society of Industrial Archaeology* 6, no. 1 (1980): 13.

14 For a general history of the project see Ornella Selvafolta, "La Galleria Vittorio
   Emanuele II," in *Costruire in Lombardia,1880–1980,* vol. 1, ed. Aldo Castellano
   and Ornella Selvafolta (Milan: Electa, 1983), 221–65.

15 Selvafolta, "La Galleria Vittorio Emanuele II," 238, 254, 263; Boriani, "Sviluppo
   urbano," 13.

16 Scotti, "Architettura in Lombardia," 179–82.

17 Etienne Dalmasso, *Milano capitale economica d'Italia*, trans. Andrea Caizzi and
   Dario Gibelli (Milan: Franco Angeli, 1972), 187–8.

18 Dalmasso, *Milano capitale economica*, 193–4.

19 "Le esposizioni milanesi del 1881 e del 1906," in Valerio Castronovo et al., *La
   Lombardia Moderna* (Milan: Electa, 1989), 105–9. For a broader cultural review
   of the event see Giovanna Rosa, *Il mito della capitale morale: Letteratura
   e pubblicistica a Milano fra Otto e Novecento* (Milan: Edizioni di Comunità,
   1982), 20–2.

20 "Le esposizioni milanesi," 105–9.

21 Vittorio Spinazzola, "La 'capitale morale': Cultura Milanese e mitologia urbana,"
   Belfagor 3 (May 1981): 317.

22 Rosa, *Il mito della capitale morale*, 145–60.

23 See Reggiori, *Milano*, 29–38; Renato Airoldi, "La Milano dell'ingegner Beruto,"
   Casabella, 451–2 (1979): 12–17; Renato Rozzi, ed., *La Milano del Piano
   Beruto (1884–1889): Società, urbanistica e architettura nella seconda metà
   dell'Ottocento,* vol. 1 (Milan: Guerini, 1992); Maurizio Boriani and Augusto
   Rossari, eds., *La Milano del Piano Beruto (1884–1889): Società, urbanistica
   e architettura nella seconda metà dell'Ottocento,* vol. 2 (Milan: Guerini, 1992).

24 Mitchell, *European Historical Statistics*, 88.

25 Florence was the capital of Italy from 1865–70.

26 Guido Zucconi, *La città contesa: Dagli ingegneri sanitari agli urbanisti (1885–
   1942)* (Milan: Editoriale Jaca, 1989), 56.

27 Paolo Mezzanotte and Giacomo Bescape, *Milano nell'arte e nella storia* (Milano:
   E. Bestetti, 1948), 271.

28 Lucio Gambi, *Milano* (Roma: Laterza, 1982), 204.

29 Gambi, *Milano*, 204.

30 Boriani, "Sviluppo urbano," 17.

31 On Vienna, see Carl E. Shorske, *Fin-de-Siècle Vienna: Politics and Culture* (1961; New York: Random House, 1981).

32 Boriani, "La costruzione della Milano moderna," 58.

33 Reggiori, *Milano*, 32.

34 Augusto Rossari, "Architettura e immagine della Città: Note a partire dal dibattito in Consiglio Comunale," in *La Milano del Piano Beruto (1884–1889): Società, urbanistica e architettura nella seconda metà dell'Ottocento*, vol. 1, ed. Maurizio Boriani and Augusto Rossari (Milan: Guerini, 1992), 277.

35 The piazza also held the Credito Italiano (Luigi Broggi, 1901) and Assicurazioni Generali (Luca Beltrami, 1899–1901). To the west of the piazza along Via Cordusio were the Palazzo delle Poste centrali (Paolo Cesa Bianchi, 1905–07, and Giannino Ferrini, 1910–12) and the Banca d'Italia (Luigi Broggi and Cesare Nava, 1907–12).

36 "[C]arattere eminentemente commerciale ...," quoted in Ornella Selvafolta, "Architettura per la nuova società: La ricerca della modernità fra Ottocento e Novecento," in Valerio Castronovo et al., *La Lombardia Moderna* (Milan: Electa, 1989),158.

37 Dalmasso, *Milano capitale economica*, 173.

38 Meriggi and Tilly, "Notables, Bourgeoisie, Popular Classes, and Politics," 279.

39 Dalmasso, *Milano capitale economica*,196–7.

40 Giancarlo Consonni and Graziella Tonon, "La Terra degli Ossimori," in *La Lombardia*, ed. Duccio Bigazzi and Marco Meriggi (Turin: Einaudi, 2001), 111.

41 "Una sensazione di tensione, di slancio verso il futuro era a quei tempi diffusa un po' dappertutto nell'aria di Milano ... Dappertutto si fabbricava, si puliva, si restaurava. Si viveva come in un'ebbrezza di rinnovamenti e di rischio. Si sentiva che la città voleva arrivare a un suo destino di metropolis." Carlo Linati, *Sulle orme di renzo: Pagine di fedeltà lombarda* (Rome: La Voce, 1919), 31.

42 Boriani, "La costruzione della Milano moderna," 60; Meriggi, "Lo 'Stato di Milano' nell'Italia unita," 33.

43 Gambi, *Milano*, 205.

44 Consonni and Tonon, "Casa e lavoro nell'area Milanese," 167–8.

45 Between 1881 and 1901 the population beyond the Spanish walls went from 143,000 to 294,000. Boriani, "La costruzione della Milano moderna," 60.

46 For a thoughtful discussion of workers' housing in this period see Selvafolta, "Housing the Urban Industrial Work Force."

47 Boriani, "La costruzione della Milano moderna," 77.

48 Boriani, "La costruzione della Milano moderna," 60.

49 Boriani, "La costruzione della Milano moderna," 56–7.

50 Guido Bezzola, "La Milano dei loisirs," in *Milano nell'Italia Liberale, 1898–1922*, ed. Giorgio Rumi, Adele Carla Buratti, and Alberto Cova (Milan: Cariplo, 1993), 121.

51 Massimo Negri, "Il mito di Milano e i riti della società borghese," in *La città bor-
    ghese: Milano, 1880–1968,* ed. Massimo Negri and Sergio Rebora (Milan: Skira,
    2002), 92–3.
52 Boriani, "Sviluppo urbano," 21.
53 Adolfo Scotto Di Luzio, "L'Industria dell'informazione: Periodici e quotidiani,
    giornalisti e imprenditori," in *La Lombardia,* 348.
54 Selvafolta, "Architettura per la nuova società," 171.
55 Meriggi and Tilly, "Notables, Bourgeoisie, Popular Classes, and Politics," 280.
56 Boriani, "Sviluppo urbano," 25.
57 Kent Roberts Greenfield, *Economics and Liberalism in the Risorgimento: A Study
    of Nationalism in Lombardy 1814–1848* (Baltimore: Johns Hopkins University
    Press, 1934, 1965), 117–18.
58 Selvafolta, "Housing the Urban Industrial Work Force," 14–16.
59 Consonni and Tonon, "Casa e lavoro nell'area Milanese," 179–81; Anna Treves,
    "La Politica antiurbana del fascismo e un secolo di resistenza all'urbanizzazione
    industriale in Italia," in *Urbanistica Fascista: Ricerche e saggi sulle città e il terri-
    torio e sulle politiche urbane in Italia tra le due guerre,* ed. Alberto Mioni (Milan:
    Angeli, 1980), 314–15.
60 Rosa, *Il mito della capitale morale,* 30.
61 Guido Baglioni, *L'ideologia della borghesia industriale nell'Italia liberale* (Turin:
    Einaudi, 1974), 388–90; Louise A. Tilly, "Structure and Action in the Making of
    Milan's Working Class," *Social Science History* 19, no. 2 (1995): 251–4.
62 Meriggi, "Lo 'Stato di Milano' nell'Italia unita," 26.
63 R.J.B. Bosworth, *Italy and the Approach of the First World War* (New York: St.
    Martin's Press, 1983), 16–18.
64 Selvafolta, "Housing the Urban Industrial Work Force," 17–18.
65 Meriggi, "Lo 'Stato di Milano' nell'Italia unita," 36; Boriani, "La costruzione
    della Milano moderna," 85–6.
66 Christine Poggi, "Mass, Pack, and Mob: Art in the Age of the Crowd," in *Crowds,*
    ed. Jeffrey T. Schnapp and Matthew Tiews (Stanford: Stanford University Press,
    2006), 170.
67 Leopoldo Marchetti, *Milano tra due guerre: 1914–1946* (Milan: Istituto ortope-
    dico "Gaetano Pini," 1963), 19.
68 Dalmasso, *Milano capitale economica,* 214.
69 Sergio Zaninelli, "Lo sviluppo industriale di Milano negli anni Venti e Trenta,"
    in *Il sogno del moderno: Architettura e produzione a Milano tra le due guerre,*
    ed. Alberto Mioni, Antonello Negri, and Sergio Zaninelli (Florence: Edifir,
    1994), 9.
70 R.J.B. Bosworth, *Mussolini* (New York: Oxford University Press, 2002), 89–90.
71 Adrian Lyttelton, *The Seizure of Power: Fascism in Italy, 1919–29* (New York:
    Scribner, 1973), 47.

72 Ivano Granata, "PNF: Organizzazione del consenso e società Milanese negli anni trenta," in *Storia di Milano*, vol. 18, pt. 1 (Rome: Istituto della Enciclopedia Italiana, 1995–96), 624.

73 Lyttelton, *The Seizure of Power*, 50; Marchetti, *Milano tra due guerre,* 18.

74 Stanley Payne, *A History of Fascism, 1914–45* (London: University College London, 1995), 93.

75 Payne, *A History of Fascism*, 99.

76 Granata, "PNF," 265.

77 Ivano Granata, "Il Regime Fascista," in *Milano durante il fascismo, 1922–45*, ed. Alberto Cova, Giogio Rumi, and Virgilio Vercelloni (Milan: Cariplo, 1994), 14.

78 Granata, "Il Regime Fascista," 45.

79 Granata, "Il Regime Fascista," 47.

80 "Milano è ad un'ore del confine. Lo straniero che vi scende, deve, come disse il Presidente del Consiglio dei Ministeri, avere nella grandezza della Metropoli Lombarda l'immagine anticipata della grandezza dell'Italia. Essa deve essere seconda Roma per grandezza politica, insubre Atene per grandezza civile." "La Milano di domani," *Il Popolo d'Italia*, 30 September 1923. For an overview of the city's inter-war history see Augusto Rossari, "Architettura e Trasformazioni Urbane dal 1920 al 1940," in *Milano contemporanea: Itinerari di architettura e urbanistica*, ed. Maurizio Boriani, Corinna Morandi, and Augusto Rossari (Milan: Maggioli, 2007), 37–61.

81 On 2 September 1923 Milan annexed the surrounding towns of Affori, Baggio, Chiaravalle Milanese, Crescenzago, Gorla-Precotto, Greco Milanese, Lambrate, Musocco, Niguarda, Trenno, and Vigentino. On 23 December of the same year, the city incorporated Ronchetto sul Naviglio and Lorenteggio. Reggiori, *Milano*, 45–6; Dario Franchi and Rosa Chiumeo, *Urbanistica a Milano in regime fascista* (Florence: La Nuova Italia Editrice, 1972), 5.

82 Robert John Mullin, "Ideology, Planning Theory and the German City in the Inter-War Years: Part I," *Town Planning Review* 53, no. 2 (1982): 119.

83 Reggiori, *Milano*, 45–6.

84 Genoa absorbed sixteen towns (174,000 residents), Naples eight, Reggio Calabria fourteen, and Venice five. Zucconi, *La città contesa,*, 139.

85 "Mussolini per la più grande Milano," *Il Popolo d'Italia*, 25 August 1923.

86 Alberto Mioni, "La Città e l'urbanistica durante il fascismo," in *Urbanistica fascista*, 26, 30; Loretto di Nucci, *Fascismo e spazio urbano: Le città storiche dell'Umbria* (Bologna: Mulino, 1992), 23.

87 Reggiori, *Milano*, 46. See also Luigi Dodi, ed., *Aspetti, problemi, realizzazioni dei Milano: Raccolta di scritti in onore di Cesare Chiodi* (Milan: Giuffre, 1957); Zucconi, *La città contesa,* 136–7.

88 Renzo Riboldazzi, *Una città policentrica: Cesare Chiodi e l'urbanistica milanese nei primi anni del fascismo* (Milan: Polipress, 2008),10.

89 For an overview of the debate surrounding the role of engineers see Zucconi, *La città contesa,* 93–131.

90 Cesare Chiodi, "Come viene impostato dalla città di Milano lo studio del suo nuovo piano di ampliamento" (Milan: Stab. Stucchi Ceretti, 1925).

91 Riboldazzi, *Una città policentrica,* 139.

92 The title *podestà* evoked the name given to the head of local governments in Italian medieval city-states. For the reorganization of municipal and provincial governments under fascism, see Ettore Rotelli, "Le trasformazioni dell'ordinamento comunale e provinciale durante il regime fascista," *Storia Contemporanea* 4, no. 1 (1973): 57–121.

93 For the history of the competition, see Reggiori, *Milano,* 53–9; Franchi and Chiumeo, 15–26.

94 "La creazione anche al centro di nuovi nuclei edilizi concepiti con unità architettonica." Bando di Concorso Nazionale per lo Studio di un Progetto di Piano regolatore e d'ampliamento per la Città di Milano, ASCM, OF, c. 1411.

95 "La indicazione delle aree riservate ai vari Uffici pubblici, governative e comunali, e agli altri edifici che sono necessari alla vita intellettuale e materiale di una grande città." Bando di Concorso Nazionale, ASCM, OF, c. 1411.

96 Additional notable participants included one of the authors of the 1912 master plan for Milan, Giovanni Masera; the director of the Pinacoteca Brera, Ettore Modigliani; a leading Milanese architect and professor at the Milan Polytechnic, Gaetano Moretti; the architect of Milan's Central Station, Ulisse Stacchini; the artist and caricaturist for *Il Popolo d'Italia,* Mario Sironi; the noted sculptor Adolf Wildt; and the Roman architect Armando Brasini. Elenco dei componente, La commissione per l'esame dei progetti di Piano regolatore del Comune di Milano, ASCM, OF, c. 1411.

97 Albertini wrote many articles about Milan's urban form. See, in particular, *The Characteristic of the Development of Milan* (Milan: Edizione del Comune, 1929) as well as G. Laura Di Leo, ed., *Cesare Albertini urbanistica: Antologia di scritti* (Rome: Gangemi, 1995).

98 Andrea Bona, "Il Club degli architetti urbanisti: Una battaglia per Milano," in *Città Immaginata e città costruita: Forma, empirismo e tecnica in Italia otto e novecento,* ed. Cristina Bianchetti (Milan: F. Angeli, 1992), 97–8.

99 "Il Fascismo, per la sua stessa concezione di vita collettiva, non è favorevole all'accentrarsi delle popolazioni nelle grandi città. Il preoccupante fenomeno dell'urbanesimo, sebbene in Italia non raggiunga limiti eccessivi, è vigilato attentamente e contenuto." Proemio di Arnaldo Mussolini per la relazione del concorso, ASCM, OF, c. 1411.

100 For a discussion of Mussolini's anti-urbanism and further references, see Anna Treves, "La politica antiurbana," 313–30; Per Binde, "Nature Versus

City: Landscapes of Italian Fascism," *Environment and Planning D: Society and Space* 17, no. 6 (1999): 761–6. Riccardo Mariani details this political shift and its relationship to housing in Italy in *Città e campagna in Italia 1917–43* (Milan: Edizioni Comunità, 1986); see in particular 11–12, 59–61, 71, 115–22. See also Benito Mussolini, *Opera Omnia*, ed. Edoardo Susmel and Dulio Susmel (Florence: La Feince, 1957): "Il Discorso dell'ascensione," 26 May 1927, 12:360–90; "Il numero come forza," 1 September 1928, 13:197–8; and "Sfolare le città," 22 November 1928, 13:256–8.

101 Robert R. Taylor, *Word in Stone: The Role of Architecture in the National Socialist Ideology* (Berkeley: University of California Press, 1974), 250–5; John Robert Mullin, "Ideology, Planning Theory and the Germany City in the Inter-War Years: Part II," *The Town Planning Review* 53, no. 3 (1982): 258–60.

102 Treves, "La Politica antiurbana," 323–5.

103 Treves, "La Politica antiurbana," 328–9.

104 Zaninelli, "Lo sviluppo industriale di Milano negli anni Venti e Trenta," 9, 17, 20.

105 "Altre hanno grande importanza per la loro efficienza e il loro compito. Quest'ultimo è il caso di Milano, fervida di vita, ricca di iniziativa, di impulsi, di attività molteplici e feconde nel campo della produzione come in quello della cultura e dell'arte. Di simili città è necessario seguire punto per punto il ritmo e l'ascensione." Proemio di Arnaldo Mussolini per la relazione del concorso, ASCM, OF, c. 1411.

106 For a more complete history of the competition and its results, see Riboldazzi, "Nihil sine studio 2000" and "Gli esiti del concorso per il nuovo Piano rego-latore," in *Una città policentrica*, 141–202, 203–69; Giuseppe De Finetti, *Milano: Costruzione di una città*, ed. Giovanni Cislaghi, Mara De Benedetti, and Piergiorgio Marabelli (Milan: Etas Kompass, 1969), 221–39; Reggiori, *Milano*, 53–9; Franchi and Chiumeo, 15–26; Piero Portaluppi and Marco Semenza, *Milano, com'è ora come sara* (Milan: Bestetti e Tumminelli, 1927). Christina Bianchetti argues that the emphasis on circulation reflected Portaluppi's under-standing of rapid movement as one of the essential features of the modern city; it also maintained the modernist interest in circulation as the basis for spatial expe-rience and fascination with a rationally conceived urban structure: "Portaluppi e Milano," in *Portaluppi: Linea errante nell'architettura del Novecento*, ed. Luca Molinari (Milan: Skira, 2003), 259.

107 The most active participants in jury were Albertini, Piacentini, Ojetti, Gorla, and Belloni. It was Ojetti who persuaded the members of the artistic subcommittee, whose advocate was Piacentini, to award "Ciò per amore" rather than "Forma urbis Mediolani" first place. Verbale della seduta 18 giugno 1927, ASCM, OF, c. 1411.

108 "Mediolani" was the name for Milan in the Middle Ages, and the group may have been referring to the Milanese poet Bonvesin da la Riva's *De magnalibus urbis Mediolani* (*Concerning the Great Works of the City of Milan*), written in 1288. For a general discussion of this plan in addition to the reference already given, see Renato Airoldi, "Forma urbis Mediolani: Un'illusione aristocratica," *Casabella* 468 (1981): 34–43.

109 Led by Giuseppe De Finetti, the group included Tomaso Buzzi, Ottavio Cabiati, Ambrogio Gadola, Emilio Lancia, Michele Marelli, Alessandro Minali, Giovanni Muzio, Alberto Alpago Novello, Piero Palumbo, Gio Ponti, and Ferdinando Reggiori. See Andrea Bona, "Città e architettura a Milano da Novecento al Razionalismo: 1921–33," 129–50; Annegret Burg, *Novecento Milanese: I Novecentisti e il rinnovamento dell'architettura a Milano fra il 1920 e il 1940* (Milan: Frederico Motta Editore, 1991).

110 Verbale della seduta 18 Giugno 1937 and Commissione per il Piano regolatore seduta del 3 October 1927, ACSM, OF, c. 1411.

111 "Il Duce approva il progetto per il Piano regolatore," *Il Popolo d'Italia*, 14 July 1927.

112 Corinna Morandi, "Per un profilo biografico di Cesare Albertini," in G. Laura Di Leo, ed., *Cesare Albertini urbanistica: Antologia di scritti* (Rome: Gangemi, 1995), 273.

113 Zucconi, *La città contesa*, 149.

114 Morandi, "Per un profilo biografico di Cesare Albertini," 273; Paolo Nicoloso, "L'urbanistica delle riviste di architettura tecnica, igiene, e amministrazione: 1921–32," in *Città immaginata e città costruita: Forma, empirismo e tecnica in Italia otto e novecento*, ed. Cristina Bianchetti (Milan: F. Angeli, 1992), 215–17; Zucconi, *La città contesa*, 155–63.

115 Indicative of this change, the population within the core of the city dropped from 102,902 in 1921 to 93,245 in 1931. Zaninelli, "Lo sviluppo industriale di Milano negli anni Venti e Trenta," 17.

116 Boriani, "La costruzione della Milano moderna," 89.

117 Boriani, "La costruzione della Milano moderna," 93.

118 Vittoria de Grazia, *Irresistible Empire: America's Advance through Twentieth-Century Europe* (Cambridge, MA: Belknap, 2005), 54–5.

119 Ernesto Cianci, *Il Rotary nella società Italiana* (Milan: Mursia, 1983), 139–41.

120 Bona, "Il Club degli architetti urbanisti," 91–111.

121 One of the most enduring criticisms of the 1934 master plan was its lack of a clear financial plan. See, for example, Franchi and Chiumeo, 29; De Finetti, *Milano*, 278. Scholars have looked at the effects of this policy on the lower classes and the poor. See Giancarlo Consonni and Graziella Tonon, "Milano: Classe e metropoli tra due economie di guerra," in *La classe operaria durante il*

fascismo, Annali, Fondazione Giangiacomo Feltrinelli 20 (1979/80); Boriani, "La costruzione della Milano moderna," 94–7.

122 "Roma mangia, ma Milano paga." Fiduciary report, 20 November 1938, Archivio Centrale dello Stato (ACS), Partito Nazionale Fascista (PNF), Situazione Politica ed Economia delle Province, Rome, b. 7.

2. Respectable Fascism

1 "Il Gruppo rionale rimane sempre una sede strettamente politica. Deve essere austero e severo, attivo in ogni branca del bene. Alcuni compiti ben definiti sono la vigilanza contro i residui atteggiamenti antinazionali, la severità contro i dissolvitori e i seminatori di discordia. Vi è infine un compito di volgarizzazione fascista e gli spunti necessari a questo fine sono forniti ogni giorno dall'azione del Duce e dei gerarchie dalla politica nazionale ed internazionale." "Stile Fascista, Gruppi rionale," *Il Popolo d'Italia*, 18 October 1929.

2 See Augusto Rossari, "Ideologia e tipizzazione," in *Architetture sociali nel Milanese, 1860–1990,* by Cesare Stevan et al. (Milan: Touring Club Italiano, 1994), 57–105.

3 Despite their importance to the Fascist Party, *case del fascio*, with the exception of Giuseppe Terragni's Casa del Fascio in Como, have been given only marginal scholarly attention; see Diane Ghirardo, "Architecture and the State: Fascist Italy and New Deal America," doctoral diss., Stanford University, 1982, 47–91. Later articles by the same author elaborate on aspects of this research, among them "Terragni, Conventions, and the Critics," in *Critical Architecture and Contemporary Culture*, ed. William J. Lillyman, Marilyn F. Moriarty, and David J. Neuman (New York: Oxford University Press, 1994), 91–103. See also Franco Biscossa, "Dalla casa del popolo alla casa del fascio," in *Case del popolo: Un architettura monumentale del moderno,* ed. Marco De Michelis (Venice: Marsilio, 1986), 175–224; Emilio Gentile, *The Sacralization of Politics in Fascist Italy*, trans. Keith Botsford (Cambridge, MA: Harvard University Press, 1996), 102–31; Flavio Mangione, *Le case del fascio in Italia e nelle terre d'Oltremare* (Rome: Ministero per i beni e le attività culturali direzione generale per gli archivi, 2003); Paolo Portoghesi, Flavio Mangione, and Andrea Soffitta, eds., *L'architettura delle case del fascio: Catalogo della mostra, Le case del fascio in Italia e nelle terre d'Oltremare* (Florence: Alinea, 2006).

4 "Teste calde, gente turbolenta con le bombe sempre in tasca che aveva troppi nemici." Piero Parini, "La Casa del Fascio di Milano," *La Rivista Illustrata del Popolo d'Italia* 2, no. 4 (1924): 28; Adrian Lyttelton, *The Seizure of Power: Fascism in Italy, 1919–29* (New York: Scribner, 1973), 38–53; Lyttelton, "Fascismo e violenza: Conflitto sociale e azione politica in Italia nel primo dopoguerra," *Storia Contemporanea* 13, no. 6 (1982): 965–83.

5 *Il Popolo d'Italia*, 6, 11, 14, 23 December 1921.

6 See Mario Missori, *Gerarchie e statuti del PNF: Gran consiglio, direttorio, nazionale, federazione provinciale* (Rome: Bonacci, 1986), 87–90. The statute is reproduced on pp. 333–51.

7 Missori, *Gerarchie e statuti del PNF*, 336.

8 Gentile, *The Sacralization of Politics*, 1–31.

9 "Oggi fra i molti altari delle molte religioni, abbiamo finalmente e stabilmente consacrati anche gli altari delle religione della patria. E intorno a questi altari noi educheremo i nostri figli. Le sede in cui ci raccoglieremo, saranno chiese per la nostra fede; e fortilizi per le nostre battaglie." "La nuova sede del Circolo 'Fabio Filzi' inaugurata alla presenza della madre dell'eroe," *Il Popolo d'Italia*, 9 October 1923. For biographical information see Manlio Morgani, "Attilio Longoni," *La Rivista Illustrata del Popolo d'Italia* 10, no. 4 (1932): 19; Ivano Granata, "Il Partitio Nazionale Fascista a Milano tra 'dissidentismo' e 'normalizzazione' (1923–1933)," in *Il fascismo in Lombardia: Politica, economia e società*, ed. Maria Louisa Betri et al. (Milan: Franco Angeli, 1989), 13.

10 Alberto C. O'Brien, "Italian Youth in Conflict: Catholic Action and Fascist Italy, 1929–1931," *The Catholic Historical Review* 68, no. 4 (1982): 625–35.

11 Biscossa, "Dalla casa del popolo alla casa del fascio," in *Case del Popolo*, 175–224; Luigi Arbizzani, Saveria Bologna, and Lidia Testoni eds., *Storie di case del popolo: Saggi, documenti e immagini d'Emilia Romagna* (Casalecchio di Reno, Bologna: Grafis, 1982), 17–31; S. Frederick Starr, *Melnikov: Solo Architect in a Mass Society* (Princeton: Princeton University Press, 1978), 130–45; Deitrich Schmidt, "From People's House to 'School of Communism': Houses for Training Programs and Recreation – The Development of the Soviet Worker's Clubs," in *Konstantin S. Mel'nikov and the Construction of Moscow*, ed. Mario Fosso, Otakar Máčel, and Maurizio Meriggi (Milan: Skira, 2000), 77–83.

12 Mabel Bezerin, *Making the Fascist Self: The Political Culture of Interwar Italy* (Ithaca: Cornell University Press, 1997), 159–60.

13 Dylan Riley, "Civic Associations and Authoritarian Regimes in Interwar Europe: Italy and Spain in Comparative Perspective," *American Sociological Review* 70, no. 2 (2005): 289–300.

14 Luigi Ganapini, "Il Partito Nazionale Fascista a Milano negli anni trenta," in Camillo Brezzi and Luigi Ganapini, *Cultura e società negli anni del fascismo* (Milan: Cordani, 1987), 302.

15 For a discussion that positions this project within contemporary cultural and political debates, see Andrea Bona, "Il Club degli architetti urbanisti: Una battaglia per Milano," in *Città immaginata e città costruita: Forma, empirismo e tecnica in Italia tra Otto e Novecento*, ed. Cristina Bianchetti (Milan: F. Angelli, 1992), 95–7.

16 "La posizione è ottima. Centrale e tuttavia non soffocata nelle strette viuzze." "Circoli rionali fascisti," *Il Popolo d'Italia*, 4 July 1922.

17 "La prima impressione era veramente disastrosa e le note di languidi valtzer di una
    vicina sala da ballo della reputazione equivoca, aggiungevano un che di sardonico
    alla infinita povertà dell'ambiente." Parini, "La Casa del Fascio di Milano," 28.
18 Parini, "La Casa del Fascio di Milano," 29.
19 "Deliberazioni del Direttorio," *Il Popolo d'Italia*, 6 May 1922.
20 "Il Fascismo costruisce – romanamente – pietra su pietra, i suoi edifici ideali."
    Mussolini, "Per la nuova sede del Fascio di Milano," *Il Popolo d'Italia*, 11 May
    1922.
21 "La nuova casa del Fascismo Milanese," *Il Popolo d'Italia*, 5 September 1923.
22 "La nuova casa del Fascismo Milanese," *Il Popolo d'Italia*, 5 September 1923.
23 "L'abbiamo voluta bella e anche architettonicamente aristocratica perché al bello
    e alle aristocrazie tendono gli sforzi del Fascismo." "La nuova Casa del Fascio
    Milanese," *Il Popolo d'Italia*, 30 October 1923.
24 *Il Popolo d'Italia* credited this statement to Mario Giampaoli. "La nuova Casa del
    Fascio," *Il Popolo d'Italia*, 9 October 1927.
25 "Venendo qui intendo anche tributare un plauso a tutti i soci dei circoli rionali
    milanese. Io ammiro che voi facciate delle belle sedi. Siamo degli artisti. Non
    amiamo le buie cantine. Lasciamo i circoli sudici ed infetti a quelli che apparten-
    gono alla bassa zoologia. Le nostre sedi non saranno mai sufficientemente belle,
    pulite, e degna. Debbono essere dei tempi, non solo del case; debbono avere linee
    armoniose e possenti. Quando il fascista entra nella sede del suo circolo deve
    entrare in una casa di bellezza perché siamo suscitate in lui emozioni di forza, di
    potenza, di beltà e di amore." "Al 'Gruppo Sciesa' una medaglia d'oro a Mataloni,"
    Il Popolo d'Italia, 30 October 1923; reprinted in Benito Mussolini, *Opera omnia*,
    ed. Edoardo Susmel and Duilio Susmel, vol. 20 (Florence: La Feince, 1957), 66.
    This address represents Mussolini's only documented commentary on the architec-
    tural form and character of *case del fascio*. The speech took place at the inaugura-
    tion of the Sciesa Group's new headquarters on Via Silvio Pellico, a narrow street
    running along one side of the Galleria Vittorio Emanuele II; at the event Mussolini
    bestowed a gold medal (Medaglia d'oro) on Jenner Mataloni, the leader of the
    group's action squad. The following year, Mataloni became president of the Sciesa
    Group, and Mussolini later appointed him director (1932–1942) of the La Scala
    opera house.
26 "La nuova Casa del Fascismo Milanese," *Il Popolo d'Italia*, 25 October 1923.
27 "Il Fascio ha quindi le cose con buon gusto, intonando mobili e uffici all'ambiente
    signorile. E ciò è bene ed è logico perché un grande Partito che ha i propri uomini
    alla direzione della cosa pubblica deve anche nelle forme esteriori prendere una
    linea di alta distinzione e signorilità." "La nuova Casa del Fascismo Milanese," *Il
    Popolo d'Italia*, 25 October 1923. See also Parini, "La Casa del Fascio a Milano,"
    27–31.

28 Gianni Mezzanotte, conversation with author,19 December 2005. The group had its first home on Via Matteo Bandello, then Bastioni di Porta Magenta. Dante Dini, "Il Gruppo Francesco Baracca del Fascio di Milano," *La Rivista Illustrata del Popolo d'Italia* 5, no. 7 (1927): 18–19.

29 For example, Mezzanotte was a member of the regulatory Building Commission (Commissione Igienico Edilizia, 1922–25) and served as a director of the Fascist Syndicate of Engineers (Sindacato Fascista Ingegneri, 1924–32) in Milan. Filomena Lerose, "Paolo Mezzanotte: Architetto del 900," master's thesis, Politecnico di Milano, Milan, 1984, 10–11. For a contemporary summary of Mezzanotte's career see Bramantino, "Il nuovo Palazzo della Borsa," *L'Illustrazione Italiana*, 24 April 1932, 551.

30 Massimiliano Savorra, *Enrico Agostino Griffini: La casa, il monumento, la città* (Napoli: Electa, 2000), 157–8.

31 "Non è dei giovanissimi: ma per età e produzione, sta giusto fra la vecchia scuola dell' anteguerra e la nuova del dopoguerra." Ferdinando Reggiori, "Valutazione estetica della nuova Borsa," *L'Ambrosiano*, 6 June 1931.

32 "Il Duce alla nuova sede del Gruppo Baracca," *Il Popolo d'Italia*, 19 April 1927.

33 Gianni Mezzanotte, interview with author, 19 December 2005. The architect Piero Portaluppi, also a member of the Baracca Group, donated his services for an adjacent building to house youth services (1937–40) and in other projects for the Fascist Party. Paolo Nicoloso, "Il contesto sociale, politico e universitario di Portaluppi," in *Piero Portaluppi: Linea errante nell'architettura del novecento*, ed. Luca Molinari (Milan: Skira, 2003): 248–9. Giuseppe Terragni also refused payment for the Casa del Fascio in Como. Diane Ghirardo, "The Politics of a Masterpiece: The Vicenda of the Decoration of the Façade of the Casa del Fascio, Como, 1936–39," *The Art Bulletin* 62, no. 3 (1980): 474.

34 R.J.B. Bosworth, *Mussolini* (New York: Oxford University Press, 2002), 176.

35 Granata, "Il Partito Nazionale Fascista," 14–23; Arnaldo Mussolini, *Scritti e discorsi di Arnaldo Mussolini* (Milan: Hoepli, 1937); Benito Mussolini, *Vita di Arnaldo* (Rome: Quaderni di Novissima, 1933); Duilio Susmel, ed., *Carteggio Arnaldo-Benito Mussolini* (Florence: La Fenice, 1954).

36 Il battistrada [Raffaello Giolli], "La Casa dei Fasci Milanese," *Problemi d'Arte Attuale* 1, no. 3 (1927): 31. Raffaello Giolli founded *Problemi d'Arte Attuale* in 1927. It was the first Italian journal devoted to contemporary art and architecture and was renamed *Poligono* in 1929.

37 "Debbono essere dei tempi, non solo del case; debbono avere linee armoniose e possenti." "Al 'Gruppo Sciesa' una medaglia d'oro a Mataloni," *Il Popolo d'Italia*, 30 October 1923; reprinted in Mussolini, *Opera Omnia*, 66.

38 "Due Cerimonie al Gruppo 'Baracca,'" *Il Popolo d'Italia*, 19 October 1926.

39 "[A]ltari delle religione della patria ... chiese per la nostra fede." "La nuova sede del Circolo 'Fabio Filzi' inaugurata alla presenza della madre dell'eroe," *Il Popolo d'Italia*, 9 October 1923.

40 "Il Duce alla nuova sede del Gruppo Baracca," *Il Popolo d'Italia*, 10 April 1927.

41 Victoria de Grazia, *The Culture of Consent: Mass Organization of Leisure in Fascist Italy* (New York: Cambridge University Press, 1981); Tracy Koon, *Believe, Obey, Fight: Political Socialization of Youth in Fascist Italy, 1922–1943* (Chapel Hill: University of North Carolina Press, 1985); David G. Horn, "L'Ente Opere Assistenziali: Strategie politiche e pratiche di assistenza," in *Il fascismo in Lombardia: Politica, economia e società*, ed. Maria Louisa Betri et al. (Milan: Franco Angeli, 1989), 479–90.

42 "È costruito da operai: e s'è voluto far si che gli operai, abituati in passato a big-hellonare o andare ad abbrutirsi nelle osterie possono trovare, invece, nella sede rionale fascista sano diletto, molti svaghi, cordiale e fraternale assistenza." "Il Duce alla nuova sede del Gruppo Baracca," *Il Popolo d'Italia*, 10 April 1927.

43 "Una vasta quanto bella palestra." "Il Duce alla nuova sede del Gruppo Baracca," *Il Popolo d'Italia*, 10 April 1927.

44 Dini, "Il Gruppo Francesco Baracca del Fascio di Milano," 19, 21.

45 "[I]l magnifico, splendente, Salone Imperiale"; "Il Duce alla nuova sede del Gruppo Baracca," *Il Popolo d'Italia*, 10 April 1927.

46 *Il Popolo d'Italia* notes the Baracca Group headquarters was the first of the twenty-eight groups to have its own headquarters. "Il Gruppo Baracca: Dov'era iscritto Arnaldo Mussolini," *Il Popolo d'Italia*, 17 February 1937. The architect's son Gianni Mezzanotte also claims that it was the first *casa del fascio* built in Milan. However, there is no mention of this in the article describing Mussolini's visit. "Il Duce all nuova sede del Gruppo Baracca," *Il Popolo d'Italia*, 10 April 1927. An article on the Indomita-Bernini Group suggests that this group was instead the first to have a purpose-built headquarters. "Indomita-Bernini: La squadra battezzata dal Duce," *Il Popolo d'Italia*, 19 January 1937.

47 See Granata, "Il Partito Nazionale Fascista," 14–22.

48 "La Nuova Casa del Fascio," *Il Popolo d'Italia*, 9 October 1927; Il battistrada [Raffaello Giolli], "La Casa dei Fasci Milanese," 29.

49 Indeed, the project attracted international attention as an example of fascist architecture. Edward Carrick, "Fascist Architecture in Italy," *The Architect's Journal* (August 1928): 186–91.

50 Granata, "Il Partito Nazionale Fascista," 14–23.

51 Gianni Mezzanotte, letter to author, 12 September 2004, and interview with author, 19 December 2005.

52 The city renamed the street when the party relocated the regional headquarters to the Palazzo Besana in 1930. "La Sede del Fascio trasferita in Piazza Belgioioso,"

Corriere della Sera, 29 March 1930. The building later housed offices for the city's welfare organization (Ente Comunale d'Assistenza). Ferdinando Reggiori, *Milano: 1800–1943* (Milan: Edizioni del Milano, 1947), 396. In the immediate post-war period the building served as the Milan headquarters for the Christian Democrat Party (Democrazia Cristiana, DC), of the center-right. It has recently been restored and is part of the nearby Catholic University (Università Cattolica).

53 Throughout the interwar period San Ambrogio played an important role as the representative symbol of Milan. The city bulletin *Milano* featured San Ambrogio on its cover in 1934 and made San Ambrogio and the Monument to the Fallen the subject of its cover in 1939. Osvaldo Lissone and Siro della Morte made both a feature of the cover for their book *La Milano voluta dal Duce e la vecchia Milano*, published in 1935. On the Monument to the Fallen see Fluvio Irace, *Giovanni Muzio 1893–1982* (Milan: Electa, 1994), 91–102.

54 "La nuova Casa del Fascio," *Il Popolo d'Italia*, 9 October 1927.

55 The building is still there, but its function has changed: after serving as a head-quarters for the Christian Democracy Party (Democrazia Cristiana, DC), it is now part of the Catholic University and underwent substantial renovations in 2001. "All'Università Cattolica l'ex sede Dc di via Nirone," *La Repubblica*, 28 November 2001.

56 "Semplice e severo ...." "La nuova Casa del Fascio in via Nirone," *Il Popolo d'Italia*, 18 June 1926.

57 These replaced the four pairs of free-standing obelisks and fasces placed along the edge of the central balcony in an early design criticized by the Building Commission (Commissione Edilizia). Sindaco to Sig. Consigliere Delegato della Società Immobiliare Casa del Fascio, 22 March 1926, prot. 160896, Archivio Storico Civico, Milano (ASCM), Ornato Fabriche (OF), serie II, c. 1201.

58 Ivano Granata, "PNF: Organizzazione del consenso e società Milanese negli anni trenta," in *Storia di Milano*, vol. 18, pt. 1 (Rome: Istituto della Enciclopedia Italiana, 1995–96), 631–5.

59 As evidence of the growing interest in architectural models from Roman antiquity, some critics claimed that the project represented the "austere character of classical *romanità*" (un austero carattere di classica romanità). "La nuova Casa del Fascio Milanese," *Il Popolo d'Italia*, 9 October 1927. Another reporter remarked that recent excavations in Ostia influenced Mezzanotte's design for the façade. "La nuova Casa del Fascio," *Il Popolo d'Italia*, 18 June 1926.

60 Richard Etlin provides the best post-war account of this project and, following Giolli, pays particular attention to the structural possibilities made possible by reinforced concrete. Etlin also notes the similarities between Mezzanotte's build-ing and Giuseppe Terragni's Casa del Fascio of Como (1933–36). Terragni started work on the project in 1928, and Mezzanotte's Casa del Fascio was one of the few

models for this building type available. Etlin, *Modernism in Italian Architecture, 1890–1940* (Cambridge, MA: MIT Press, 1991), 463–6.

61 Etlin, *Modernism*, 462.

62 Mezzanotte also provided offices for the Gruppo degli Studenti Universitario Fascisti, Gruppo dei Postelegrafico, Gruppo dei Ferrovieri Fascisti, Commando degli Avanguardisti, Balilla, and Direzione dell'Ente Provinciale Sportivo. "La nuova Casa del Fascio," *Il Popolo d'Italia*, 9 October 1927.

63 Mussolini is reported to have explained: "Se il salone è stretto, ingranditelo con gallerie ai fianchi." Il battistrada [Raffaello Giolli], "La Casa dei Fasci Milanese," 29. Mussolini's participation is also noted in "La nuova Casa del Fascio," *Il Popolo d'Italia*, 9 October 1927.

64 Etlin, *Modernism,* 463–8.

65 Il Gruppo 7, "Architecture" and "Architecture II: The Foreigners," trans. Ellen Shapiro, *Oppositions* 6 (Fall 1976): 86–102; "Architecture III: Unpreparedness – Incomprehension – Prejudices" and "Architecture IV: A New Archaic Era," trans. Ellen Shapiro, *Oppositions* 12 (Spring 1978): 88–98.

66 For a review of the general trajectory of their argument and its contradictory impulses, see Dennis Doordan, *Building Modern Italy: Italian Architecture, 1914–36* (Princeton: Princeton University Press, 1988), 45–63.

67 David Rifkind, *The Battle for Modernism: Quadrante and the Politization of Architectural Discourse in Fascist Italy* (Vicenza/Venice: CISA Andrea Palladio/ Marsilio, 2013).

68 "Il Fascismo ... è sopratutto un fede." "Statuto del PNF" (1926), reproduced in Mario Missori, *Gerarchie e statuti del PNF*, 355.

69 "In questa casa aperta alle glorie e alle fortune del Fascismo Milanese i camerati ricordano con orgoglio riconoscente e memore i gloriosi caduti Fascisti che nel nome d' Italia suggellarono nel sangue la grandezza e la nobil-ita della fede comune." The thirteen were: Aldo Sette, Franco Baldini, Ugo Pepe, Eliseo Bernini, Edoardo Crespi, Emilio Tonoli, Cesare Melloni, Paolo Grassigli, Enzo Meriggi, Vittorio Agnusdei, Loris Socrate, Blce Avignone, and Giuseppe Ugolini. "I segni tangibili della Vittoria," *Il Popolo d'Italia*, 30 October 1927.

70 Also present at this event was the president of the Institute of Culture, Dino Alfieri, who later became a principal organizer of the seminal Exhibition of the Fascist Revolution (Mostra della Rivoluzione Fascista, Rome, 1932) and Minister of Popular Culture (1936–39). "La visita di Arnaldo Mussolini alla nuova Casa del Fascio," *Il Popolo d'Italia*, 11 October 1927; Maria Luisa Betri, "Tra politica e cultura: La Scuola Mistica Fascista," in *Il fascismo in Lombardia: Politica, economia e società*, ed. M.L. Betri et al. (Milan: Franco Angeli, 1989), 381–2.

71 For more on Belloni and Giampaoli, see Granata, "Il Partito Nazionale Fascista," 31–9.

72 Granata, "Il Partito Nazionale Fascista," 36.

73 Betri, "Tra politica e cultura," 377–98.

74 Granata, "Il Partito Nazionale Fascista," 45.

75 Granata, "Il Partito Nazionale Fascista," 49.

76 "La Sede del Fascio trasferita in Piazza Belgioioso," *Corriere della Sera*, 29 March 1930.

77 "Il Palazzo Besana era più adatto per tradizione e per maestosità a sede della Federazione." Stralcio della relazione di consegna, September 1930, and Appunti colloquio con il Segretario Federale Amministrativo, Ravasco, 7 June 1934, Archivio Centrale dello Stato, Rome (ACS), Partito Nazionale Fascista (PNF), Servizi Varie, f. 103, b. 1200.

78 "La Sede del Fascio trasferita in piazza Belgioioso," *Corriere della Sera*, 29 March 1930. See, for example, *Il Popolo d'Italia*, 29 October 1924.

79 Mussolini issued this directive to all regional authorities in 1927. Renzo De Felice, *Mussolini. Il fascista: L'organizzazione dello stato fascista, 1925–1929* (Turin: Einaudi, 1968), 298–301.

80 "La nuova sede della Federazione fascista," *Il Popolo d'Italia*, 18 May 1930.

81 "[S]calone monumentale." "La nuova sede della Federazione fascista," *Il Popolo d'Italia*, 18 May 1930.

82 "Il tempio mistico ove gli spiriti dei Tredici indimenticabili verranno esaltati in muto raccoglimento." "La nuova sede della Federazione fascista," *Il Popolo d'Italia*, 18 May 1930.

83 The chapel was designed by Rezzani, one of the engineers responsible for the restructuring of the palazzo and a member of the Baracca Group, and Mazzucotelli, likely the celebrated Italian metalworker Alessandro Mazzucotelli (1865–1938). "La nuova sede della Federazione fascista," *Il Popolo d'Italia*, 18 May 1930.

84 "L'inaugurazione della Casa del Fascio," *Il Popolo d'Italia*, 21 May 1930.

85 Ganapini, "Il Partito Nazionale Fascista," 304.

86 De Felice quotes Mussolini as saying, "Il Partito deve svolgere nel contempo una intensa opera di propaganda allo scopo di specificare quanto è stato fatto in Italia per allegerire la crisi, predisponendo le opere pubbliche e l'assistenza, la quale deve avere il carattere non di elemosina, ma quello di un'opera di solidarietà umana, nazionale, fascista": *Mussolini. Il duce: Gli anni del consenso, 1929–36,* 2nd ed. (Turin: Einaudi, 1996), 227.

87 "La popolazione operaia si trova così sotto l'incubo della disoccupazione, … commenti tutt'altro che favorevoli verso il Governo Fascista, che è accusato di lasciare troppo braccio agli industriali ai danni della classe operaia." Sesto San Giovanni,

4 November 1931, ACS, PNF, Situazione Politica ed Economica delle Province (Milano), b. 7.

88 De Felice, *Mussolini. Il duce*, 88.

89 Horn, "L'Ente Opere Assistenziali," 480–6.

3. The Commercial City

1 "La sistemazione della Borsa si presentava, d'altra parte, intimamente connessa a tutta una serie di altri problemi, primo fra cui quello riguardante la organica e razionale sistemazione edilizia del centro della città." Angelo Salmoiraghi to Giuseppe Belluzzo, Ministero dell'Economia Nazionale, 15 December 1925, Archivo Storico della Camera di Commercio (ASCC), Milan, s. 1442, f. 4/8/b/1.

2 From the late 1920s, banks and other financial institutions built a number of new buildings in the city's centre. The relationships between these buildings, the individuals that encouraged their construction, and government policy offer a fruitful area for further research. These buildings include Piero Portaluppi's Banca Commerciale (1928–32), Giovanni Greppi's Banca Popolare (1928–31), Gio Ponti and Emilio Lancia's Banca Unione (1931–32), Marcello Piacentini's Banca Agricola (1934), Giovanni Muzio and G. Greppi's Casa di Risparmio delle Provincie (1936–41), and Giovanni Maggi's Palazzo della Banca Nazionale (1940). A general history of some of these projects can be found in Ornella Selvafolta, "Grandi architetture, grandi trasformazioni," in *Milano durante il fascismo, 1922–45*, ed. Giorgio Rumi, Alberto Cova, and Virgilio Vercelloni (Milan: Cariplo, 1994), 306–13.

3 Early discussion about the need to build a larger Stock Exchange and Commodities Exchange dates from at least 1916; ASCC, s. 1433, f. 2/4/1.

4 Salmoiraghi to Belluzzo, 15 December 1925, ASCC, s. 1442, f. 4/8. For the location of Milan's other markets in this period, see Gianni Mezzanotte, "La Borsa di Milano," in *Costruire in Lombardia, 1880–1980*, vol. 1, ed. Aldo Castellano and Ornella Selvafolta (Milan: Electa, 1980), 222.

5 "[U]n fabbricato a carattere industriale di più recente costruzione"; E.N.W. [E.N. Winderling], "Il Palazzo delle Borse di Milano," *Rassegna di Architettura*, no. 3 (1932): 97.

6 Giuseppe de Finetti, "Relazione sulla sistemazione nella sede attuale della 'Cooperativa' in 'Milano di una Borsa Valori e di una Borsa Merci,'" n.d., ASCC, s. 1442, f. 4/8/c,.

7 "Della sistemazione edilizia della parte più vitale della grande metropoli lombarda un organico sviluppo avvenire del centro cittadino per la formazione della nuova 'City'"; Salmoiraghi to Belluzzo, 15 December 1925, ASCC, s. 1442, f. 4/8.

8   "[L]a organica e razionale sistemazione edilizia del centro della città"; Angelo
    Salmoiraghi to Giuseppe Belluzzo, Ministero dell'Economia Nazionale, 15
    December 1925, ASCC, s. 1442, f. 4/8/b/1.

9   "[C]on grande porticati destinati ad accogliere i frequentatori"; memorandum, 25
    November 1935, ASCC, s. 1444, f. 4/21/c.

10 Various figures are offered in correspondence from the spring and summer of
    1930. See Tarlarini to Podestà, 4 August 1930, and memorandum, 25 November
    1935, ASCC, s. 1444, f. 4/21/c.

11 Mezzanotte, "La Borsa di Milano," in *Costruire in Lombardia*, 226. On Milan's
    central station see Gianfranco Angeleri and Cesare Columba, *Milano Centrale:
    Storia di una stazione* (Rome: Edizione Abete, 1985).

12 In the summer of 1928, Paolo Mezzanotte presented his plans for the Exchange;
    Presidenza del Consiglio, ASCC, s. 1444, f. 4/17. Even though Mezzanotte had
    arrived at what the president and vice-president of the council described as the "pro-
    getto definitivo" in 1928, some members of the organization had doubts about it and
    suggested holding a national competition; Estratto del Processo Verbale del Adunanza
    Plenaria, 2 October 1928. ASCC, s. 1444, f. 4/22. During this same period, the minis-
    ter of the economy was in the process of reorganizing the council, and the uncertainty
    surrounding the design may have been in part a result of changing leadership. Images
    related to this stage of the project were published in Raffaello Giolli, "Il Palazzo della
    Borsa di Milano," *Poligono: Rivista mensile d'arte* 8 (December 1929): 90–3.

13 "Il grandioso Palazzo della Borsa sta per essere ultimato," *Il Popolo d'Italia*, 26
    June 1931.

14 Cesare De Seta, *Architetti Italiani del Novecento*, rev. ed. (Rome: Laterza, 1987),
    81, 84.

15 Mezzanotte collected prints and drawings of eighteenth- and nineteenth-century
    neoclassicists; of these, many were by Cagnola; see Filomena Lerose, "Paolo
    Mezzanotte: Architetto del 900," master's thesis, Politecnico di Milano, 1984, 11.

16 "[C]orretta e severa"; Mezzanotte, "Luigi Cagnola," *Architettura e Arti Decorative*
    2, no. 8 (1927–28): 348, 337–56.

17 "[S]uperiore volontà dominatrice"; Mezzanotte, "Luigi Cagnola," 348.

18 Mezzanotte wrote numerous articles on Milanese architecture and made engrav-
    ings of the streets and buildings of Milan; many of these engravings were pub-
    lished in local architectural journals. His library, now part of the Mezzanotte
    Archive, contains a large number of books on the history and architecture of
    Milan as well as a collection of architectural treatises, including several editions
    of Vitruvius and an eighteenth-century edition of Palladio. Mezzanotte wrote, with
    Giacomo Bescapè, the comprehensive *Milano nell'arte e nella storia* (Milan:
    E. Bestetti, 1948) as well as the five chapters devoted to the architectural history
    of Milan in *La storia di Milano* (Milan: Treccani, 1959).

19 The architects Agnoldomenico Pica and Franco Albini, both members of Mezzanotte's studio in this period, participated in the design of the Commodities Exchange. Pica worked on its courtyard and the elevation along Via delle Orsole, and Albini helped to design its façade. Gianni Mezzanotte, "La Borsa di Milano: Architettura e urbanistica nella città in espansione" in *La Borsa di Milano: Dalle origini a Palazzo Mezzanotte* (Milan: Frederico Motta, 1993), 58. Albini to Mezzanotte, n.d., Archivio Paolo Mezzanotte (APM), Milan.

20 "[C]hiesastico e di rusticano Lombardo"; Arturo Tofanelli, "Il Palazzo delle Borse a Milano," *Il Lavoro Fascista*, 17 September 1932. The same text is included in Fausto M. Bongioanni, "Il nuovo Palazzo delle Borse a Milano," *Il Sole*, 27 October, 1932.

21 Milan, founded as the Celtic Insubres city Mediolanum around the start of the fourth century BCE, came under Roman dominion in 222 BCE and was the most important city in the Western Roman Empire from the end of the third century to the start of the fifth. Repeated invasions in the following centuries destroyed much of the city's Roman patrimony, and it was not until the twentieth century that archeologists began to map out the plan of the city during Roman times

22 Soprintendenza alle Antichità to Tarlarini, 15 November 1929, ASCC, f. 4/89, s. 1458.

23 "Una grande piazza coperta"; Gino Giulini, "Il nuovo Palazzo delle Borse di Milano," *Le Vie d'Italia e dell'America Latina* 28 (1932): 974. For the Silk and Silkworm Cocoon Exchange, Mezzanotte adapted the Palazzo Turati.

24 An arcade connects Via Gaetano Negri and Via Meravigli; Ferdinando Reggiori, *Milano, 1800–1943* (Milan: Edizioni del Milano, 1947), 216.

25 "Prevedeva la costituzione di una piazza molto capace, chiusa al traffico dei veicoli, e circondata da palazzi a porticati e sottopassaggi"; Tarlarini to Podestà, 2 June 1930, ASCC, s. 1444, fasc. 4/21/a,. See also Prefetto Presidente to Podestà, 15 April 1930, ASSC, s. 1444, fasc. 4/21/a.

26 "[A]ntico e razionalissimo modello del Mercato Italico ed Mediterraneo"; Arturo Tofanelli, "Il Palazzo delle Borse a Milano," *Il Lavoro Fascista*, 17 September 1932.

27 Ufficio Urbanistico to Mezzanotte, 31 October 1927, ASCC, s. 1444, fasc. 4/21/a.

28 Ivano Granata, "Il regime fascista: Peculiarità Milanese," in *Milano durante il fascismo*, 66.

29 De Capitani to Salmoiraghi, 15 December 1925, ASCC, s. 1443, f. 4/12/a/1.

30 Mezzanotte, "La Borsa di Milano," in *Costruire in Lombardia,* 273; Mezzanotte, "La Borsa di Milano," in *La Borsa di Milano,* 52. In the records held at the ASCC the project is consistently listed as the first version and is given the more precise date of 24 December 1928. Paolo Mezzanotte to on. Consiglio Provinciale dell'Economia, 21 July 1930, ASCC, s. 1444, f. 4/21/a; and Paolo Mezzanotte to Commissione Edilizia di Milano, 12 July 1938, ASCC, s. 1444, f. 4/21/c.

31 Tarlarini to Podestà, 4 August 1930, ASCC, s. 1444, f. 4/21/a.

32 Paolo Mezzanotte [?] to Podestà, 14 January 1930, ASCC, s. 1444, f. 4/21/a. See
    also Dario Franchi and Rosa Chiumeo, *Urbanistica a Milano in regime fascista*
    (Florence: La Nuova Italia Editrice, 1972), 69–76.

33 Franchi and Chiumeo, *Urbanistica a Milano*, 72–3.

34 Franchi and Chiumeo, *Urbanistica a Milano*, 74.

35 Tarlarini to Podestà, 4 August 1930, ASCC, s. 1444, f. 4/21/a.

36 See letters to Tarlarini as well as Siragusa and the *podestà* in ASCC, s. 1444, f. 4/21/a.

37 "L'inconveniente principale nei riguardi del Palazzo delle Borse ad un'area tri-
    angolare antiestetica e di forma al tutto contraria alle norme urbanistiche creando
    così una brutta visuale all'uscita monumentale del Palazzo." Paolo Mezzanotte to
    on. Consiglio Provinciale dell'Economia, 30 April 1930, ASCC, s. 1444, f. 4/21/a.

38 Tarlarini to Podestà, 4 August 1930, ASCC, s. 1444, f. 4/21/a.

39 Daniele Bardelli and Pietro Zuretti, "L'amministrazione comunale nel periodo
    podestarile ," in *Storia di Milano,* vol. 18 (Rome: Istituto della Enciclopedia
    Italiana, 1995–96), 658; Prefetto to Ministero del Interno, 9 November 1934,
    Archivio Centrale dello Stato, Rome (ACS), Ministero del Interno, Podestà e
    Consulte Municipali, b. 197.

40 Granata, "Il regime fascista," 101.

41 Sergio Zaninelli, "Lo sviluppo industriale di Milano negli anni Venti e Trenta," in
    Il sogno del moderno: Architettura e produzione a Milano tra le due guerre, ed.
    Alberto Mioni, Antonello Negri, and Sergio Zaninelli (Florence: Edifir, 1994),18.

42 See Vittorio Vidotto, *Roma contemporanea* (Rome: Laterza, 2001), 179–83, 208.

43 Paolo Nicoloso, *Mussolini architetto: Propaganda e paesaggio urbano nell'Italia
    fascista* (Turin: Einaudi, 2008), 20–5.

44 "Con una superficie totale ridotta a poco più di 2,000 metri quadrati ... maestoso
    arcone"; "Il grandioso Palazzo della Borsa sia per essere ultimato," *Il Popolo
    d'Italia*, 26 June 1931. *Il Lavoro Fascista* also lamented the loss of the original
    project: "se l'avessero lasciato costruire secondo il primitivo progetto, avremmo
    oggi un Palazzo più bello, più accessibile, più degnamente disposto ed ambientato,
    più omogeneo e più utile." Tofanelli, "Il Palazzo delle Borse a Milano."

45 Reggiori, "Valutazione estetica della nuova Borsa," *L'Ambrosiano*, 4, 6, 11 June
    1931; Giuseppe De Finetti, Giovanni Muzio, and Alberto Alpago Novello, *Memoria
    sui progetti per il Piano regolatore di Milano, 1928–1929* (Milan: Omenoni, 1930).

46 "La quale, cosi come appare nell'ultima edizione ufficiale, se è cattiva dal punto
    di vista planimetrico e viario, peggiore sarà nell'aspetto ambientale ed estetico."
    Reggiori, "Valutazione estetica," *L'Ambrosiano*, 11 June 1931.

47 "La questione della piazza avanti alla Borsa è divenuta tra gli interessati e gli stu-
    diosi argomenti scottanti." Alberto Calza-Bini, 14 October 1931, ASCC, s. 1444,
    f. 4/21/b.

48 Prefetto Presidente, Giuseppe Siragusa to Ministro delle Finanze and Ministro delle Corporazione, 27 October 1932, ASCC, s. 1458, f. 4/93; *Corriere della Sera*, 27 October 1932; *Il Popolo d'Italia*, 27 October 1932; *Il Sole*, 27 October 1932.

49 Giuseppe Pagano, "La pietra trasparente nell'edilizia moderna," *L'Ambrosiano*, 29 January 1932; ger. [Gerbi], "Novità e mezzi tecnici della nuova Borsa di Milano," *L'Ambrosiano*, 23 February 1932. See also Mezzanotte to Pagano, 11 February 1932, and Pagano to Mezzanotte, 13 February 1932, ASCC, s. 1457, f. 4/86.

50 Bardelli and Zuretti, "L'amministrazione comunale," 659–60.

51 Reggiori, *Milano*, 84.

52 Although *Corriere della Sera* published possible solutions in June 1932 and August 1937, none of these were carried out. In August 1939 *Il Popolo d'Italia* and *Corriere della Sera* published the city's plan for the Piazza degli Affari: "La sistemazione di Piazza degli Affari," *Il Popolo d'Italia*, 10 August 1939; and "Questo sarà l'assetto di Piazza degli Affari," *Corriere della Sera*, 10 August 1939.

53 "Questo sarà l'assetto," *Corriere della Sera*, 10 August 1939.

54 Franchi and Chiumeo, *Urbanistica a Milano*, 74.

55 Mezzanotte to Podestà, 13 November [?] 1930, Archivio Civico, Milan, Atti di Protocollo, cat 9-1, 1932, prot. 169287; E.N.W. [E.N. Winderling], "Il Palazzo delle Borse di Milano."

4. Fascist Authority

1 "La Giustizia deve presiedere alla vita degli uomini, questa non può non avere carattere universale." Arnaldo Mussolini, "I Giovani," *Il Popolo d'Itala*, 11 November 1930.

2 New law courts were built in Trieste (Enrico and Umberto Nordio, 1912–1929), Messina (Marcello Piacentini, 1923–29), Catania (Franceso Fichera, 1936–53), Palermo (Gaetano and Ernesto Rapisardi, 1938–57), Lecco (Mario Cereghini, 1938–41), and Pisa (Gaetano and Ernesto Rapisardi, 1935–58).

3 Sites considered by the City Technical Commission (Commissione Tecnica Comunale) prior to 1923 include the area of the ex-Zecca between Via Moscova, Via Manion, and Via Parini; the ex-penitentiary of Porta Nuova; the Caserma Principe Eugenio Savioa on Corso di P. Vittoria; the expansion of the tribunal in Piazza Beccaria; the Vetra Quarter; the Collegio di S. Luca in Corso Italia; the Caserma di S. Marina; and the Collegio Reale delle Fanciulle in Via Passione. Salva Bullara, *Il Palazzo di Giustizia a Milano* (Milan: Industria Grafica 'Italia Ars,' 1925), 11.

4 "Il Palazzo di Giustizia," *Il Popolo d'Italia*, 13 March 1930.

5 *L'Edilizia pubblica e privata nell'attività dell'amministrazione comunale a Milano nel trentennio 1923–25* (Milan: Comune di Milano, 1926), 22; Mangiagalli to Mussolini, 8 December 1923, Archivio Centrale dello Stato, Rome (ACS), Direzione Generale, Ministero del Interno, anni 1922–24, b. 2109.

6 Dario Franchi and Rosa Chiumeo, *Urbanistica a Milano in regime fascista* (Florence: La Nuova Italia Editrice, 1972), 62; "Ancora del Palazzo di Giustizia," *Il Popolo d'Italia*, 23 August 1930.

7 Mussolini to Mangiagalli, 24 August 1924, ACS, Segreteria Particolare del Duce (SPD), 536.663.

8 "Le proteste furono molte e vibrate quando si voleva mandare – e non solo topo-graficamente – la giustizia al Macello, sotto la giunta Mangiagalli." "Il Palazzo di Giustizia," *Il Popolo d'Italia*, 21 August 1930.

9 See ACS, Presidenza del Consiglio dei Ministri, anno 1925, b. 1236, f. 1/1.

10 Vice Podestà Dorici to Carlo Roncoroni, Camera dei Deputati, 11 April 1932, Archivio Civico, Milan (ACM), Piano Regolatore (PR), 1932, f. 362.

11 "Ancora del Palazzo di Giustizia," *Il Popolo d'Italia*, 23 August 1930.

12 Piero Portaluppi and Marco Semenza, *Milano, com'è ora, come sarà* (Milan: Bestetti e Tumminelli, 1927), 262.

13 "La grande Piazza sarà fiancheggiata da grandi palazzi collegati con porticati al Palazzo di Giustizia, così da costruire un tutto armonico e chiuso." Portaluppi and Semenza, *Milano, com'è ora, come sarà*, 263.

14 The group's members were Alberto Alpago Novello, Giusepe De Finetti, Tomaso Buzzi, Ottavio Cabiati, Guido Ferrazza, Ambrogio Gadola, Emilio Lancia, Michele Marelli, Piero Palumbo, Gio Ponti, and Ferdinando Reggiori.

15 Appunti della Sotto Commissione Artistica, 7, Archivio Storico Civico, Milan (ASCM), Ornato Fabbriche (OF), c. 1411.

16 Appunti della Sotto Commissione Artistica, 9, ASCM, OF, c. 1411.

17 "Una nuova convenzione tra Stato e Comune per la costruzione dei pubblici edi-fici," *Corriere della Sera*, 20 June 1931.

18 Inconveniently, this decision was made in the midst of the competition for the Palace of Justice held in 1929. "Concorso per il progetto del Palazzo di Giustizia in Milano," *Rassegna di Architettura*, no. 5 (1930): 161. Franchi and Chiumeo indicate that Marcello Piacentini was responsible for pushing this change through: *Urbanistica a Milano*, 66.

19 Schuster to Visconti di Modrone, 8 May 1930, ACM, PR, 1932, f. 362.

20 Cesare Albertini, "Le Comunicazioni col Palazzo di Giustizia," *Milano*, February 1934, 55–8.

21 Franchi and Chiumeo, *Urbanistica a Milano*, 65.

22 Eberhard Schroeter, "Rome's First National State Architecture: The Palazzo delle Finanze," in *Art and Architecture in the Service of Politics*, ed. Henry

Millon and Linda Nochlin (Cambridge, MA: MIT Press, 1978), 131; Terry Kirk, "The Political Topography of Modern Rome, 1870–1936: Via XX Settembre to Via del'Impero," in *Rome: Continuing Encounters between Past and Present*, ed. Dorigen Caldwell and Lesley Caldwell (London: Ashgate, 2011), 106–7; Bruno Regni and Marina Sennato, "Marcello Piacentini (1881–1960)," *Storia dell'Urbanistica* 3, no. 5 (1983): 13.

23 "La concezione architettonica, semplice e severa, dovrà rispondere all'alto scopo cuì il Palazzo e destinato, essere degno della Città di Milano e dell'Epoca Fascista in cui sorge." "Concorso per il progetto del Palazzo di Giustizia in Milano," ASCM, Archivio Giuseppe Rivolta (AGR), c. 41/L/3.

24 Ironically, the term "severe" repeated the language used decades earlier in the competition brief for the Palace of Justice in Rome. Terry Kirk, "Roman Architecture before the Lateran Pact: Architectural Symbols of Reconciliation in the Competitions for the Palazzo di Giustizia, 1883–87," in *Guglielmo Calderini: La costruzione di un architettura nel progetto di una capitale*, ed. Fedora Boco (Perugia: Accademia di Belle Arti di Perugia, 1996), 84. For Calderini see also Fedora Boco, Terry Kirk, and Giorgio Muratore, *Guglielmo Calderini: Dai desegni dell'Accademia di Belle Arti di Perugia, un architetto nell'Italia in costruzione* (Perugia: Accademia di Belle Arti di Perugia, Guerra, 1995).

25 Paolo Nicoloso, "I concorsi di architettura durante il fascismo," *Casabella* 683 (November 2000): 4–7; Nicoloso, *Gli architetti di Mussolini: Scuole, e sindacato, architetti e massoni, professori e politici negli anni del regime* (Milan: Franco Agnelli, 1999), 153–9; Giorgio Ciucci, *Gli architetti e il fascismo* (Turin: Einaudi, 1989), 129–51.

26 "Fu bandita male, con strane incertezze, senza un regolamento ben preciso che la inquadrasse, senza garanzie per i concorrenti, meno ancora per i vincitori, con premi modesti, senza render noto, preventivamente, i nomi dei giudici." F.R. [Ferdinando Reggiori], "Esito del concorso per il Palazzo di Giustizia di Milano," *Architettura e Arti Decorative* 1, no. 3 (1930): 128; "Concorso per il progetto del Palazzo di Giustizia in Milano," *Rassegna di Architettura*, 161–9.

27 "Il Palazzo di Giustizia," *Corriere della Sera*, 23 March 1930. The jury included Giuseppe Baselli, Giuseppe Tarlarini, the city councilor and president of the Building-Hygiene Commission (Commissione Edilizia-Igiene) Diego Brioschi, Luigi Belletti, head of the city planning office Cesare Albertini, the representative of the head of the Court of Appeals Edoardo Della Sala Spada, Livio Larmberti Bocconi, Francesco Casalegno, Giannino Ferrini, Ignazio Regondi, Giovanni Broglio, the architect Ulise Stacchini, Luigi Gianturco, Eliseo Antonio Porro, Luigi Pellegrini, the artist Mario Sironi, De Capitani d'Arzago (*podestà* until 19 November 1929), Deputy *Podestà* Giuseppe Gorla, Manlio Pozzi, Giuseppe Rivolta, vice-president of the Provincial Economic Council Carlo Tarlarini, the city councilor Cesare Dorici, Carlo Peverelli, and Milziade Baccani. Verbale delle

Sedute della Giuria, 4, 29 November, 13, 16 December 1929, ACM, Servizi e Lavori Pubblici (LLPP), f. 205, 1934. Piacentini's role as a member of the jury is mentioned in Nicoloso, *Gli architetti di Mussolini*, 156.

28 "Il Palazzo di Giustizia," *Corriere della Sera*, 23 March 1930.

29 "Concorso per il progetto del Palazzo di Giustizia in Milano," *Rassegna di Architettura*, 161–9; and F.R. [Ferdinando Reggiori], "Esito del Concorso per il Palazzo di Giustizia di Milano," 122–30.

30 "L'architettura delle fronti è ispirata a molta – forse eccessiva – semplicità … L'aggetto della fronte principale a forma di abside semi-circolare non è troppo felice, anche perchè sminuisce anziché accrescere l'impronta di grandiosità, che si vorrebbe attribuita all' ingresso principale del Palazzo verso il Corso di Porta Vittoria." "Concorso per il progetto del Palazzo di Giustizia in Milano, Relazione della Giuria," 16 December 1929, ACM, LLPP, 1934, f. 205.

31 "Senza tuttavia raggiungere quell'impronta di pubblico edificio, che sarebbe desiderata." "Concorso per il progetto del Palazzo di Giustizia in Milano, Relazione della Giuria," 16 December 1929, ACM, LLPP, 1934, f. 205.

32 Deputy *Podestà* Fausto Gallavresi headed the commission. Its members included Teodoro Tufaroli, Cesare Dorici, Luigi Belletti, Livio Lamberti Bocconi, Diego Brioschi, Milziade Baccani, Luigi Gianturco, Omodei Zorini, Spada della Sala, and president of the tribunal Fracassi. Primo Riunione della Commissione per il Costruendo Palazzo di Giustizia di Milano, 18 April 1930, ACM, LLPP, 1934, f. 205.

33 Primo Riunione della Commissione per il Costruendo Palazzo di Giustizia di Milano, 18 April 1930, ACM, LLPP, 1934, f. 205.

34 Giuseppe Baselli of the Office of Technical Services would oversee the project. Primo Riunione della Commissione per il Costruendo Palazzo di Giustizia di Milano, 18 April1930, ACM, LLPP, 1934, f. 205.

35 Podestà to Prima Presidente della Corte d'Appello, 18 August 1930, ACM, LLPP, 1934, f. 205; "Una nuova convenzione tra Stato e Comune per la costruzione dei pubblici edifici," *Corriere della Sera*, 20 June 1931. Once it was under-way, Mussolini used this project, like the many other public works initiatives throughout Italy, to boost employment, particularly in the winter months. See, for example, telegrams from Mussolini to Prefect of Milan, 10 March, 19, 26, December 1932, ACS, SPD, 536.663; Piacentini and Dorici to Mussolini, 12 August 1932, ACS, Presidenza del Consiglio dei Ministri, anno 1931–33, b. 1379, f. 1/1–3, 1/1–4.

36 Primo Presidente to Podestà, 24 July, 18 August, 3 September 1930, ACM, LLPP, 1934, f. 205. See, for example, "Il problema del Palazzo di Giustizia," *Corriere della Sera,* 12 March 1930; "Il Palazzo di Giustizia," *Il Popolo d'Italia*, 21 August 1930; "Ancora del Palazzo di Giustizia," *Il Popolo d'Italia*, 23 August 1930; "Ancora il Palazzo di Giustizia," *Corriere della Sera*, 27 August 1930.

37 Daniele Bardelli and Pietro Zuretti, "L' amministrazione comunale nel periodo podestarile," in *Storia di Milano*, vol. 18, pt. 1 (Rome: Istituto della Enciclopedia Italiana, 1995–96), 657.

38 "Una nuova convenzione tra Stato e Comune per la costruzione dei pubblici edifici," *Corriere della Sera*, 20 June 1931; Vita Comunale, *Milano*, June 1931, 326.

39 "Il podestà a Roma," *Il Popolo d'Italia*, 29 August 1931; Vice Podestà Dorici to Carlo Roncoroni, Camera dei Deputati, 11 April 1932, ACM, PR, fasc. 362, 1932.

40 Verbale della Seduta Podestarile del Giorno, 5 November 1931, ACM, Segreteria Generale (SG), 1941, f. 47. The announcement to the *consulta* was made on 14 October 1931. Reggiori, *Milano,* 347.

41 Ing. Capo to Podestà, 6 December 1930; Piacentini to Dorici, 8 December 1930. ACM, LLPP, 1934, f. 205.

42 Mario Lupano, *Marcello Piacentini* (Bari: Laterza, 1991), 185.

43 This is one of several instances where Piacentini translated his participation on a jury into a commission. Nicoloso, *Gli architetti di Mussolini*, 156–7.

44 Piacentini had already submitted drafts to the podestà, magistracy, and head of the Milan Court of Appeals. Piacentini to Podestà Pesenti, 30 January 1936, ACM, SG, 1942, f. 10; "Il nuovo Palazzo di Giustizia a Milano," *Il Popolo d'Italia,* 9 February 1932; "Come sarà il nuovo Palazzo di Giustizia," *Corriere della Sera*, 9 February 1932; "Il progetto di Marcello Piacentini per il nuovo Palazzo di Giustizia di Milano," *L'Illustrazione Italiana*, 14 February 1932, 205–7; "Il Palazzo di Giustizia," *Milano*, February 1932, 82–8.

45 "S.E. Capo del Governo ha approvato il progetto dell'edificio che risulta grandioso e razionale ad un tempo, degno quindi della Giustizia, del Regime, e di Milano." *Podestà* Visconti di Modrone and deputy *podestà* Pini and Dorici were also present. "Vita Comunale," *Milano*, February 1932, 106.

46 Piacentini to Pesenti, 30 January 1936, ACM, SG, 1942, f. 10; Piacentini to Pesenti, 30 January 1936, ACM, SG, 1942, f. 10; Pesenti to Piacentini, 25 April 1936, ACM, SG, 1941, f. 47.

47 The piers are faced with highly polished plum marble, and bands of reflective dark grey and white stone cover the floor. From either side of the atrium, long low stairs of dark grey diorite provide public access to the second storey. For an overview of the project see, Raffaele Calzini, "Il Palazzo di Giustizia di Milano," special issue, *Architettura*, nos. 1–2 (1942): 1–78.

48 Gian Capo, "Il Palazzo di Giustizia," *Milano*, February 1932, 83, 84.

49 "Tutto il piano di terra, infatti è internamente sistemato in modo da poter essere percorso dai veicoli: Si potrà cosi giungere in automobile presso le scale e i numerosi ascensori che condurranno alle varie destinazioni, senza dover attraversare altri locali o fare lunghi tragitti a piedi." Gian Capo, "Il Palazzo di Giustizia,"

Milano, February 1932, 85. For a discussion of the history of the corridor in western architecture see Mark Jarzombeck, "Corridor Spaces," *Critical Theory* 36, no. 4 (2010): 728–70.

50 "Il progetto di Marcello Piacentini per il nuovo Palazzo di Giustizia di Milano," *L'Illustrazione Italiana*, 14 February 1932, 205. Piacentini's sketches, and notebooks show that the architect was working through his ideas for the Palace of Justice at the same time that he was working on the Città Universitaria in Rome and the Piazza della Vittoria in Brescia. Some of his sketches are reproduced in Sandro Scarrocchia, *Albert Speer e Marcello Piacentini: L'architettura del totalitarismo* (Skira: Milan, 1999), 143; and Lupano, *Marcello Piacentini*, figs. 122, 176.

51 "[L]a mania del fastoso, del ricco, dell'esuberante." Piacentini, *Il volto di Roma* (Roma: Edizione della Bussola, 1944), 142.

52 Kirk, "Roman Architecture before the Lateran Pact," 83–125.

53 "Semplicissima e chiara." Piacentini, *Il volto di Roma*, 139, 142.

54 "L'architettura del Palazzo di Giustizia di Roma riabilitata dall'architettura del Palazzo di Giustizia di Milano," *L'Italia Letteraria*, 21 June 1936, 5.

55 Ojetti's letter responded directly to the recent publication of Piacentini's project for the Città Universitaria in *Architettura*. Ojetti, letter to Piacentini, in *Pegaso*, February 1933. Republished and translated by Laura Neri, "Arches and Columns: The debate between Piacentini and Ojetti, 1933," *Modulus* (1982): 7–8.

56 For example, he invited prominent architects such as Giuseppe Pagano, editor of *Casabella* and a vocal advocate of avant-garde architecture, as well as Giovanni Michelucci, the author of the controversial new train station in Florence (1932–34), to participate in his project for the Città Universitaria in Rome.

57 Piacentini's list included the Palazzo Chigi, Palazzo Madama, Palazzo Montecitorio, Palazzo Mattei, and Palazzo Sacchetti. Piacentini, letter to Ojetti in *La Tribuna*, 2 February 1933, republished and translated by Neri, "Arches and Columns," 9.

58 Piacentini, letter to Ojetti, in Neri, "Arches and Columns," 10–11.

59 Piacentini, letter to Ojetti, in Neri, "Arches and Columns," 12.

60 Pesenti Memorandum, 27 September 1933, ACM, LLPP, 1936, f. 166; Giovanna Ginex et al., "Il Palazzo di Giustizia di Milano: Le opere decorative," in *Gli Annitrenta: Arte e cultura in Italia* (Milan: Mazzotta, 1985), 53–5. Podestà Visconti di Modrone led the jury, which included G. Radice Fossati, M. Piacentini, Gaetano Moretti, Francesco Messina (a sculptor from the Brera), and Michele Guerrisi (a representative from the Fine Arts Syndicate). Deliberazione del Podestà, 3 October 1934, and notes from a meeting held 17 November 1934, ACM, LLPP, 1936, f. 166. The city awarded thirty thousand lire to Eros Pellini, Aldo Andreani, Vico Consorti, Italo Griselli, Tullio Petri, and Alberto Bazzoni. Verbale del Podestà, 17 November, 1934. ACM, LLPP, 1936, f. 166.

61 See Paolo Nicoloso, *Mussolini architetto: Propaganda e paesaggio urbano nell'Italia fascista* (Turin: Einaudi, 2008), 251–4.

62 "Due tempii eccezionale, quello dellá giustizia romana e della religione imperiale," Pesenti to Piacentini, 9 November 1937, ACM, SG, 1941, f. 47.

63 The idealist philosopher and leading fascist intellectual Giovanni Gentile similarly isolated the three great periods of Italian history as imperial, papal, and fascist Rome when working with Piacentini on the project for the 1942 Universal Exposition. Giovanni Gentile, "Roma Eterna/L'idea di Roma," *Civilta* 2 (21 June 1940): 4–8.

64 Terry Kirk, "Church, State, and Architecture: The Palazzo di Giustizia of Nineteenth-Century Rome," PhD diss., Columbia University, New York, 1997, 330.

65 Albert C. O'Brian, "Italian Youth in Conflict: Catholic Action and Fascist Italy, 1929–1931," *Catholic Historical Review* 68, no.4 (1982): 625–35.

66 Alberto Bazzoni, Alfredo Biagini, Timo Bortolotti, Remo Brioschi, Luigi Broggini, Anselmo Bucci, Guido Cadorin, Corrado Cagli, Massimo Campigli, Arnaldo Carpanetti, Carlo Carrà, Giannino Castiglioni, Giovanni Colacicchi, Primo Conti, Arturo Dazzi, Ercole Drei, Ferruccio Ferrazzi, Lucio Fontana, Achille Funi, Nino Galizzi, Italo Griselli, Bruno Innocenti, Giannino Lambertini, Leone Lodi, Giacomo Manzù, Antonio Maraini, Vitaliano Marchini, Marino Marini, Arturo Martini, Piero Marussig, Giacomo Maselli, Fausto Melotti, Francesco Messina, Enzo Morelli, Cipriano Efisio Oppo, Eros Pellini, Siro Penagini, Carlo Pini, Carlo Pizzi, Giovanni Prini, Domenico Rambelli, Romano Romanelli, Guilio Rosso, Alberto Salietti, Antonio Giuseppe Santagata, Enrico Saroldi, Attilio Selva, Pio Semeghini, Gino Severini, Mario Sironi, Ivo Soli, Ottavio Steffenini, Silvano Tajuti, M. Giovanni Tolleri, Mario Tozzi, Gian Filippo Usellini, Gianni Vagnetti, Corrado Vigni, Francesco Wildt, and Silvio Zaniboni. The decorative program has been treated in Ginex et al., "Il Palazzo di Giustizia di Milano," 53–7; and Ginex, "Il dibato critico e istituzionale sul muralismo in Italia," in *Muri ai pittori: Pittura murale e decorazione in Italia, 1930–50*, ed. Vittorio Fagone, Giovanna Ginex, and Tulliola Sparagni (Milan: Mazzotta, 1999), 25–45. For a broader discussion on the role of mural art in this period see also Romy Golan, *Muralnomad: The Paradox of Wall Painting, Europe 1927–1957* (New Haven: Yale University Press, 2009).

67 "Ho sempre pensato che il Palazzo Comunale di Siena figurerebbe non bene se non vi avesse dipinto Simone Maritini, e così tutti i Palazzi della Rinascenza, da Schifanoia alla Farnesina, sarebbero freddi e aridi e non affermerebbero sufficientemente la loro epoca, se spogliati degli affreschi che ne rivestono le pareti." Piacentini to Calzini, 2 January 1942, Fondo Marcello Piacentini, Biblioteca della Facoltà di Architettura, Università degli Studi, Florence (FMP), b. 111.

68 For example, he again called on Ercole Drei, the author of the *quadriga* for the Palace of Justice in Messina, and he had collaborated with Arturo Dazzi on the Monument to Victory in Bolzano (1930–2) and on the Monument to the Fallen in Genova (1931).

69 "Sara di carattere strettamente inerente alla Giustizia e potrà anche essere ispirato a soggetti biblici o a fatti storici." Contract with sculptor Silvio Zaniboni, 15 October 1938, ACM, LLPP, 1942, f. 62.

70 Preda to Scotti, 22 July 1939, ACM, SG, 1942, f. 10.

71 Marla Susan Stone, *The Patron State: Culture and Politics in Fascist Italy* (Princeton: Princeton University Press, 1998), 1–10.

72 Bottai to Grandi, 17 September 1940, FMP, b. 95.1.

73 Atti del Comune di Milano, 8 February 1938, ACM, PR Demanio Urbanistica, 1939, f. 200.

74 Construction was completed in 1937. Bruno Moretti, *Case d'abitazione in Italia* (Milan: Hoepli, 1939), 170–3; n.d.r., "Palazzo per abitazione e uffici in Milano," *Rassegna di Architettura*, no. 3 (1938): 97–101.

75 Edificio per la Nuovo Questura/Stato di Fatto e di Diritto Milano, Segretario Generale, 20 September 1946; Centro Studi Archivio della Comunicazione (CSAC), Parma, Archivio Giuseppe De Finetti (AGD), Questura; "La Nuova Sede della Questura," *Il Popolo d'Italia*, 7 December 1938; "Il nuovo Palazzo della Questura," *Corriere della Sera*, 11 July 1939; Ferdinando Reggiori, "Il nuovo programma edilizio dell'Amministrazione Provinciale di Milano," *Rassegna di Architettura*, no. 3 (1939): 105–14.

76 "La scelta della località per erigere il nuovo edificio non fu razionale ma accidentale, e venne influenzata da interessi del momento, diretti ed indiretti ..." Deputazione Provinciale Verbale della Seduta del 18 Settembre 1946, CSAC, AGD, Questura.

77 Pesenti to Piacentini, 31 August 1937, ACM, PR Demanio Urbanistico, 1939, f. 199. See also Elisabetta Susani, "La resistenza al moderno: L'architettura maggiore," in *Milano dietro le quinte: Luigi Lorenzo Secchi* (Milan: Electa, 1999), 67–87. Susani discusses Piacentini's involvement with the project on p. 77.

5. Urban Networks

1 "Le Case del Fascio rappresentano l'organo sociale per eccellenza del Fascismo. In queste case 'politiche' il popolo partecipa della vita pubblica, stabilisce i contatti con le gerarchie, trova la sede più opportune per le riunione e gli esercizi fisici—infine vi ricorre, nei momenti meno fortunate, per trovare aiuto e conforto. Istituzione originale, dove si sono sapute risolvere le varie sedi della vita civile e politica, la 'Casa del Fascio' e fra le manifestazioni più evidenti e più diffuse

del nuovo clima italiano. Da tali presupposti, la progettazione e l'attuazione di una 'Casa del Fascio' deriva un impegno preciso che si deve risolvere in manifestazioni dell'architettura italiana più alta e caratteristica del nostro tempo." "La nuova sede del Gruppo Rionale Fascista 'Fabio Filzi' a Milano," *Edilizia Moderna* 29 (October–December 1938): 26.

2 There is an extensive bibliography on this building in both Italian and English. See Diane Ghirardo, "Italian Architects and Fascist Politics: An Evaluation of the Rationalist's Role in Regime Building," *Journal of the Society of Architectural Historians* 39, no. 2 (1980): 109–27; Sergio Poretti, "1928, 1932–36, Casa del Fascio di Como," in *Giuseppe Terragni: Opera competa*, ed. Giorgio Ciucci (Milan: Electa, 1996), 392–3.

3 Diane Ghirardo, "Terragni, Conventions, and the Critics," in *Critical Architecture and Contemporary Culture*, ed. William J. Lillyman, Marilyn F. Moriarty, and David J. Neuman (New York: Oxford University Press, 1994), 93–6.

4 "Il Fascismo è una casa di vetro in cui tutti possono guardare." Giuseppe Terragni, "La costruzione della Casa del Fascio di Como," *Quadrante* 35–36 (October 1936; repr., Como: Tipografia Editrice Cesare Nani, 1994): 6. Terragni took these words from Mussolini's address to party leaders in Milan in July 1929 following the scandals of 1928. Renzo De Felice, *Mussolini. Il duce: Gli anni del consenso, 1929–36*, 2nd ed. (Turin: Einaudi, 1996), 203.

5 "[I]n questo primo tempo – soltanto in periferia; poiché, qui, esse potranno effettivamente assolvere – per ragioni di ambiente – il loro compito sociale di grande portata." "La convocazione dei Fiduciari alla Casa del Fascio," *Il Popolo d'Italia*, 6 January 1929.

6 In addition to the three examples discussed in some detail, others include the Delcroix Group (Mario Cereghini, 1936), the D'Annunzio Group (Renzo Gerla, 1937–38), and the Mario Asso Group (1938). Groups that had plans under way for new headquarters in the final years of the regime include the Beretta Group, the Indomita-Bernini Group (G. Nerlo, 1939), and the Piave Group (1941).

7 Simonetta Falasca-Zamponi, *Fascist Spectacle: The Aesthetics of Power in Mussolini's Italy* (Berkeley: University of California Press, 1997), 100–18.

8 Although he was regarded with derision by members of Mussolini's government, Starace was endorsed by Arnaldo Mussolini, and fiduciary reports indicate that the new party secretary had strong local support, perhaps because he had helped to run the Fascist Party in Milan following Federal Secretary Giampaoli's dismissal a few years before. Antonio Spinosa, *Starace: L'uomo che inventò lo stile fascista* (Milan: Mondadori, 2002), 64; Estratto della Relazione del Mese di Dicembre 1931, Archivio Centrale dello Stato, Rome (ACS), Partito Nazionale Fascista (PNF), Situazione Politica e Economia Province (Milano), b. 6.

9 Albert C. O'Brian, "Italian Youth in Conflict: Catholic Action and Fascist Italy, 1929–1931," *The Catholic Historical Review* 68, no. 4 (October 1982): 625–35. Lavishly illustrated limited edition publications such as *Il Fascio primogenito* (Milan: Officine Grafiche Esperia, 1937) documented the party's activities.

10 The Milan-based architect Giulio Ulisse Arata and the Bolognese architect Alberto Legnani completed the jury. Carlo Savoia, "La Casa del Fascio," *L'Assalto*, 21 May 1932.

11 Peressutti and Rogers won with their *casa del fascio* for a town of ten thousand inhabitants, while Banfi and Belgiojoso won with their project for a town of thirty thousand inhabitants. The projects are mentioned briefly in Serena Maffioletti, *BBPR* (Bologna: Zanichelli, 1994), 18–19. Less enthusiastically, the jury awarded the prize for the *casa del fascio* for a large city to Renzo Bianchi of the School of Architecture in Turin. "Il Littoriale di Architettura e la relazione della Giuria," *L'Assalto*, 26 May 1932.

12 Ezio Bonfanti, *Città, museo, e architettura: Il gruppo BBPR nella cultura architet-tonica italiana 1932–1970* (Florence: Vallecchi, 1973).

13 "Il Segretario del Partito e il Ministro dell'Educazione Nazionale sono già al cor-rente di quanto di sta facendo." "Casa del Fascio 'tipo,'" *L'Assalto*, 2 April 1932.

14 Savoia, "La Casa del Fascio," *L'Assalto*, 21 May 1932.

15 "L'operaio, lo studente, il contadino, l'impiegato." Carlo Savoia, "La Casa del Fascio," *L'Assalto*, 26 May 1932.

16 "[L]'intima semplicità degli esterni." "Il Littoriale di Architettura e la relazione della Giuria," *L'Assalto*, 26 May 1932.

17 Ghirardo, "Terragni, Conventions, and the Critics," 93–6.

18 "[È] un idea non solo pratica ma corrispondente alla religione fascista del 'pre-sente.'" Giuseppe Pagano, "Un concorso di giovani," *Casabella* 5 (June 1932): 24.

19 Portaluppi collaborated in that same year with Banfi, Belgiojoso, Peressutti, and Rogers at the V Triennale in Milan. Pier Maria Bardi, "Nouvelles tendances dans les ècoles d'architecture Italiennes," *L'Architecture d'aujourd'hui* 10 (December–January 1933): 95.

20 Emilio Gentile, "Fascism as Political Religion," *Journal of Contemporary History* 25 nos. 2–3 (1990): 240.

21 Ivano Granata, "PNF: Organizzazione del consenso e società Milanese negli anni trenta," *Storia di Milano*, vol. 18, pt. 1 (Rome: Istituto della Enciclopedia Italiana, 1995–96), 637.

22 Renzo de Felice argues that the regime enjoyed broad support from 1929 to 1934, "the years of consensus": *Mussolini. Il duce*, 55. This assessment has been widely supported in the literature on Italian fascism, and there was little active resistance to the regime in these years. However, Simona Colarizi points to some of the difficulties of ascertaining the nature of popular support for fascism in

L'opinione degli Italiani sotto il Regime, 1929–42 (Rome: Laterza, 1991). In addition, Paul Corner argues that many Italians – largely for economic reasons – had little choice other than to support the regime; he asserts that "consensus" would be better described as "conformism": "Italian Fascism: Whatever Happened to Dictatorship?," *Journal of Modern History* 74, no.4 (2002): 325–51.

23 "57,000 kg. di pane distribuito, 29,000 litri di latte, 19,000 kg. riso, 700 kg. di olio e 24,000 kg. di carbone, premi di nuzialità, sussidi alle famiglie prolifiche, e assistenza medica a migliaia di persone." a.c., "La nuova sede del Gruppo Filzi," *Milano*, April 1938, 165.

24 In addition to the articles cited below, see Eugenio Faludi, *Architetture di Eugenio Faludi* (Milan: Officine Grafiche Esperia, 1939), 20–1.

25 Ravasco to Marinelli, 18 August 1937, 19 April 1938, ACS, PNF, Servizi Varie, Serie II, b. 1200, f. 102.

26 Ravasco to Marinelli, 18 August 1937, 19 April 1938, ACS, PNF, Servizi Varie, Serie II, b. 1200, f. 102.

27 a.c., "La nuova sede del Gruppo Filzi," 167.

28 Ruth Ben-Ghiat, *Fascist Modernities: Italy, 1922–1945* (Los Angeles: University of California Press, 2001), 70–4; Philip Cannistraro, *La fabbrica del consenso: Fascismo e mass media* (Rome: Laterza, 1975), 273–322.

29 Cannistraro, *La fabbrica del consenso*, 225–71.

30 "Gli ambienti e gli impianti sono stati studiati per provvedere nel miglior modo all'educazione delle masse, all'amministrazione più esauriente delle attività politiche, alla tutela forza fisica e all' esaltazione delle virtù atletiche." a.c., "La nuova sede del Gruppo Filzi," 166.

31 "L'Italia Fascista affida a voi giovani la sua grandezza e il suo futuro: preparatevi a servirla in ogni tempo col cuore con la mente e con le armi." a.c., "La nuova sede del Gruppo Filzi," 167.

32 In the spring of 1934 the Milan Federation decided to expand the project from two thousand to at least three thousand square meters. The sites initially proposed were too small. Ravasco to Marinelli, 28 March 1934; memorandum, 18 April 1934; Ravasco to Marinelli, 5 February 1935; ACS, PNF, Servizi Varie, Serie II, b. 1197.

33 Ravasco to Marinelli, 31 October 1935, ACS, PNF, Servizi Varie, Serie II, b. 1197.

34 Ravasco to Marcello Visconti di Modrone, 5 February 1935; Ravasco to Visconti di Modrone, 2 March 1935; Starace to Visconti di Modrone, 18 June 1935; ACS, PNF, Servizi Varie, Serie II, b. 1197. Ravasco also complained to Marinelli about the municipal government's tendency to procrastinate in order to avoid committing resources. Ravasco to Marinelli, 4 June 1935, ACS, PNF, Servizi Varie, Serie II, b. 1197.

35 Ravasco to Marinelli, 31 October 1935; Ravasco to Marinelli, 9 December 1936; ACS, PNF, Servizi Varie, Serie II, b. 1197. Appunti colloquio del 20 gennaio 1936, ACS, PNF, Servizi Varie, Serie II, b. 1197.

36 "Codesta Federazione dovrà predisporre un piano completo per assicurare che
    ogni Gruppo Rionale abbia … la propria sede decorosa, per quanto modesta,
    e proporzionata a tutte le necessità." Marinelli to Parenti, 26 April 1934, ACS,
    PNF, Servizi Varie, Serie II, b. 1201, f. 106.

37 "Il Gruppo Mussolini avrà una nuova sede," *Il Popolo d'Italia,* 17 May 1936;
    Memorandum, 11 September 1934, ACS, PNF, Servizi Varie, Serie II,
    b. 1199, f. 88.

38 Marinelli to Parenti, 26 April 1934, ACS, PNF, Servizi Varie, Serie II,
    b. 1201, f. 106.

39 Pesenti to Starace, 31 January 1938, ACS, PNF, Servizi Varie, Serie II,
    b. 1201, f. 106.

40 Pesenti to Starace, 31 January 1938, ACS, PNF, Servizi Varie, Serie II,
    b. 1201, f. 106.

41 Ravasco to Podestà, 25 November 1937, and Podestà to Fiduciario, 18 December
    1937, Archivio Storico Civicio, Milan (ASCM), Archivio Giuseppe Rivolta
    (AGR), c. 16.10.

42 Pesenti's letter listed the groups that purchased property from the city as the
    Mussolini, Tonoli, Oberdan, Filzi, Crespi, and Montegani groups. Groups
    renting city-owned property included the Beretta, Baldini, Bonservizi-Tonoli,
    Pepe, Indomita-Bernini, Mameli, Delcroix, Loris, and Gandolfo groups.
    Pesenti to Starace, 31 January 1938, ACS, PNF, Servizi Varie, Serie II, b. 1201,
    f. 106.

43 "Questi provvedimenti rientrano, in sostanza, nella collaborazione generale che
    il Comune presta per tutte le istituzioni del Regime." Scotti to Prefetto, 28 March
    1939, ASCM, AGR, c. 16.10.

44 Daniele Bardelli and Pietro Zuretti, "L'amministrazione comunale del periodo
    podestarile," in *Storia di Milano,* vol. 18, pt. 1 (Rome: Istituto della Enciclopedia
    Italiana, 1995–6), 659.

45 Carlo Ceschi, *Teoria e storia del restauro* (Rome: M. Bulzoni, 1970), 112.

46 Ravasco to Marinelli, 31 October·1935, ACS, PNF, Servizi Varie, Serie II,
    b. 1197.

47 Paolo Nicoloso, "Il contesto sociale, politico e universitario di Portaluppi," in
    Piero Portaluppi: Linea errante nell'architettura del novecento, ed. Luca Molinari
    (Milan: Skira, 2003), 241–9.

48 In April 1936 Portaluppi presented five versions of the project for review, labeled
    A, B, C, D, and E. Of these only B, C, and D remain in the national archives.
    "Incastonamento dell'edificio antico nella moderna struttura," Schema C, ACS,
    PNF, Servizi Varie, Serie II, b. 1197.

49 The federation initially agreed on the least obtrusive solution possible: modest
    additions to either side of the Palazzo Castani. "La Casa del Fascio si trasferisce,"
    Corriere della Sera, 17 June 1936.

50 In June 1936 local papers mentioned the possible enlargement of the site. Site
    plans were published in July of the same year. "La Casa del Fascio si trasferisce
    nel palazzo di piazza San Sepolcro," *Corriere della Sera*, 17 June 1936;
    "La nuova Casa del Fascio," *L'Ambrosiano*, 7 July 1936; "La Casa del Fascio
    nella nuova sede di piazza San Sepolcro," *Il Popolo d'Italia*, 7 July 1936.
51 "'Tutto di questo va bene, ma quando si comincia? Perché questo e il più impor-
    tante.'" Rossi, "Vecchia Guardia, a Noi! Il Capo fra gli arditi e i legionari della
    Vigila in piazza San Sepolcro," Fondazione Piero Portaluppi (FPP), Milan. The
    same account is given in "Annuali del Fascismo," November 1936, P. Portaluppi
    album, FPP. *Corriere della Sera* published a photograph of the model: "Mussolini
    darà oggi il 'via' ai lavori per la futura Casa del Fascio," *Corriere della Sera*, 1
    November 1936.
52 The site plans blocked out the Palazzo Castani as the "building that remains," the
    properties to either side of the palazzo as "buildings to rebuild right away," and
    the area behind this as far as the new artery as "buildings to rebuild in the future."
    "La futura Casa del Fascio," *Corriere della Sera*, 3 July 1936; "La nuova Casa
    del Fascio," *L'Ambrosiano*, 7 July 1936; "La Casa del Fascio nella nuova sede di
    piazza San Sepolcro," *Il Popolo d'Italia*, 7 July 1936.
53 Ravasco to Marinelli, 14 November 1936, ACS, PNF, Servizi Varie, Serie II, b.
    1197. Mussolini contributed token amounts of 75,000 and 25,000 lire. Marinelli
    to Parenti, 9 December 1936, and "Il Messaggero," 17 February 1937, ACS, PNF,
    Servizi Varie, Serie II, b. 1197. The industrialist Giuseppe Frua donated 50,000
    lire. Frua to Mussolini, 1 July 1936, ACS, PNF, Servizi Varie, Serie II, b. 1197.
    Ravasco also compiled a list of possible donors, many of whom were associated
    with local industrial concerns, to solicit directly. Ravasco to Marinelli, 1 July
    1936, 3 February 1937, ACS, PNF, Servizi Varie, Serie II, b. 1197. Funding for
    the project continued to be a concern, particularly in light of the federation's plans
    to complete the second structure. Ravasco to Marinelli, 25 January 1939, ACS,
    PNF, Servizi Varie, Serie II, b. 1197. For a summary of donations see Contributi e
    Impegni al 31 Dicembre 1937, ACS, PNF, Servizi Varie, Serie II, b. 1197.
54 Records show that the Breda Company gave 45,000 lire, the Stigler Company
    gave 50,000, and the founder of the Chini Company Giovanni Chini donated
    300,000. Members of the Filzi Group contributed 90,000 lire. ACS, PNF, Servizi
    Varie, Serie II, b. 1200; Gruppo Rionale to Mussolini, 20 March 1938, ACS, PNF,
    Servizi Varie, Serie II, b. 1200, f. 102.
55 Pirelli gave a sum of one million lire to Mussolini in honour of Italy's "victory" in
    the Ethiopian campaign in June 1936. Of this sum, Mussolini designated 400,000
    lire to support the party's charitable work and directed 600,000 to the construc-
    tion of the new Filzi Group headquarters. Newspaper clipping dated 3 June 1936;
    ACS, PNF, Servizi Varie, Serie II, b. 1200. Pirelli increased his commitment to

the construction to 850,000 lire "in honor of the arrival of the Duce in Milan" in November 1936. Ravasco to Marinelli, 9 November 1936, ACS, PNF, Servizi Varie, Serie II, b. 1200, f. 102.

56 "La nuova sede del Circolo 'Fabio Filzi' inaugurata alla presenza della madre dell'Eroe," *Il Popolo d'Italia*, 9 October 1923. For a general discussion of the Pirelli Company in these years see *Pirelli, 1914–80: Strategia aziendale e relazione industriali nella storia di una multinazionale* (Milan: F. Angeli, 1985), 50–85.

57 Ravasco to Marinelli, 1 April 1939, Mario Asso, ACS, PNF, Servizi Varie, Serie II, b. 1202.

58 Nicoli Tullio, Relazione Tecnica, 30 August 1937; Marinelli to Ravasco, 14 December 1937; Ravasco to Marinelli, 20 December 1937, ACS, PNF, Servizi Varie, Serie II, b. 1200, f. 102.

59 Ravasco to Marinelli, 25 July 1939, ACS, PNF, Servizi Varie, Serie II, b. 1200, f. 102.

60 Ravasco to Marinelli, 10 October 1939, ACS, PNF, Servizi Varie, Serie II, b. 1200, f. 102.

61 Ravasco to Marinelli, 7 January 1937, ACS, PNF, Servizi Varie, Serie II, b. 1200, f. 88; "Il Duce rende omaggio ai Caduti fascisti," *Il Popolo d'Italia*, 3 November 1936. Mussolini made a similar request after reviewing Gio Ponti's initial proposal for the Torre Littoria adjacent to the Palazzo dell'Arte in the Parco Sempione. Paolo Nicoloso, *Mussolini architetto: Propaganda e paesaggio urbano nell'Italia fascista* (Turin: Einaudi, 2008), 22.

62 Marco Dezzi Bardeschi, "Milano, 1918–1940: Il progetto del nuovo e l'eredita della storia," in *Milano durante il fascismo, 1922–45*, ed. Giorgio Rumi, Virgilio Vercelloni, and Alberto Cova (Milan: Caripolo, 1994), 217–52.

63 "Francamente moderna … violento." Soprintendente to Ministero dell'Educazione Nazionale, 12 November 1937, Archivio Soprintendenza Beni Artistici e Architettonici, Milan (ASBAAM), E/3/1103.

64 "Forma e dimensioni." Soprintendente to Ministero dell'Educazione Nazionale, 12 November 1937, ASBAAM, E/3/1103.

65 Giovannoni (1873–1947) was one of the leading figures of architectural culture in the interwar period, and his influence was immense. He was president of the Associazione Artistica tra i Cultori dell'Architettura, played a central role in the establishment (in 1920) and leadership of the nation's first architecture school, the Scuola Superiore di Architettura in Rome, and founded, with Marcello Piacentini, the journal *Architettura e Arti Decorative* in 1921. His theories on urban planning were indebted to Camillo Boito and formed the basis for urban plans throughout Italy in this period. Alberto Calza-Bini (1908–57) was also the director of *Architettura e Arti Decorative*, which became the official journal of the Syndicate in 1927 and a guarded supporter of modernism.

66 "[I]l problema dell'ambientamento posto dal particolare carattere della Storica Piazza." Bottai to Chierici, 20 April 1938, ASBAAM, f. E/3/1103. Giovanonni wrote: "per banalità di linee assolutamente inadequato all'importanza ed al significato che l'edificio dovrebbe assumere; e nell'ibrido innesto della torre con l'edificio settecentesco ravvisa un' offeso al carattere della piazza." Giovanonni to Bottai, 21 March 1938, ACS, Antichità e Belle Arti (AABBAA), Pubblica Istruzione (PI), div. II, b. 248,1934–40. Piacentini and Calza-Bini likewise criticized the proposal and suggested that Portaluppi restudy the tower with greater attention to the historical and architectural importance of the Piazza. Calza-Bini to Bottai, 31 March 1938, ACS, AABBAA, PI, div. II, b. 248, 1934–40.

67 D. Medina Lasansky, *The Renaissance Perfected: Architecture, Spectacle and Tourism in Fascist Italy* (University Park, PA: Penn State University Press, 2004), 184–5.

68 Ravasco to Bottai, 4 May 1938, ACS, PNF, Servizi Varie, Serie II, b. 1197; Chierici to Bottai, 4 May 1938, "Zona che ha vincoli monumentali"; Portaluppi to Chierici, 27 July 1938, ASBAAM, E/3/1103.

69 Marinelli to Ravasco, 9 March 1937; Ravasco to Marinelli, 27 April 1937; ACS, PNF, Servizi Varie, Serie II, b. 1197. Ravasco to Bottai, 4 May 1938, ACS, PNF, Servizi Varie, Serie II, b. 1197. Ravasco to Parenti, 2 May 1938, ACS, PNF, Servizi Varie, Serie II, b. 1197. Pesenti to Bottai, 4 May 1938, ASCM, AGR, c. 61, 10. Marinelli to Bottai, 16 May 1938, ACS, PNF, Servizi Varie, Serie II, b. 1197. For a review of this episode see also Ferruccio Luppi, "Sede della Federazione dei Fasci Milanesi," in *Piero Portaluppi: Linea errante nell'architettura del novecento*, ed. Luca Molinari (Milan: Skira, 2003), 132–3.

70 Bottai approved the project on 25 August 1938. Bottai to Cherici, 25 August 1938, ASBAAM, E/3/1103.

71 Maurizio Boriani, Corinna Morandi, and Augusto Rossari, eds., *Milano contemporanea: Itinerari di architettura e urbanistica* (Milan: Maggioli, 2007), 122.

72 A short biography of Bacciocchi is available in *Gli Annitrenta: Arte e cultura in Italia* (Milan: Mazzotta, 1982), 544.

73 "Gruppo Rionale Filzi," *Il Popolo d'Italia*, 22 January 1937.

74 "[U]n maggiore carattere di italianità." Nicoli Tullio, Relazione Tecnica, 30 August 1937, ACS, PNF, Servizi Varie, Serie II, b. 1200, f. 102.

75 Lodi was a member of the group. *La nuova sede del Gruppo Fabio Filzi*, Milan, n.d. [ca. 1940]; "Gruppo Fascista Fabio Filzi," *L'Ascesa*, 1938. Archivio Leone Lodi (ALL), Milan.

76 "Il Fascismo stabilisce l'uguaglianza verace e profonda in tutti gli individui di fronte alla nazione … L'obbiettivo della nostra marcia sul terreno economico è la realizzazione di una più alta giustizia sociale per il popolo Italiano." *La nuova*

sede del Gruppo Rionale Fabio Filzi (Milan: Same, n.d. [ca. 1940]), ALL. This inscription does not appear in any period photographs. However, this plaque is now covered, suggesting an explicitly fascist inscription.

77 The group occupied the neoclassical early-nineteenth-century Palazzo Besana from 1930 to 1931 and a palazzo on Via Santo Spirito from 1931 to 1939, which was remodelled for the group by Paolo Vietti Violi. From 1939 to the collapse of fascism, the group occupied the sixteenth-century Palazzo Erba Odescalchi on Via Unione, which was renovated by the engineer Leopoldi Valentini and the Novecento Milanese architect Giovanni Greppi, both of whom were members of the group. "Documento nuovo sede" and Ravasco to Marinelli, 26 January 26, 1938, ACS, PNF, Servizi Varie, Serie II, b. 1200, f. 103.

78 Gianni Mezzanotte, "La Borsa di Milano," in *Costruire in Lombardia, 1880–1980*, vol. 1, ed. Aldo Castellano and Ornella Selvafolta (Milan: Electa, 1980), 237.

79 Gardini to Podestà, 23 June 1937, ASCM, AGR, c. 16, 10. On this building see Costruzioni-Casabella [pseudo.], "La nuova sede del Gruppo Crespi a Milano," *Costruzioni-Casabella* 149 (May 1940): 16–23; "La sede del Gruppo Rionale Fascista 'P.E. Crespi' a Milano," *Architettura*, nos. 9–10 (1941): 380–3. On Varisco see Stefania Cottini, "Tito Bassanesi Varisco Architetto," master's thesis, Politecnico di Milano, 2000.

80 This area, which now holds the Milan Fair Grounds, served as the site of the unrealized Rationalist housing and community project Green Milan (Milano Verde) designed by Franco Albini, Ignazio Gardella, and Giuseppe Pagano among others. The Baracca Group sponsored the project in 1938. Giusppe Pagano, "Proposta di Piano regolatore per la Zona Sempione-Fiera, a Milano," *Casabella-Costruzioni* 132 (December 1938): 2–23. The role of the Baracca Group in the cultural life of the city merits further study.

81 "Come sarà in piazza San Sepolcro la monumentale Casa del Fascio," *Corriere della Sera*, 23 February 1939 and ACS, PNF, Servizi Varie, Serie II, b. 1197.

82 Earlier plans had indicated that this memorial chapel would be part of or adjacent to the restored Room of the Sansepolcristi on the opposite side of the building and on axis with the nave of San Sepolcro. a.c.r. [Antonio Cassi-Ramelli], "Una Villa a Merate – il Palazzo dei Fasci e una casa di abitazione a Milano," *Rassegna di Architettura*, no. 10 (1940): 269; Ferdinando Poch, "La nuova sede del Fascio primogenito," *Milano*, March 1930, 120; "La storica Sala dei Sansepolcristi è stata oggi simbolicamente consegnata alla Federazione Fascista," March 1939, ASCM, AGR, c. 61.10.

83 The winged victories represented: 24 May 1915–4 November 1918 – Victory of War or the First World War (*La Vittoria delle armi*); 23 March 1919 – The Victory of the Spirit or the Foundation of the Fascist Party (*La Vittoria dello Spirito*); 28 October 1922 – The Victory of Boldness or the March on Rome (*La Vittoria*

dell'audacia); 9 May 1936 – The Victory of the People or the Declaration of Empire (*La Vittoria del Popolo*). Ravasco Memorandum, n.d., ACS, PNF, Servizi Vari, Serie II, b. 1197. The sculptures were by Arch. [Aldo?] Andreani and were approved by Marinelli on 30 March 1939. Marinelli to Ravasco, 30 March 1939, ACS, PNF, Servizi Varie, Serie II, b. 1197.

84 "La nuova sede della Federazione," *L'Ambrosiano*, 23 February 1939; Poch, "La nuova sede del Fascio primogenito," 122.

85 "... questa nuova concezione dell'individuo e dello stato si manifesta colle grandi adunate di masse eterogenee di cittadini ..." Savoia, "La Casa del Fascio," *L'Assalto*, 26 May 1932.

86 "La nuova sede del Gruppo 'Mussolini' a Milano," *Case d'Oggi*, October 1938, n.p.

87 "Cerimonie e delle celebrazioni." a.c.r. [Antonio Cassi-Ramelli], "Le Case del Fascio Milanese nell'Anno XVI," *Rassegna di Architettura*, no. 9 (1938): 393.

88 Emilio Gentile, *The Sacralization of Politics in Fascist Italy*, trans. Keith Botsford (Cambridge, MA: Harvard University Press, 1996), 21, 136–9.

89 Marinelli to Ravasco, 28 September 1938, ACS, PNF, Servizi Varie, Serie II, b. 1202.

90 "Generazioni nate e maturate nel solco lasciato e segnato dagli Eroi scomparsi." a.c.r. [Antonio Cassi-Ramelli], "Una Villa a Merate," 303. The members of the group were Gianni Albricci, Mario Tevarotto, Marco Zanuso, Luigi Mattoni, Gianluigi Reggio, and Mario Salvedè. See also Costruzioni [pseudo.], "Sacrario dei Caduti Fascisti nella nuova Federazione di Milano," *Costruzioni-Casabella* 157 (January 1941): 44–5.

91 "I progetti per la cappella votiva nella nuova Casa del Fascio esaminato dal Segretario del Partito," *L'Italia*, 28 April 1939; "Il Segretario del Partito alla Fiera e alla Casa del Fascio," *Il Popolo Lombardia*, 29 April 1939.

92 The sculpture by Fontana and the rough stone walls are the only elements of the *sacrario* that remain. For a more detailed history of Fontana's project see Paolo Campiglio, *Lucio Fontana: La scultura architettonica negli anni Trenta* (Nuoro: Ilisso, 1995), 111–18; Cecilia De Carli, "Fontana e gli architetti: Un inedito," *Arte Christiana* 68 (March–April 1989): 157–62.

93 Paolo Nicoloso, *Mussolini architetto*, 281; Carla Quinto, "L'eredità architettonica del fascismo. Gli edifice e loro riutilizzo nel dopoguerra," master's thesis, Università degli Studi di Trieste, 2012.

6. Museum, Monument, and Memorial

1 "In un regime totalitario come deve essere necessariamente un regime sorto da un rivoluzione trionfante, la stampa è un elemento di questo regime, una forza al servizio di questo regime: un regime unitario, la stampa non può essere estranea a questo unità." Address to journalists in Rome, 10 October 1928, in

Benito Mussolini, *Opera omina*, ed. Edoardo Susmel and Duilio Susmel, vol. 23 (Florence: La Feince, 1957), 230–4.

2 "Il giornale della Rivoluzione Fascista inizia oggi il XXV anno di vita gettando le fondamenta della nuova sede," *Il Popolo d'Italia*, 15 November 1938. The same day *Corriere della Sera* ran an abbreviated announcement without a photo. "L'annuale del 'Popolo d'Italia,'" *Corriere della Sera*, 15 November 1938.

3 Fulvio Irace provides an excellent discussion of this building as part of his analysis of Muzio's engagement with public buildings in Milan in the 1930s: *Giovanni Muzio, 1893–1982* (Milan: Electa, 1994), 148–61.

4 "Il giornale della Rivoluzione Fascista inizia oggi il XXV anno di vita gettando le fondamenta della nuova sede," *Il Popolo d'Italia*, 15 November 1938.

5 Italy entered the First World War on 16 April 1915. After the editorial offices were transferred to Via Lovanio the property housed the Mystical School of Fascism (Scuola Mistica Fascista). The site was declared a national monument in April 1939. Ministero dell'Educazione Nazionale to Soprintendente, 13 April 1939, Archivio Soprintendenza Beni Artistici e Architettonici, Milan (ASBAAM), E/3/1103. Severino Pagani, *Milano: Guida turistica della città e dintorni* (Milan: Casa Editrice Ceschina, 1939), 82.

6 Mabel Bezerin, *Making the Fascist Self: The Political Culture of Interwar Italy* (Ithaca: Cornell University Press, 1997), 173.

7 For a history of the journal see Giorgio Pini, *Filo diretto con Palazzo Venezia* (Bologna: Cappelli, 1950); Philip Cannistraro, "La Stampa," in *La fabbrica del consenso: Fascismo e mass media* (Bari: Laterza, 1975), 173–224; Paolo Murialdi, "La stampa quotidiana del regime fascista," in *La stampa Italiana nell'età fascista*, ed. Nicola Tranfaglia, Massimo Legnani, and Paolo Murialdi (Bari: Laterza, 1980), 221–5; Marco Tarchi, ed., *Il Popolo d'Italia, antologia, 1914–1917* (Florence: L. Landi, 1982).

8 Salvatore Lupo, "Il Popolo d'Italia," in Victoria de Grazia and Sergio Luzzatto, *Dizionario del Fascismo*, vol. 2 (Turin: Einaudi, 2005), 408; Philip Cannistraro and Brian Sullivan, *The Duce's Other Woman* (New York: Morrow, 1993), 125; R.J.B. Bosworth, *Mussolini* (New York: Oxford University Press, 2002), 107.

9 Including Agostino Lanzillo, Guido Dorso, and Sergio Panunzio. For a history of *La Voce* and the participation of some of its leading members in Mussolini's *Popolo d'Italia*, see Walter Adamson, *Avant-garde Florence: From Modernism to Fascism* (Cambridge, MA: Harvard University Press, 1993), 102–43, 198–9, 201, 224–5. Masthead slogans translated in Bosworth, *Mussolini*, 105. For more about the founding of the journal see Bosworth, *Mussolini*, 105–6.

10 Cannistraro and Sullivan, *The Duce's Other Woman*, 194.

11 Giorgio Rumi, "'Il Popolo d'Italia,'" in *1919–1925, Dopoguerra e fascismo: Politica e stampa in Italia*, ed. Brunello Vigezzi (Bari: Editori Laterza, 1965), 467.

12 Bosworth, *Mussolini*, 133, 166.

13 Manilo Morgani, "Dalla 'tenda' al palazzo," *La Rivista Illustrata del Popolo d'Italia* 2, no. 1 (1924): 12; "La nuova sede del 'Popolo d'Italia' che il 'fondatore' Presidente del Consiglio – inaugurà domani," *Il Popolo d'Italia*, 23 December 1923.

14 Mussolini's office even retained its original telephone. Pini, *Filo diretto*, 7.

15 Emily Braun and Cioni Carpi, "Illustrations of Propaganda: The Political Drawings of Mario Sironi / Illustrazioni di propaganda: I disegni politici di Mario Sironi," *Journal of Decorative and Propaganda Arts* 3 (Italian Theme Issue) (Winter 1987): 86–96. See also Braun, *Mario Sironi and Italian Modernism: Art and Politics under Fascism* (Cambridge, MA: Cambridge University Press, 2000), 132–40.

16 Murialdi, "La stampa quotidiana," 59.

17 Murialdi, "La stampa quotidiana," 60.

18 "[D]i carattere schivo e riservato." Pini, *Filo diretto*, 7; Murialdi, "La stampa quotidiana," 130, 188.

19 Innovations adopted by Italian journals in this period included new layouts and typesets that were easier to read, photographic illustrations, and greater coverage of sporting, arts and cultural events. Murialdi, "La stampa quotidiana," 116, 189.

20 Braun, *Mario Sironi and Italian Modernism*, 134.

21 Pini participated in the fascist movement while a student in Bologna and served as the editor for the Bologna-based party-controlled paper *L'Assalto* until 1928, when he transferred to Genoa to edit the *Giornale di Genova*. He also wrote several books on Mussolini and fascism, including *Benito Mussolini* (Bologna: L. Cappelli, 1926) and *Storia del Fascismo* (Rome: Libr. del Littorio, 1928). See Pini, *Filo diretto*, 19–36; Edoardo Savino, *La nazione operante*, 3rd ed. (Novara: Istituto Geografico de Agostini, 1937), 583.

22 "Escludere i disegni enfatici e retorici per far posto a quelli di contenuto mordente e persuasivo (sollecitare disegni di Sironi)." Pini, *Filo diretto*, 60.

23 Murialdi, "La stampa quotidiana," 222.

24 "Fare del *Popolo d'Italia* un quotidiano che dia al lettore, oltre l'indirizzo politico fondamentale, tutte le informazioni e le immagini della vita quotidiana, in grado non meno completo degli altri più attrezzati e diffusi giornali italiani." Pini, *Filo diretto*, 59.

25 Marco Tarchi, "La voce di Mussolini nella fabbrica del consenso 'Il Popolo d'Italia,' 1914–1943," in *Il Popolo d'Italia: Antologia, 1914–1917* (Florence: L. Landi, 1982), 87–8; Murialdi, "La stampa quotidiana," 189.

26 Tarchi, "La voce di Mussolini," 94.

27 Sketches prepared by architect Luciano Baldessari for a new building on the same site from 1935 indicate that the project predates Pini, although in his memoires Pini takes credit. Zita Mosca Baldessari, ed., *Luciano Baldessari* (Milan: Mondadori, 1985), 76; Fluvio Irace, *Giovanni Muzio*, 153; Pini, *Filo diretto*, 176.

28 Reggiori, *Milano, 1800–1943* (Milan: Edizioni del Milano, 1947), 289.

29 For a history of the site and the structure demolished in 1939, see Paolo
   Mezzanotte and Giacomo Bescape, *Milano nell'arte e nella storia* (Milan: E.
   Bestetti, 1948), 911–12. The site measured approximately four thousand square
   metres. Giovanni Muzio, "Il nuovo Palazzo del 'Popolo d'Italia,'" *La Rivista
   Illustrata del Popolo d'Italia* 18, no. 11 (1939): n.p.

30 The journal purchased the site around 1930. Albertini's preferred solution
   designated a significant section of the former Polytechnic site for public use.
   Cesare Albertini, "Si chiacchiera ancora del Piano regolatore," *Milano*, February
   1930, 52–5.

31 Ugo Ojetti served as president of the organization at its founding. Irace, *Giovanni
   Muzio*, 17.

32 "Oggi a noi sembra necessario una reazione alla confusione ed all'esasperato
   individualismo dell'architettura odierna, ed il ristabilimento del principio di
   ordine per il quale l'architettura, arte eminentemente sociale, deve in un paese
   anzitutto essere continua nei suoi caratteri stilistici, per esser suscettibile di dif-
   fusione e formare con il complesso degli edifici un tutto armonico ed omogeneo."
   Muzio, "L'Architettura a Milano intorno all'Ottocento," in *Giovanni Muzio,
   opere e scritti*, ed. Giuseppe Gambirasio and Bruno Minardi (Milan: F. Angeli,
   1982), 233.

33 The letter was written shortly after the appointment of two new deputy *podestà*,
   Innocenzo Pini and Cesare Dorici. Muzio perhaps hoped that new leadership
   would rekindle interest in the urban fabric. Giovanni Muzio to Podestà[?],
   September 1930, Archivio Giovanni Muzio, Milan, AGM.

34 Giovanni Muzio, "Forme nuove di città moderne," presented at a conference
   held by the Engineers Syndicate (Sindacato Ingegneri di Milano) on 12 June
   1930. Archivio Giovanni Muzio. Later published in *Atti del Sindacato Fascista
   Ingegneri di Milano*, no. 9 (1930): 7.

35 "[A]ppare sfondata nei suoi attuali margini al sud e diviene una serie allungata e
   bistorta di incroci, di smussi e di cantonate dove invano si tenterebbe poi con aiuole
   e 'suppellettili stradali' di comporre una simmetria." Giuseppe De Finetti, Giovanni
   Muzio, and Alberto Alpago Novello, *Memoria sui progetti per il Piano regolatore
   di Milano, 1928–1929* (Milan: Libreria Editrice degli Omenoni, 1930), 55.

36 For Modigliani's involvement in other initiatives see Andrea Bona, "Il Club
   degli architetti urbanisti: Una battiglia per Milano," in *Città immaginata e città
   costruita: Forma, empirismo e tecnica in Italia Otto e Novecento*, ed. Cristina
   Bianchetti (Milan: F. Angeli, 1992).

37 Ettore Modigliani to Prefetto di Milano, 22 June 1931, Archivio Centrale dello
   Stato, Rome (ACS), Pubblica Istruzione (PI), Antichità e Belle Arti (AABBAA),
   1934–40, b. 247.

38 Reggiori, *Milano*, 287. In the late nineteenth century the debates over the appropriate treatment of the towers were taken up by many of the leading cultural

figures in Milan, including Camillo Boito. The history of the towers and the arches was used as evidence in the 1930s to support preserving the monument in its entirety. Ettore Modigliani to Ministero dell'Educazione Nazionale Direzione Generale per le Antichita' e Belle Arti, 31 January 1931, ACS, AABBAA, PI, 1934–40, b. 247.

39 Ettore Modigliani to Ministero dell'Educazione Nazionale Direzione Generale per le Antichita' e Belle Arti, 31 January 1931, ACS, PI, AABBAA, 1934–40, b. 247.

40 Reggiori, *Milano*, 292.

41 Reggiori, *Milano*, 292.

42 Paolo Nicoloso, *Mussolini architetto: Propaganda e paesaggio urbano nell'Italia fascista* (Turin: Einaudi, 2008), 252–3.

43 Reggiori, *Milano*, 91.

44 "Il Piano regolatore di Milano e le opere previste per il quadriennio 1939–42 XVII–XXI E.F.," *Rassegna di Architettura,* no. 11 (1938): 471. The city again proposed moving the arches. "Le direttive del Duce per la più potente e più bella Milano," *Corriere della Sera*, 11 December 1938.

45 Gino Chierici to Ministero dell'Educazione Nazionale, Direzione Generale Antichità e Belle Arti, 12 December 1939, ACS, PI, AABBAA, 1934–40, b. 247.

46 Chierici to Ministero dell'Educazione Nazionale, Direzione Generale Antichità e Belle Arti, 13 December 1939, ACS, PI, AABBAA, 1934–40, b. 247.

47 Giuseppe De Finetti, "Projetto di una piazza. La Piazza Cavour in Milano," in *Milano: Costruzione di una città*, ed. Giovanna Cislaghi, Mara De Benedetti, and Piergiorgio Marabelli (Milan: Etas Kompass, 1969).

48 Although *Il Popolo d'Italia*'s headquarters on the corner of Via Moscova had been expanded and updated numerous times, these cosmetic changes did not fundamentally alter the operational or symbolic functions of the complex. Notably, in 1934 Rationalist architect and designer Giuseppe Pagano redesigned the offices of the director (Vittorio), editor-in-chief (Giuliani), and administrative director (Barella). Pagano was in charge of the artistic division of the Mystical School of Fascism (Scuola Mistica Fascista) of which Vittorio (Vito) Mussolini was president. It was likely this connection that led to the commission. Alberto Bassi and Laura Castagno, *Giuseppe Pagano* (Roma: Laterza, 1994), 97–101; Antonino Saggio, *L'opera di Giuseppe Pagano tra politica e architettura* (Bari: Dedalo, 1984), 13–16. See also Maria Luisa Betri, "Tra politica e cultura: La Scuola mistica fascista," in Il *fascismo in Lombardia: Politica, economia e società*, ed. Maria Luisa Betri et al. (Milan: Franco Angeli, 1989), 377–98.

49 Irace, *Giovanni Muzio*, 139.

50 Muzio, with Sironi, designed the *Il Popolo d'Italia* pavilion at the Milan Trade Fair (Fiera Campionaria di Milano) in 1928. Barella had also hired the pair

to design the Italian press and book exhibits for the 1928 Press Exhibition (Internationale Presse-Ausstellung) in Cologne and the installation of the Italian Pavilion for the 1929 International Exposition (Exposiciòn Internacional) in Barcelona. Braun, *Mario Sironi and Italian Modernism*, 142–5; Irace, *Giovanni Muzio*, 139.

51 Scholars have debated Sironi's role in the design of the façade and elsewhere. Fabio Benzi argues that Sironi actively participated in the design process, and he connects several undated and unnamed sketches by Sironi to this project. Benzi, *Sironi: Il mito dell'architettura* (Milan: Mazzotta, 1990), 91–3. Elena Pontiggia and Andrea Sironi have refuted many of Benzi's claims; see Pontiggia, "Le decorazioni scultoree per il Palazzo del 'Popolo d'Italia'"; Sironi, "L'officina," in *Sironi: La grande decorazione*, ed. Sironi (Milan: Electa, 2004), 453–7. Correspondence between Mario Sironi and Muzio shows that the two were in regular contact during the design and construction of the building and collaborated on many aspects of the decorative program. There is no specific mention of the sculptures for the façade; however, the ongoing collaboration between the two and the integral relationship between the architectural and decorative programs strongly suggests that this aspect of the project was done together.

52 "[I]lusterà le origini e lo sviluppo del giornale e della Rivoluzione." "Un grande quotidiano moderno," *Il Popolo d'Italia*, 15 November 1938.

53 Benzi, *Sironi*, 92.

54 "Ricorderanno ogni giorno ai milanesi che nel giornale del Duce arde e vigila sempre lo spirito della Rivoluzione Fascista." Giovanni Muzio, "Il nuovo Palazzo del 'Popolo d'Italia,'" *La Rivista Illustrata del Popolo d'Italia* 18, no. 11 (1939): n.p.

55 "Una parte del edificio, e precisamente quella d'angolo tra piazza Cavour e Via Senato, sarà riservata alle scritte luminose per la segnalazione di avvenimenti politici, sportive, ecc." "Un grande quotidiano moderno," *Il Popolo d'Italia*, 15 November 1938.

56 For example, Oscar Nitzche made the facade of his project for the Maison de la Publicitè (1934–6) in Paris a glowing grid of screens announcing news and events. Alvar Aalto also planned to project the front page of the newspaper on the façade of the Turun Sanomat Building (1927).

57 "L'Annuale del 'Popolo d'Italia,'" *Corriere della Sera*, 15 November 1938.

58 For more on this theme in early modern Italy, see Yvonne Elet, "Seats of Power: The Outdoor Benches of Early Modern Florence," *Journal of the Society of Architectural Historians* 61, no. 4 (2002): 444–69.

59 The word *arengario* comes from the verb *arringare* ("to address"). In the Middle Ages it referred to the government building from which officials addressed the public. The term was revived in fascist Italy.

60 Aldo Gini, "Gli impianti tecnici della nuova sede," *La Rivista Illustrata del Popolo d'Italia* 18, no. 11 (1939): n.p.

61 "[T]ecnicamente attrezzata meglio di qualunque sede di qualsiasi giornale
   europeo." Pini, *Filo diretto*, 177. "[G]iudica anche migliore di quella del New
   York Times." Pini, *Filo diretto*, 222.

62 "La fedele ricostruzione degli ambienti dove il Duce e Arnaldo hanno lavorato.
   Sarà anche ricostruito il salone Bonservizi. In questi ambienti saranno conservate
   le memorie principali e più significative dell'attività giornalistica del Duce e del
   Suo indimenticabile Fratello ... Il Sacrario sarà posto al piano terreno. Al primo
   piano sarà ricostruita la sala 'XXVIII Ottobre' dove il Duce concepì organizzò e
   diresse la Marcia su Roma. La Galleria storica illustra le principali date della vita
   del giornale e custodirà le memorie più care." "Un grande quotidiano moderno," *Il
   Popolo d'Italia*, 15 November 1938. For an analysis of the role of the *dopolavoro*
   in fascist Italy see Vittoria de Grazia, *The Culture of Consent: Mass Organization
   of Leisure in Fascist Italy* (Cambridge: Cambridge University Press, 1981).

63 "L'annuale del 'Popolo d'Italia,'" *Corriere della Sera*, 15 November 1938.

64 The journal headquarters on Via Lovanio also had a room dedicated to Nicola
   Bonservizi, a fascist delegate to France mortally wounded in Paris by Enrico
   Bonomini on 20 February 1924. He died in Milan on 26 March and Mussolini
   attended his funeral. The Room of Arnaldo was notable in early plans for its curved
   wall. Plan dated March 1939, AGM. For an overview of some of the symbolic intentions of the building, see Manlio Morgagni, "Il 'Popolo d'Italia' avrà la sua grande e
   moderna sede," *La Rivista Illustrata del Popolo d'Italia* 18, no. 11 (1939): n.p.

65 Plan dated March 1939, AGM; plan dated 12 May 1939; Archivio Civico del
   Comune, Milan, (ACM), Palazzo dei Giornali, Anno 1962 Atti di Proto. 40689.

66 This exhibition has been the focus of numerous scholarly works. The fundamental study on it is Libero Andreotti, "Art and Politics in Italy: The Exhibition
   of the Fascist Revolution, 1932," doctoral diss., MIT, 1989. Subsequent studies
   include Jeffrey Schnapp, "Epic Demonstrations: Fascist Modernity and the 1932
   Exhibition of the Fascist Revolution," in *Fascism, Aesthetics, and Culture*, ed.
   Richard Golsan (Hanover: University Press of New England, 1992), 1–37; Marla
   Susan Stone, *The Patron State: Culture and Politics in Fascist Italy* (Princeton:
   Princeton University Press, 1998), 128–76; and Claudio Fogu, *The Historic
   Imaginary: The Politics of History in Fascist Italy* (Toronto: University of Toronto
   Press, 2003).

67 "È il motivo, solenne e guerriero, che si svolgerà lungo tutta la Mostra, a
   dimostrare come un giornale diretto da un Uomo di genio, dalla volontà acuminata
   e della passione incandescente, possa veramente costruire la storia." Dino
   Alfieri and Luigi Freddi, eds., *Mostra della Rivoluzione Fascista: Guida storica*
   (Bergamo: Officine dell'Istituto Italiano d'Arti Grafiche, 1933; repr., Milan:
   Industrie Grafiche Italiane, 1982), 81.

68 Stone, *The Patron State*, 135.

69 A recreation of the "rugged den" on Via Paolo da Cannobio from which Mussolini directed the fascist movement and his journal was the focal point of the Hall of Honour (Salone d'Onore) designed by Mario Sironi. The disorder, simple furnishings, revolver, and standard bearing a skull and crossbones behind the desk captured the revolutionary moment in the history of the journal's and the party's leadership. Mussolini's office on Via Lovanio was presented in the following room. The more elegant furnishings and artfully placed images behind the desk – a dramatic portrait of Mussolini, a photograph of the masses gathered in the Campidoglio in Rome, and a reproduction of a Renaissance-styled painting of the Italian poet Dante projected an image of controlled confidence. This collection of images also paired images of secular authority (Campidoglio) with those of rhetorical authority (Dante) and suggested that Mussolini was the natural inheritor of these traditions in the making of a new and authentically Italian state.

70 Braun, *Mario Sironi and Italian Modernism*, 151.

71 Dinale and Alfieri, *Mostra della Rivoluzione Fascista*, 211.

72 Atrio d'Ingresso, 7 April 1941, AGM.

73 Sketches show that they explored the possibility of low-relief sculptures or other decorative panels for the ceiling in July 1941. Il Sofito, Atrio d'Ingresso, 23 July 1941, AGM. Sironi and Muzio continued to revise the decorative program for the atrium as late as 1942. AGM.

74 "Dominate, al centro del tutto l'edificio, la Sala del Duce." Muzio, "Il nuovo Palazzo del 'Popolo d'Italia,'" n.p.

75 Mario Sironi, *Scritti editi e inediti*, ed. Ettore Camasasca (Milan: Feltrinelli, 1980), 310.

76 "Questo secolo del Fascismo ce ne per voi e per quelli che verranno dopo di voi." Variante del una parete del Sala del Duce, 6 May 1942, AGM.

77 The use of porphyry may also have been a reference to ancient Rome. Porphyry was the material favoured for imperial projects in antiquity. Its use here also suggests that Sironi sought to reuse ideas explored in the 1934 competition for the Palazzo del Littorio in Rome, where his team had used porphyry to face the curved façade of their Project A (A. Carminati, P. Lingeri, E. Saliva, L. Vietti, N. Nizzoli). David Rifkind, conversation with author, October 2006. Muzio would also indicate porphyry for the sculpted columnar balcony of the Arengario (now Palazzo del Turismo, 1935–43) in Milan. Massimiliano Savorra, "Piazza Duomo," in *Piero Portaluppi: Linea errante nell'architettura del novecento*, exhibition catalogue, ed. Luca Molinari (Milan: Skira, 2003), 134.

78 Braun's discussion of Sironi's sculptures for the palazzo offers a succinct assessment of their iconography and place in Sironi's oeuvre: *Mario Sironi and Italian Modernism*, 202–5. Pontiggia offers a more detailed reading of the iconography: "Le decorazioni Scultoree," 401–24.

79 "[S]enza inutile cerimonie, senza strombazzamenti." Marcello Morabito, "Il 'Popolo d'Italia' nella sua nuova sede Milanese," *Milano*, November 1942, 474–6. Photos of the building as it neared completion can be found in Morabito, "Il 'Popolo d'Italia' nella sua nuova sede Milanese," and "La nuova sede del Popolo d'Italia," *Edilizia Moderna* 37–39 (1942): 47.

80 In 1937 *Podestà* Guido Pesenti had held a competition to create a master plan for the new piazza and manage the refurbishment of the southern and western edges of Piazza del Duomo. Architects Piero Portaluppi, Ernrico Agostino Griffini, Pier Giulio Magistretti, and Giovanni Muzio formed an unlikely but politically power-ful team and won the competition in the fall of 1938. Savorra, "Piazza Duomo," in *Piero Portaluppi*, 134–7; Savorra, "Una Scenografia Mancata: L'arengario e la piazza del Duomo a Milano negli anni trenta," in *L'architettura nelle città Italiane del XX secolo: Dagli anni venti agli anni ottanta,* ed. Vittorio Franchetti Pardo (Milan: Jaca Book, 2003); Irace, *Giovanni Muzio*, 124–32. Portaluppi spent sev-enteen hours working on designs for the Palazzo del Fascio in 1942. Fondazione Piero Portaluppi, Milan.

81 Murialdi, "La stampa quotidiana," 248–9.

Epilogue

1 Alberto Mioni, "Le città e l'urbanistica durante il fascismo," in *Urbanistica Fascista: Ricerche e saggi sulle città e il territorio e sulle politiche urbane in Italia tra le due guerre,* ed. Alberto Mioni (Milan: Angeli: 1980), 44.

2 See, for example, Dawn Ades et al., eds., *Art and Power: Europe under the Dictators, 1930–45* (London: Thames and Hudson, 1995); Timothy Colton, *Moscow: Governing the Socialist Metropolis* (Cambridge, MA: Belknap, 1995); Robert R. Taylor, *The Word in Stone: The Role of Architecture in the National Socialist Ideology* (Berkeley: University of California Press, 1974); Gabriel Ureña, *Arquitectura y urbanística civil y militar en el período de la autarquía (1936–1945): Análisis, cronología y textos* (Madrid: Istmo, D.L. 1979). Capital cities are also the primary focus of studies analysing democratic nations and postcolonial nations; see, for example, Lawrence J. Vale, *Architecture, Power and National Identity* (New Haven: Yale University Press, 1992).

3 Taylor, *The Word in Stone*, 49–52, 258, 263–8; John Robert Mullin, "Ideology, Planning Theory and the German City in the Inter-War Years: Part II," *Town Planning Review* 53, no. 3 (1982): 262.

4 Evan B. Bukey, "Hitler's Hometown under Nazi Rule: Linz, Austria, 1938–45," *Central European History* 16, no. 2 (1983): 172, 186; Joshua Hagen, "Parades, Public Space, and Propaganda: The Nazi Culture Parades in Munich," *Geografiska Annaler: Series B, Human Geography* 90, no. 4 (2008): 349–67.

5 Milano Verde (Franco Albini, Ignazio Gardella, Giulio Minoletti, Giuseppe Pagano, Giancarlo Palanti, Giangiacomo Predaval, and Giovanni Romano) was a self-sufficient middle-class residential community set within parkland to be developed just beyond the Spanish Walls. The fascist-controlled Baracca Group sponsored the project. The Quattro Città Satelliti (Franco Albini, Piero Bottoni, Renato Camus, Ezio Cerutti, Franco Fabbri, Cesare Mazzocchi, Maurizio Mazzocchi, Giulio Minoletti, Giancarlo Palanti, Mario Pucci, and Aldo Putelli) was a project for four independent satellite cities housing factory workers and linked to industrial complexes overseen by Giuseppe Gorla, vice-president of the IFACP (Istituto Fascista autonomo delle case popolari). For a contemporary account of Milano Verde see "Proposta di piano regolatore per la zona Sempione-Fiera a Milano," *Casabella-Costruzioni* 132 (December 1938): 2–23.

6 Leopoldo Marchetti, *Milano tra le due guerre, 1914–1946* (Milan: Strenna dell'Istituto Ortopedico "Gaetano Pini," 1963), 114.

7 Corinna Morandi, "Boom economico ed edilizio contro il piano Razionalista: Grandi progetti contro il piano della città conflittuale," in *Milano contemporanea: Itinerari di architettura e urbanistica*, ed. Maurizio Boriani, Corinna Morandi, and Augusto Rossari (Milan: Maggioli, 2007), 64. See also Patrizia Gabellini, Corinna Morandi, and Paola Vidulli, *Urbanistica a Milano, 1945–1980* (Rome: Edizione delle Autonomie, 1980).

8 For an overview of the post-war period see Vittorio Gregotti, *New Directions in Italian Architecture*, trans. Giuseppina Salvadori (New York: George Braziller, 1968) and Manfredo Tafuri's classic *History of Italian Architecture, 1944–1985*, trans. Jessica Levine (Cambridge, MA: MIT Press, 1989), 3–33. See also Matilde Baffa, Corinna Morandi, Sara Protasoni, and Augusto Rossari, eds.; *Il Movimento di Studi per L'Architettura, 1945–1961* (Rome: Laterza, 1995); and on Milan, Maurizio Grandi and Attilio Pracchi, *Milano: Guida all'architettura moderna* (Bologna: Zanichelli, 1980), 229–49.

9 The project is presented in *Casabella* 194 (1946). See also Giancarlo Consonni, "Il Piano AR per Milano e la Lombardia, 1944–45," in *Piero Bottoni: Opera completa, catalogo della mostra*, ed. Giancarlo Consonni, Lodovico Meneghetti, and Graziella Tonon (Milan: Fabbri, 1990), 326–9.

10 Morandi, "Boom economico," 68–9.

11 Morandi, "Boom economico," 70.

Selected Bibliography

The following bibliography includes the books and articles most frequently cited and those that were of particular importance in framing my ideas. It is by no means a complete record of all of the works cited or consulted.

Archives and Special Collections

Archivio Centrale dello Stato, Rome
Archivio Civico, Milan
Archivio di Stato, Milan
Archivio Giovanni Muzio, Milan
Archivio Giuseppe De Finetti, Centro Studi Archivio della Comunicazione, Parma
Archivio Giuseppe Rivolta, Archivio Storico Civico del Comune, Milan
Archivio Leone Lodi, Milan
Archivio Paolo Mezzanotte, Milan
Archivio Soprintendenza Beni Artistici e Architettonici, Milan
Archivio Storico Civico, Milan
Archivio Storico della Camera di Commercio, Milan
Archivio Tito Bassanesi Varisco, Milan
Civica Raccolta delle Stampe Achille Bertarelli, Milan
Civico Archivio Fotografico e Biblioteca, Milan
Fondazione Piero Portaluppi, Milan
Fondo Marcello Piacentini, Biblioteca della Facoltà di Architettura, Università degli Studi, Florence

Periodicals and Newspapers Consulted from 1922 to 1943

L'Ambrosiano
Architettura

L'Assalto
Casabella
Casa d'Oggi
Corriere della Sera
L'Illustrazione Italiana
Milano
Il Popolo d'Italia
Il Popolo d'Lombardia
Quadrante
Rassegna di Architettura
La Rivista Illustrata del Popolo d'Italia

Primary Sources

a.c. "La nuova Sede del Gruppo Filzi." *Milano*, April 1938, 165–7.

a.c.r. [Antonio Cassi-Ramelli]. "Le Case del Fascio Milanese nell'Anno XVI." *Rassegna di Architettura*, no. 9 (1938): 383–93.

Albertini, Cesare. *Cesare Albertini urbanista: Antologia di scritti.* Edited by G. Laura Di Leo. Rome: Gangemi, 1995.

– *The Characteristic of the Development of Milan.* Milan: Edizione del Comune, 1929.

Alfieri, Dino, and Luigi Freddi, eds. *Mostra della Rivoluzione Fascista: Guida storica.* Bergamo: Officine dell'Istituto Italiano d'Arti Grafiche, 1933. Repr., Milan: Industrie Grafiche Italiane, 1982.

Baedeker, Karl. *Italy: Handbook for Travellers by Karl Baedeker, First Part: Northern Italy*, 13th ed. Leipzig: Karl Baedeker, 1906.

Bardi, Pier Maria, "Nouvelles tendances dans les ècoles d'architeture Italiennes." *L'Architecture d'aujourd'hui* 10 (1933): 95–8.

Bullara, Salva. *Il Palazzo di Giustizia a Milano.* Milan: Industria Grafica "Italia Ars," 1925.

Calzini, Raffaele. "Il Palazzo di Giustizia di Milano." *Architettura*, nos. 1–2 (1942): 1–78.

Capo, Gian. "Il Palazzo di Giustizia." *Milano,* February 1932, 82–8.

Carrick, Edward. "Fascist Architecture in Italy." *The Architect's Journal* (August 1928): 186–91.

Chiodi, Cesare. "Come viene impostato dalla città di Milano lo studio del suo nuovo piano di ampliamento." Milan: Stab. Stucchi Ceretti, 1925.

"Concorso per il progetto del Palazzo di Giustizia in Milano." *Rassegna di Architettura*, no. 5 (1930): 162–7.

Costruzioni [pseudo.]. "Sacrario dei Caduti Fascisti nella nuova Federazione di Milano." *Costruzioni-Casabella* 157 (January 1941): 44–5.

Costruzioni-Casabella [pseudo.]. "La nuova sede del Gruppo Crespi a Milano."
    Costruzioni-Casabella 149 (May 1940): 16–23.
De Finetti, Giuseppe, Giovanni Muzio, and Alberto Alpago Novello. *Memoria sui*
    progetti per il piano regolatore di Milano, 1928–1929. Milan: Libreria Editrice
    degli Omenoni, 1930.
L'Edilizia pubblica e privata nell'attività dell'Amministrazione Comunale a Milano
    nel trentennio 1923–25. Milan: Comune di Milano, 1926.
Enciclopedia Italiana di scienze, lettere ed arti. Vols. 1–36. Rome: Istituto Giovanni
    Treccani, 1929–39.
Faludi, Eugenio. *Architetture di Eugenio Faludi.* Milan: Officine Grafiche Esperia,
    1939.
Il Fascio primogenito. Milan: Officine Grafiche "Esperia," 1937.
[F.R.] Ferdinando Reggiori. "Esito del concorso per il Palazzo di Giustizia di
    Milano." *Architettura e Arti Decorative,* no. 3 (1930): 122–30.
Gerla, Renzo. "Tre nuovi palazzi milanesi." *Milano,* September 1931, 469–72.
Guida di Milano. Milan: Savallo, 1922–43.
Giolli, Raffaello. "Il Palazzo della Borsa di Milano." *Poligono: Rivista mensile*
    d'arte 8 (December 1929): 90–3.
– [Il battistrada]. "La Casa dei Fasci Milanese." *Problemi d'Arte Attuale* 1, no. 3
    (1927): 29–31.
Lissone, Osvaldo, and Siro della Morte. *La Milano voluta dal Duce e la vecchia*
    Milano. Milan: Officine Grafiche 'Esperia,'1935.
Morabito, Marcello. "Il *Popolo d'Italia* nella sua nuova sede Milanese." *Milano,*
    November 1942, 474–6.
Mussolini, Arnaldo. *Carteggio Arnaldo-Benito Mussolini.* Edited by Duilio Susmel.
    Florence: La Fenice, 1954.
– *Scritti e discorsi di Arnaldo Mussolini.* Vols. 1–5. Milan: Hoepli, 1937.
Mussolini, Benito. *Opera omnia.* Vols. 1–44. Edited by Edoardo Susmel and Duilio
    Susmel. Florence: La Feince, 1957.
– *Vita di Arnaldo.* Rome: Quaderni di Novissima, 1933.
Muzio, Giovanni. *Giovanni Muzio: Opere e scritti.* Edited by Giuseppe Gambirasio
    and Bruno Minardi. Milan: F. Angeli, 1982.
– "Forme nuove di città moderne." *Atti del Sindacato Fascista Ingegneri di Milano* 9
    (1930): 3–8.
– *Giovanni Muzio.* Preface by Piero Torriano. Milan: Maestri dell'architettura, 1931.
– "Il nuovo Palazzo del 'Popolo d'Italia.'" *La Rivista Illustrata del Popolo d'Italia*
    18, no. 11 (1939): n.p.
n. d. r. "Palazzo per abitazioni e uffici in Milano." *Rassegna di Architettura,* no. 10
    (1938): 97–101.
"La nuova sede del Gruppo Rionale Fascista 'Fabio Filzi' a Milano." *Edilizia*
    Moderna 29 (October–December 1938): 26–33.

"Il nuovo Palazzo della Borsa Valori e Titoli di Milano." *Rassegna di Architettura*, no. 1 (1929): 3–8.

Pagano, Giuseppe. "Un concorso di giovani." *Casabella* 5 (June 1932): 19–24.

– "Proposta di piano regolatore per la zona Sempione-Fiera a Milano." *Casabella-Costruzioni* 132 (December 1938): 2–23.

"Il Palazzo di Giustizia." *Milano*, February 1932, 82–8.

Parini, Piero. "La Casa del Fascio di Milano." *La Rivista Illustrata del Popolo d'Italia* 2, no. 4 (1924): 27–31.

Piacentini, Marcello. *Architettura d'oggi*. Roma: P. Cremonese, 1930.

– *Architettura moderna*. Edited by Mario Pisani. Venice: Marsilio, 1996.

– *Il Palazzo di Giustizia di Milano*. Milan: Garazanti Editore, 1942.

"Il Piano regolatore di Milano e le opere previste per il quadriennio 1939–42 E.F." *Rassegna di Architettura*, no. 11 (1938): 463–73.

Pica, Agnoldomenico. *Nuova architettura Italiana*. Milan: Ulrico Hoepli, 1936.

Pini, Giorgio. *Filo diretto con Palazzo Venezia*. Bologna: Cappelli, 1950.

P.L. "Il Nuovo Palazzo di Giustizia di Milano." *Edilizia Moderna*, 37–9 (April–December 1942): 35–45.

P.M. [Paolo Mezzanotte]. "La Casa del Fascio di Milano." *Architettura e Arte Decorative* 2, no. 7 (1928): 319–26.

Poch, Ferdinando. "La nuova sede del Fascio primogenito." *Milano*, March 1939, 120–2.

Portaluppi, Piero. *Aedilita*. Vols. 1, 2. Milan: Bestetti e Tumminelli, 1924, 1930.

Portaluppi, Piero, and Marco Semenza. *Milano, com'è ora, come sarà*. Milan: Bestetti e Tumminelli, 1927.

"Il Progetto di Marcello Piacentini per il nuovo Palazzo di Giustizia di Milano." *L'Illustrazione Italiana*, 14 February 1932, 205–7.

Reggiori, Ferdinando. "Il nuovo programma edilizio dell'Amministrazione Provinciale di Milano." *Rassegna di Architettura*, no. 3 (1939): 105–14.

– "Valutazione estetica della nuova Borsa." *L'Ambrosiano*, 4 June 1931.

– "Valutazione estetica della nuova Borsa." *L'Ambrosiano*, 6 June 1931.

– "Valutazione estetica della nuova Borsa." *L'Ambrosiano*, 11 June 1931.

Ricordo di Milano: 32 Vedute (Milan: C. Capello, 192-?).

Savino, Edoardo. *La Nazione operante*. 3rd ed. Novara: Istituto Geografico de Agostini, 1937.

Savoia, Carlo. "La Casa del Fascio." *L'Assalto*, 21 May 1932.

"La sede del Gruppo Rionale Fascista 'P.E. Crespi' a Milano." *Architettura*, nos. 9–10 (1941): 380–3.

Sironi, Mario. *Scritti editi e inediti*. Edited by Ettore Camesasca. Milan: Feltrinelli, 1980.

Terragni, Giuseppe. "La costruzione della Casa del Fascio di Como." *Quadrante* 35–36 (October 1936): 5–27. Facsimile of the original Como: Tipografia Editrice Cesare Nani, 1994.

Tofanelli, Arturo. "Il Palazzo delle Borse a Milano." *Il Lavoro Fascista*, 17
   September 1932.
E.N.W. [E.N. Winderling]. "Il Palazzo delle Borse di Milano." *Rassegna di*
   Architettura, no. 3 (1932): 97–118.

Secondary Sources

Adamson, Walter L. *Avant-garde Florence: From Modernism to Fascism.*
   Cambridge, MA: Harvard University Press, 1993.
.– "Avant-Garde Modernism and Italian Fascism: Cultural Politics in the Era of
   Mussolini." *Journal of Modern Italian Studies* 6, no. 2 (2001): 230–48. http://
   dx.doi.org/10.1080/13545710110047001.
– "Fascism and Culture: Avant-Gardes and Secular Religion in the Italian Case."
   Journal of Contemporary History 24, no. 3 (1989): 411–35. http://dx.doi.org/
   10.1177/002200948902400302.
Ades, Dawn, Tim Benton, David Elliott, and Ian Boyd White, eds. *Art and Power:*
   Europe under the Dictators 1930–45. Exhibition catalogue. London: Thames and
   Hudson, 1995.
Adler, Frank. *Italian Industrialists from Liberalism to Fascism: The Political*
   Development of the Industrial Bourgeoisie, 1906–1934. Cambridge: Cambridge
   University Press, 1995. http://dx.doi.org/10.1017/CBO9780511572593.
Affron, Mathew, and Mark Antliff, eds. *Fascist Visions: Art and Ideology in France*
   and Italy. Princeton: Princeton University Press, 1997.
Gli Annitrenta: Arte e cultura in Italia. Exhibition catalogue. Milan: Mazzotta, 1982.
Antliff, Mark. "Fascism, Modernism, and Modernity." *Art Bulletin* 84, no. 1 (2002):
   148–69. http://dx.doi.org/10.2307/3177257.
Antonini, Ezio, et al. *La Borsa di Milano: Dalle origini a Palazzo Mezzanotte.*
   Milan: Frederico Motta, 1993.
Aquarone, Alberto. *L'organizzazione dello Stato totalitario.* Turin: Einaudi, 1965.
Arbizzani, Luigi, Saveria Bologna, and Lidia Testoni, eds. *Storie di case del popolo:*
   Saggi, documenti e immagini d'Emilia Romana. Casalecchio di Reno, Bologna:
   Grafis, 1982.
Arendt, Hannah. *The Origins of Totalitarianism.* New York: Harcourt Brace, 1975.
Argan, Giulio Carlo. *L'arte moderna, 1770–1970.* Florence: Sansoni, 1970.
Baffa, Matilde, Corinna Morandi, Sara Protasoni, and Augusto Rossari, eds. *Il*
   Movimento di Studi per L'Architettura, 1945–1961. Rome: Laterza, 1995.
Barocchi, Paola. *Storia moderna dell'arte in Italia.* Vol. 3, pt. 2. *Dal Novecento ai*
   dibattito sulla figura e sul monumentale, 1925–45. Turin: Einaudi, 1990.
Baxa, Paul. "Piacentini's Window: The Modernism of the Fascist Master Plan of
   Rome." *Contemporary European History* 13, no. 1 (2004): 1–20. http://dx.doi.org/
   10.1017/S0960777303001449.

– *Roads and Ruins: The Symbolic Landscape of Fascist Rome*. Toronto: University of Toronto Press, 2010.

Ben-Ghiat, Ruth. *Fascist Modernities: Italy, 1922–1945*. Los Angeles: University of California Press, 2001.

Benzi, Fabio. *Sironi: Il mito dell'architettura*. Milan: Mazzotta, 1990.

Betri, Maria Luisa, Alberto De Bernardi, Ivano Granata, and Nanda Torcellan, eds. *Il fascismo in Lombardia: Politica, economia e società*. Milan: Franco Angeli, 1989.

Bezerin, Mabel. *Making the Fascist Self: The Political Culture of Interwar Italy*. Ithaca: Cornell University Press, 1997.

Bianchetti, Cristina, ed. *Città immaginata e città costruita: Forma, empirismo e tecnica in Italia Otto e Novecento*. Milan: F. Angeli, 1992.

Bigazzi, Duccio, and Marco Meriggi, eds. *La Lombardia*. Turin: Einaudi, 2001.

Bilancioni, Guglielmo. *Aedilitia di Piero Portaluppi*. Milan: CittàStudi, 1993.

Binde, Per. "Nature versus City: Landscapes of Italian Fascism." *Environment and Planning D: Society & Space* 17, no. 6 (1999): 761–75. http://dx.doi.org/10.1068/d170761.

Bologna, Giulia. *Milano: Palazzo di Giustizia*. Milan: Biblioteca Trivulziana, 1988.

Bonfanti, Ezio. *Città, museo, e architettura: Il gruppo BBPR nella cultura architettonica italiana 1932–1970*. Florence: Vallecchi, 1973.

Boriani, Maurizio, Remo Dorigati, Valeria Erba, Marina Molon, and Corinna Morandi. *La costruzione della Milano moderna: Casa e servizi in un secolo di storia cittadina*. Milan: Clup, 1982.

Boriani, Maurizio, Corinna Morandi, and Augusto Rossari, eds. *Milano contemporanea: Itinerari d'architettura e urbanistica*. Rev. ed. Milan: Maggioli, 2007.

Boriani, Maurizio, and Augusto Rossari, eds. *La Milano del Piano Beruto (1884–1889): Società, urbanistica e architettura nella seconda metà dell'Ottocento*. Vol. 2. Milan: Guerini, 1992.

Bosworth, R.J.B. *Italy and the Approach of the First World War*. New York: St. Martin's Press, 1983.

– *Mussolini*. New York: Oxford University Press, 2002.

Braun, Emily. *Mario Sironi and Italian Modernism: Art and Politics under Fascism*. Cambridge, MA: Cambridge University Press, 2000.

– "Political Rhetoric and Poetic Irony: The Uses of Classicim in the Art of Fascist Italy." In *On Classic Ground: Picasso, Lèger, de Chirico and the New Classicism, 1910–1930*, edited by Elizabeth Cowling and Jennifer Mundy, 345–58. London: Tate Gallery, 1990.

– "Speaking Volumes: Giorgio Morandi's Still Lifes and the Cultural Politics of Strapaese." *Modernism/Modernity* 2, no. 3 (1995): 89–116. http://dx.doi.org/10.1353/mod.1995.0050.

– ed. *Racemi d'oro: Il mosaico di Sironi nel palazzo del Informazione*. Bergamo: Immobilare Metanopoli, 1992.

Brezzi, Camillo, and Luigi Ganapini, eds. *Cultura e società negli anni del fascismo.* Milan: Cordani, 1987.

Brunetti, Fabrizio. *Architetti e fascismo.* Florence: Alinea Editrice, 1993.

Burg, Annegret. *Novecento Milanese: I Novecentisti e il rinnovamento dell'architettura a Milano fra il 1920 e il 1940.* Milan: Frederico Motta Editore, 1991.

Cannistraro, Philip. *La fabbrica del consenso: Fascismo e mass media.* Bari: Laterza, 1975.

Cannistraro, Philip, and Brian Sullivan. *Il Duce's Other Woman.* New York: Morrow, 1993.

Castellano, Aldo, Flavio Crippa, Franco Della Peruta, Franco Loi, Giuliana Ricci, Marco Rosci, Aurora Scotti, Angelo Turchini, and Paola Venturelli. *La Lombardia delle riforme.* Milan: Electa, 1987.

Castellano, Aldo, and Ornella Selvafolta, eds. *Costruire in Lombardia, 1880–1980.* Vols. 1–5 Milan: Electa, 1983–90.

Castronovo, Valerio, Enrico Decleva, Roberto Mainardi, Gianfranco Miglio, Antonello Negri, Bruno Pianta, Aurora Scotti, Ornella Selvafolta, and Giorgio Vecchio. *La Lombardia Moderna.* Milan: Electa, 1989.

Cederna, Antonio. *Mussolini urbanista: Lo sventramento di Roma negli anni del consenso.* Bari: Laterza, 1979.

Ceschi, Carlo. *Teoria e storia del restauro.* Roma: M. Bulzoni, 1970.

Cianci, Ernesto. *Il Rotary nella società Italiana.* Milan: Mursia, 1983.

Ciucci, Giorgio. *Gli architetti e il fascismo: Architettura e città.* Turin: Einaudi, 1989.

– "Gli studi sulla città e l'architettura a Roma durante il fascismo una proposta di bibliografia ragionata." *Roma Moderna e Contemporanea* 2, no. 3 (1994): 587–604.

– "Italian Architecture during the Fascist Period: Classicism between Neoclassicism and Rationalism, The Many Souls of the Classical." *Harvard Architectural Review* 6 (1987): 77–87.

– ed. *Giuseppe Terragni: Opera completa.* Milan: Electa, 1996.

Ciucci, Giorgio, and Franceso Dal Co, eds. *Architettura Italiana del '900.* Milan: Electa, 1993.

Cohen, Jean-Louis, ed. *Les Années 30: L'architecture et les arts de l'espace entre industrie et nostalgie.* Exhibition catalogue. Paris: Éditions du Patrimoine, 1997.

Colarizi, Simona. *L'opinione degli Italiani sotto il regime, 1929–42.* Rome: Laterza, 1991.

Consonni, Giancarlo, and Graziella Tonon. "Milano: Classe e metropoli tra due economie di Guerra." In *Annali (Fondazione Giangiacomo Feltrinelli).* Milan: Feltrinelli, 1979/80, 405–510.

Corner, Paul. "Italian Fascism: Whatever Happened to Dictatorship?" *Journal of Modern History* 74, no. 2 (2002): 325–51. http://dx.doi.org/10.1086/343410.

Cottini, Stefania. "Tito Bassanesi Varisco Architetto." Master's thesis, Politecnico di Milano, 2000.

Crane, Sheila. *Mediterranean Crossraods: Marseille and Modern Architecture.* Minneapolis: University of Minnesota Press, 2011.

Cresti, Carlo. *Architettura e fascismo.* Florence: Vallecchi, 1986.

Crispolti, Enrico, ed. *Arte e fascismo in Italia e in Germania.* Milan: Feltrinelli, 1974.

Dalmasso, Etienne. *Milano capitale economica d'Italia.* Translated by Andrea Caizzi and Dario Gibelli. Milan: Franco Angeli, 1972.

Danesi, Silvia. and Luciano Patetta, eds. *Il Razionalismo e l'architettura in Italia durante il fascismo.* Exhibition catalogue, 3rd ed. Milan: Electa, 1996.

De Felice, Renzo. *Mussolini. Il rivoluzionario, 1883–1920.* Turin: Einaudi, 1965.

– *Mussolini. Il fascista: la conquista del potere, 1921–1925.* Turin: Einaudi, 1966.

– *Mussolini. Il fascista: l'organizzazione dello Stato fascista, 1925–1929.* Turin: Einaudi, 1968.

– *Mussolini. Il duce: Gli anni del consenso, 1929–36.* 2nd ed. Turin: Einaudi, 1996.

– *Mussolini. Il duce: Lo Stato totalitario, 1936–1940.* Turin: Einaudi, 1981.

– *Mussolini. L'alleato, 1940–1945.* Turin: Einaudi, 1990.

De Finetti, Giuseppe. *Milano: Costruzione di una città.* Edited by Giovanni Cislaghi, Mara De Benedetti, and Piergiorgio Marabelli. Milan: Etas Kompass, 1969.

de Grazia, Victoria. *The Culture of Consent: Mass Organization of Leisure in Fascist Italy.* New York: Cambridge University Press, 1981. http://dx.doi.org/10.1017/CBO9780511528972.

– *How Fascism Ruled Women: Italy, 1922–1945.* Berkeley: University of California Press, 1992.

de Grazia, Victoria, and Sergio Luzzatto. *Dizionario del fascismo.* Vols. 1, 2. Turin: Einaudi, 2005.

De Michelis, Marco, ed. *Case del popolo: Un architettura monumentale del moderno.* Venice: Marsilio, 1986.

De Rose, Arianna Sara. *Marcello Piacentini: Opere 1903–1926.* Modena: Franco Cosimo Panini, 1995.

De Seta, Cesare. *Architetti Italiani del Novecento.* Rev. ed. Rome: Laterza, 1987.

– *La cultura architettonica in Italia tra le due guerre.* 2nd ed. Naples: Electa, 1988.

Di Nucci, Loreto. *Fascismo e spazio urbano: Le città storiche dell'umbria.* Bologna: Mulino, 1992.

Dodi, Lugi. *Aspetti, problemi, realizzazioni di Milano: Raccolta di scritti in onore di Cesare Chiodi.* Milan: Giuffrè, 1957.

– "L'urbanistica milanese dal 1860 al 1945." Special issue, *Urbanistica* 25, nos. 18–19 (1956): 24–39.

Doordan, Dennis. *Building Modern Italy: Italian Architecture 1914–36.* Princeton: Princeton University Press, 1988.

– "The Political Content in Italian Architecture during the Fascist Era." *Art Journal* 43, no. 2 (1983): 121–31. http://dx.doi.org/10.2307/776648.

Ernesti, Giulio, ed. *La costruzione dell'utopia: Architetti e urbanisti nell'Italia fascista*. Rome: Edizioni Lavoro, 1988.

Etlin, Richard. *Modernism in Italian Architecture, 1890–1940*. Cambridge, MA: MIT Press, 1991.

Fagone, Vittorio, Giovanna Ginex, and Tulliola Sparagni, eds. *Muri ai pittori: Pittura murale e decorazione in Italia, 1930–50*. Milan: Mazzotta, 1999.

Falasca-Zamponi, Simonetta. *Fascist Spectacle: The Aesthetics of Power in Mussolini's Italy*. Berkeley: University of California Press, 1997.

Fogu, Claudio. *The Historic Imaginary: The Politics of History in Fascist Italy*. Toronto: University of Toronto Press, 2003.

Folli, Maria Grazia, ed. *Tra Novecento e Razionalismo: Architetture milanesi, 1920–1940*. Milan: Clup, 1991.

Franchi, Dario, and Rosa Chiumeo. *Urbanistica a Milano in regime fascista*. Florence: La Nuova Italia Editrice, 1972.

Gabellini, Patrizia, Corinna Morandi, and Paola Vidulli. *Urbanistica a Milano, 1945–1980*. Rome: Edizioni delle autonomiè, 1980.

Gambirasio, Giuseppe, and Bruno Minardi, eds. *Giovanni Muzio: Opere e scritti*. Milan: F. Angeli, 1982.

Gentile, Emilio. *The Sacrilization of Politics in Fascist Italy*. Translated by Keith Botsford. Cambridge, MA: Harvard University Press, 1996. Originally published as *Il culto del littorio: La Sacralizzazione della politica nell'Italia Fascista*. Rome: Laterza, 1993.

– *Storia del Partito fascista*. Rome: Laterza, 1989.

– *La via Italiana al totalitarismo: Il Partito e lo Stato nel regime*. Roma: La Nuova Scientifica, 1995.

Ghirardo, Diane. "Architecture and the State: Fascist Italy and New Deal America," Doctoral diss., Stanford University, 1982.

– *Building New Communities: New Deal America and Fascist Italy*. Princeton: Princeton University Press, 1989.

– "Città Fascista: Surveillance and Spectacle." *Journal of Contemporary History* 31, no. 2 (1996): 347–72. http://dx.doi.org/10.1177/002200949603100207.

– "Italian Architects and Fascist Politics: An Evaluation of the Rationalist's Role in Regime Building." *Journal of the Society of Architectural Historians* 39, no. 2 (1980): 109–27. http://dx.doi.org/10.2307/989580.

– "The Politics of a Masterpiece: The *Vicenda* of the Decoration of the Façade of the Casa del Fascio, Como, 1936–39." *Art Bulletin* 62, no. 3 (1980): 466–78. http://dx.doi.org/10.2307/3050031.

– "Surveillance and Spectacle in Fascist Ferrara." In *The Education of the Architect: Historiography, Urbanism and the Growth of Architectural Knowledge*, edited by Martha Pollack, 325–62. Cambridge, MA: MIT Press, 1997.

– "Terragni, Conventions, and the Critics." In *Critical Architecture and Contemporary Culture*, edited by William J. Lillyman, Marilyn F. Moriarty, and David J. Neuman, 91–103. New York : Oxford University Press, 1994.

Grandi, Maurizio, and Attilio Pracchi. *Milano: Guida all'architettura moderna.* Bologna: Zanichelli, 1980.

Greenfield, Kent Roberts. *Economics and Liberalism in the Risorgimento: A Study of Nationalism in Lombardy 1814–1848.* Rev. ed. Baltimore: Johns Hopkins University Press, 1965.

Gregotti, Vittorio. *New Directions in Italian Architecture.* Translated by Giuseppina Savaldori. New York: George Braziller, 1968.

Griffin, Roger. "The Primacy of Culture: The Current Growth (or Manufacture) of Consensus within Fascist Studies." *Journal of Contemporary History* 37, no. 1 (2002): 21–43. http://dx.doi.org/10.1177/00220094020370010701.

Golsan, Richard. *Fascism, Aesthetics, and Culture.* Hanover: University Press of New England, 1992.

Henneberg, Krystyna von. "Monuments, Public Space, and the Memory of Empire in Modern Italy." *History & Memory* 16, no. 1 (2004): 37–85. http://dx.doi.org/10.2979/HIS.2004.16.1.37.

Hobsbawm, Eric, and Terence Ranger. *The Invention of Tradition.* Rev. ed. Cambridge: Cambridge University Press, 2005.

Insolera, Italo. *Roma Moderna: Un secolo di storia urbanistica, 1870–1970.* Turin: Einaudi, 1993.

Irace, Fluvio. *Giovanni Muzio, 1893–1982.* Milan: Electa, 1994.

Kirk, Terry. *The Architecture of Modern Italy.* Vols. 1, 2. New York: Princeton Architectural Press, 1973.

Koon, Tracy. *Believe, Obey, Fight: Political Socialization of Youth in Fascist Italy, 1922–1943.* Chapel Hill: University of North Carolina Press, 1985.

Kostof, Spiro. *The Third Rome, 1870–1950: Traffic and Glory.* Exhibition catalogue. Berkeley: UC Berkeley Art Museum, 1973.

Lasansky, D. Medina. *The Renaissance Perfected: Architecture, Spectacle and Tourism in Fascist Italy.* University Park, PA: Penn State University Press, 2004.

– "Urban Editing, Historic Preservation, and Political Rhetoric: the Fascist Redesign of San Gimignano." *Journal of the Society of Architectural Historians* 63, no. 3 (2004): 320–53. http://dx.doi.org/10.2307/4127974.

Lazzaro, Claudia, and Roger J. Crum. *Dontatello among the Blackshirts: History and Modernity in the Visual Culture of Fascist Italy.* Ithaca: Cornell University Press, 2005.

Lerose, Filomena. "Paolo Mezzanotte: Architetto del 900." Master's thesis, Politecnico di Milano, 1984.

Lupano, Mario. *Marcello Piacentini.* Bari: Laterza, 1991.

Lupo, Salvatore. *Il fascismo: La politica in regime totalitario*. Rome: Donzelli, 2000.

Luzzatto, Sergio. "The Political Culture of Fascist Italy." *Contemporary European History* 8, no. 2 (1999): 317–34. http://dx.doi.org/10.1017/S0960777399002088.

Lyttelton, Adrian. *The Seizure of Power: Fascism in Italy, 1919–29*. New York: Scribner, 1973.

– "Fascismo e violenza: Conflitto sociale e azione politica in Italia nel primo dopoguerra." *Storia Contemporanea* 13, no. 6 (1982): 965–83.

Mangione, Flavio. *Le case del fascio in Italia e nelle terre d' Oltremare*. Rome: Ministero per i beni e le attività culturali direzione generale per gli archivi, 2003.

Marchetti, Leopoldo. *Milano tra due guerre: 1914–1946*. Milan: Istituto ortopedico "Gaetano Pini," 1963.

Mariani, Riccardo. *Città and campagna in Itala 1917–43*. Milan: Edizioni Communità, 1986.

– *Fascismo e città nuove*. Milan: Feltrinelli, 1976.

Meeks, Carroll. *Italian Architecture, 1750–1914*. Yale University Press, 1966.

Meriggi, Marco, and Louise A. Tilly. "Notables, Bourgeoise, Popular Classes, and Politics: The Case of Milan at the End of the Nineteenth Century." *Social Science History* 19, no. 2 (1995): 275–87. http://dx.doi.org/10.2307/1171515.

Mezzanotte, Gianni. *Architettura neoclassica in Lombardia*. Napoli: Edizioni Scientifice Italiane, 1966.

Mezzanotte, Paolo, and Giacomo Bescape. *Milano nell'arte e nella storia*. Milano: E. Bestetti, 1948.

"Milano: Città piano progetti." Special issue, *Casabella* 451/452 (October/November 1979).

Millon, Henry. "The Role of History of Architecture in Fascist Italy." *Journal of the Society of Architectural Historians* 24, no. 1 (1965): 53–9. http://dx.doi.org/10.2307/988281.

Millon, Henry, and Linda Nochlin, eds. *Art and Architecture in the Service of Politics*. Cambridge, MA: MIT Press, 1978.

Mioni, Alberto, ed. *Urbanistica fascista: Ricerche e saggi sulle città e il territorio e sulle politiche urbane in Italia tra le due guerre*. Milan: Angeli, 1980.

Mioni, Alberto, Antonello Negri, and Sergio Zaninelli, eds. *Il Sogno del moderno: Architettura e produzione a Milano tra le due guerre*. Florence: Edifir, 1994.

Missori, Mario. *Gerarchie e statuti del PNF: Gran consiglio, direttorio nazionale, federazione provinciale*. Rome: Bonacci, 1986.

Molinari, Luca, ed. *Piero Portaluppi: Linea errante nell'architettura del Novecento*. Exhibition catalogue. Milan: Skira, 2003.

Mosse, George. *The Nationalization of the Masses: Political Symbolism and Mass Movements in Germany from the Napoleonic Wars through the Third Reich*. New York: Howard Fertig, 1975.

Mullin, Robert John. "Ideology, Planning Theory and the German City in the Inter-War Years: Part I." *Town Planning Review* 53 (April 1982): 115–30.

– "Ideology, Planning Theory and the German City in the Inter-War Years: Part I." *Town Planning Review* 53 (July 1982): 257–72.

Muzio: L'architettura di Giovanni Muzio. Exhibition catalogue. Milan: Abitare Segesta, 1994.

Negri, Massimo, and Sergio Rebora, eds. *La città borghese: Milano, 1880–1968.* Exhibition catalogue. Milan: Skira, 2002.

Neri, Laura. "Arches and Columns: The Debate between Piacentini and Ojetti, 1933." *Modulus* (1982): 7–17.

Nicoloso, Paolo. *Gli architetti di Mussolini: Scuole, e sindacato, architetti e massoni, professori e politici negli anni del regime.* Milan: Franco Agnelli, 1999.

– *Architetture per un'identità Italiana: Progetti e opera per fare gli italiani fascisti.* Udine: Gaspare Editore, 2012.

– "I concorsi di architettura durante il fascismo." *Casabella* no. 683 (November 2000): 4–7.

– *Mussolini architetto: Propaganda e paesaggio urbano nell'Italia fascista.* Turin: Einaudi, 2008.

Pansera, Anty. *Storia e cronaca della Triennale.* Milan: Longanesi, 1978.

Pardo, Vittorio Franchetti, ed. *L'architettura nelle città Italiane del XX secolo: Dagli anni venti agli anni ottanta.* Milan: Jaca Book, 2003.

Patetta, Luciano. "Cultura urbanistica e architettura nella Milano degli anni '30." *Casabella* 451–52 (October–November 1979): 47.

Payne, Stanley G. *A History of Fascism, 1914–45.* London: University College London, 1995.

Pirelli, 1914–80: Strategia aziendale e relazione industriali nella storia di una multinazionale. Ires/Cgil della Lombardia "Bruno di Pol," 4–5. Milan: F. Angeli, 1985.

Pisani, Mario. *Architetture di Marcello Piacentini: Le opere maestre.* Rome: Clear, 2004.

Poli, Stefano. "Eugenio Giacomo Faludi, 1896–1981." Master's thesis, Polytecnico di Milano, 2000.

Portoghesi, Paolo, Flavio Mangione, and Andrea Soffitta, eds. *L'architettura delle case del fascio: Catalogo della mostra, Le case del fascio in Italia e nelle terre d'Oltremare.* Exhibition catalogue. Florence: Alinea, 2006.

Reggiori, Ferdinando. *Milano, 1800–1943.* Milan: Edizioni del Milano, 1947.

Regni, Bruno, and Marina Sennato. "Marcello Piacentini (1881–1960)." *Storia dell'Urbanistica* 3, no. 5 (1983): 7–22.

Riboldazzi, Renzo. *Una città policentrica: Cesare Chiodi e l'urbanistica milanese nei primi anni del fascismo.* Milan: Polipress, 2008.

Rifkind, David. *The Battle for Modernism: Quadrante and the Politization of Architectural Discourse in Fascist Italy.* Vicenza/Venice: CISA Andrea Palladio/ Marsilio, 2013.

Riley, Dylan. "Civic Associations and Authoritarian Regimes in Interwar Europe: Italy and Spain in Comparative Perspective." *American Sociological Review* 70, no. 2 (2005): 288–310. http://dx.doi.org/10.1177/000312240507000205.

Rosa, Giovanna. *Il mito della capitale morale: Letteratura e pubblicistica a Milano fra Otto e Novecento.* Milan: Edizioni di Comunità, 1982.

Rotelli, Ettore. "Le trasformazioni dell'ordinamento comunale e provinciale durante il regime fascista." *Storia Contemporanea* 4, no. 1 (1973): 57–121.

Rozzi, Renato, ed. *La Milano del Piano Beruto (1884–1889): Società, urbanistica e architettura nella seconda metà dell'Ottocento.* Vol. 1. Milan: Guerini, 1992.

Rumi, Giorgio, Alberto Cova, and Adele Carla Buratti, eds. *Milano nell'Italia Liberale, 1898–1922.* Milan: Cariplo, 1993.

Rumi, Giorgio, Virgilio Vercelloni, and Alberto Cova eds. *Milano durante il fascismo, 1922–45.* Milan: Caripolo, 1994.

Sabatino, Michelangelo. "Back to the Drawing Board? Revisiting the Vernacular Tradition in Italian Modern Architecture." *Annali di architettura: Rivista del Centro Internazionale di Studi di Architettura Andrea Palladio* 16 (2004): 169–85.

– *Pride in Modesty: Modernist Architecture and the Vernacular Tradition in Italy.* Toronto: University of Toronto Press, 2010.

Saggio, Antonino. *L'opera di Giuseppe Pagano tra politica e architettura.* Bari: Dedalo, 1984.

Sarti, Roland. *Fascism and the Industrial Leadership in Italy, 1919–40.* Berkeley: University of California Press, 1971.

Savorra, Massimilano. *Enrico Agostino Griffini: La casa, il monumento, la città.* Naples: Electa, 2000.

Scarrocchia, Sandro. *Albert Speer e Marcello Piacentini: L'architettura del totalitarismo.* Milan: Skira, 1999.

Schnapp, Jeffrey T., ed. *A Primer of Italian Fascism.* Lincoln: University of Nebraska Press, 2000.

– "Housing the Urban Industrial Work Force: Milan, Italy, 1860–1914." *Journal for the Society of Industrial Archaeology* 6, no. 1 (1980): 9–24.

Shorske, Carl E. *Fin-de-Siècle Vienna: Politics and Culture.* New York: Random House, 1981. First published 1961 by Alfred A. Knopf.

Sica, Paolo. *Antologia di urbanistica dal Settecento a oggi.* Bari: Laterza, 1980.

Sironi, Andrea, ed. *Sironi: La grande decorazione.* Milan: Electa, 2004.

Spinosa, Antonio. *Starace: L'uomo che inventò lo stile fascista.* Milan: Mondadori, 2002.

Stevan, Cesare, Sergio Boidi, Cecilia Colombo, Augusto Rossari, and Angelo
    Torricelli. *Architetture sociali nel Milanese, 1860–1990*. Milan: Touring Club
    Italiano, 1994.
Stone, Marla Susan. *The Patron State: Culture and Politics in Fascist Italy*.
    Princeton: Princeton University Press, 1998.
Storia di Milano. Vols. 15, 16, 18. Rome: Istituto della Enciclopedia Italiana,
    1995–96.
Susani, Elisabetta. *Milano dietro le quinte: Luigi Lorenzo Secchi*. Milan: Electa,
    1999.
Tafuri, Manfredo. *History of Italian Architecture, 1944–1985*. Translated by Jessica
    Levine. Cambridge, MA: MIT Press, 1989.
Tannenbaum, Edward R. *The Fascist Experience: Italian Society and Culture,
    1922–45*. New York: Basic Books, 1972.
Tarchi, Marco, ed. *Il Popolo d'Italia: Antologia, 1914–1917*. Florence: L. Landi,
    1982.
Taylor, Robert R. *The Word in Stone: The Role of Architecture in the National
    Socialist Ideology*. Berkeley: University of California Press, 1974.
Tranfaglia, Nicola, Massimo Legnani, and Paolo Murialdi, eds. *La stampa Italiana
    nell'età fascista*. Bari: Laterza, 1980.
Vannelli, Valter. *Economia dell'architettura in Roma fascista*. Rome: Kappa, 1981.
Veronesi, Giulia. *Difficoltà politiche dell'architettura in Italia 1920–1940*. Milan:
    Tamburini, 1953.
Vidotto, Vittorio. "Palazzi e Sacrari." *Roma Moderna e Contemporanea* 11, no. 3
    (2003): 583–99.
– *Roma contemporanea*. Bari: Laterza, 2001.
Vigezzi, Brunello, ed. *1919–1925 Dopoguerra e fascismo: Politica e stampa in Italia*.
    Bari: Editori Laterza, 1965.
Visser, Romke. "Fascist Doctrine and the Cult of the Romanità." *Journal of
    Contemporary History* 27, no. 1 (1992): 5–22. http://dx.doi.org/10.1177/
    002200949202700101.
Zevi, Bruno. *Storia dell'architettura moderna*. Turin: Einaudi, 1950.
Zucconi, Guido. *La città contesa: Dagli ingegneri sanitari agli urbanisti (1885–1942)*.
    Milan: Editoriale Jaca Book, 1989.

Index